Also by this author:

Curling Wisps & Whispers of History – Vol. 1: Thanet to Tasmania

LucyAnn Curling

Curling Wisps and Whispers of History

Vol. 2: Kent to Kefalonia

Ōzaru Books

Curling Wisps & Whispers of History – Vol. 2: Kent to Kefalonia
by LucyAnn Curling

Published by Ōzaru Books, an imprint of BJ Translations Ltd
Street Acre, St Nicholas-at-Wade, Birchington, CT7 0NG, UK
https://ozaru.net/ozarubooks

This edition published 31 January 2023
ISBN: 978-1-915174-07-9

Contents

Author's note

In material quoted directly from original manuscripts the spellings follow the originals and may vary from current use.

Readers should also note that appendices are numbered according to the chapters they relate to, for example Chapter 9 has two related appendices which are numbered 9a and 9b, but as Chapter 10 has no appendices the appendix numbering sequence goes from 9b to 11.

List of illustrations

3

Introduction

This second book of our family's story begins by focusing in the first three chapters on Charles James Napier. As I wrote in Volume 1, *Thanet to Tasmania*, 'So closely involved was Napier in the Curling family's story that he must be considered an honorary member of the family.' He certainly treated the Curling family like members of his extended family. His lasting influence on the Curling fortunes begins with his marriage in 1827 to widow Elizabeth Kelly, née Oakley, sister of our 4× great-grandmother, Catharine Oakley. Events leading up to the Napier marriage are important in the Curling story too.

Full transcriptions of the letters are provided so that the writings of the Curling family are all together in one collection. Transcripts from original manuscripts are in italic. Transcripts taken from existing published works by other authors are in regular font. The transcripts are as exact as I have been able to make them. In letters of the period punctuation marks were rare, spelling was still fluid and use of capital letters random; for example John Pitt Kennedy writes 'hitherto our friends have not shown any great signs of Industry since the allotment of their Farms', capitalizing common nouns, while Edward tells Napier that local government 'will not authorize any expenses particularly as the general is fully aware of the situation', omitting a capital for 'General' (Sir Frederick Adam).

A major part of this volume is based on a work journal, held in the British Library,[1] which Edward Curling kept in the period October 1828 to March 1830. The entries mostly record the annual round of farming routines and many are in note form. While endeavouring to paraphrase the journal coherently, I have used copious direct quotations. Spellings of names, particularly of places, but also of people, continue to be 'fluid' even in the twenty-first century. When place names come up in my own text I use the modern Greek transliteration as far as possible but it should be born in mind that even in Greek there are two modern versions of the island's name, Κεφαλονιά or Κεφαλληνία,[2] transliterated Kefalonia or Kefallinia, and it is still regularly spelt Cephalonia in the Roman alphabet. The Greek for 'Saint Nicholas' is 'Agios Nikolaos', but Edward mostly (not always) refers to it as St Nicolo, a hybrid English/Italian phrase which he would have picked up locally and in all quotations the spellings are as in the original manuscript.

Where words were difficult to discern in the original I have put the most likely interpretation in square brackets. Occasionally it has not been possible to do that, and there is instead an ellipsis in square brackets. Short phrases from the journal are given in the body text, and longer quotations in separate, indented paragraphs.

---

[1]   BL Add MS 49114, ff. 1–22b
[2]   See Wikipedia's page: https://en.wikipedia.org/wiki/Cephalonia

Acknowledgements

In writing this second book I have had wonderful help from many people. In Kefalonia, Elias Toumasatos, then librarian at the Korgialenios Library in Argostoli, directed me to *Foreign Communities on Kefalonia* by local historian Angelos Debonos now, sadly, deceased. Angelos and his wife twice welcomed me warmly to their home in Argostoli. His book, written in Greek, includes a chapter on the Maltese Colony. Elaine Vallianou did me a very professional translation job.

On my most recent visit in 2022 I stayed in Sarakiniko Cottage, right by the promontory which Napier wrote about. My host was Babis Simotas. Driving is no longer an option for me, so Babis arranged for Polydoros Stellatos to drive me to remote locations. Babis also arranged a meeting with the mayor of Argostoli, Mr Tsilimidos who, with Polydoros interpreting, kindly gave me an interview and then arranged for me to speak with the Librarian at the Korgialenios Library, Mrs Antonelou. I needed copyright permission to use the photograph of Napier's house (**Napier's house on Maitland Square**, Fig. 8) Mrs Antonelou passed on my request to Theotocoula Moulinos at the Korgialenios Museum who granted it. Special thanks are due to Polydoros for his patience and interest in the project. Thanks too to his father Marinos Stellatos for guidance to the ruins of old villages. Cecilia and Rees Jenkins invited me to lunch and introduced me to friends interested in Kefalonian history – and Celia's photo, 'Cattle in Kefalonia', Fig. 20 exactly captured my mental image of Edward Curling's little herd. Shirley Ogden alerted me to the book *Odysseus' Ithaca* by Nikolas G Livadas which has valuable information about Kefalonia's many earthquakes. In Athens, my dear friends Alison and Costas Scourti helped me with Greek language usage and Alison accompanied me on museum and gallery forays in search of objects and paintings for illustrations. Warmest thanks to all of you.

I can now claim to have a bespoke 'publication team': my publisher, the hugely knowledgeable, ever patient Ben Jones, of Ozaru Books; the Wordsmith, Caroline Petherick, my truly swift and supremely competent editing genius; and Tanya Izzard, my indexer who completed the index for this second volume in three weeks – it took me five months to do the index for volume 1 (and even then Ben had to finish it off for me). My mentor, Tim Albert, has continued to cheer/goad me on, as have my lovely family without whom there would be no point in the exercise.

I'm fortunate to have had access to so many insights into the lives and the social history of my ancestors' times. And I am extremely grateful for the care with which their manuscripts have been preserved by skilled and knowledgeable archivists.

Finally, a big Thank You to you, the reader, for opening the book. I hope you find something of interest in it. Any errors and omissions which you find are mine, and I would be grateful to know about them.

Chapter 1 – First love is the truest

To Charles Napier, family was the dearest thing. He may have been far away from home for much of his life but wherever he was he wrote copious, lengthy and intimately personal letters to his mother and siblings, and later to his children, and they replied to him. His sister Emily was passionately fond of him. She made no secret of the fact that he was the favourite of her five brothers – to a degree that some of her letters to him seem to the modern eye to border on the incestuous, albeit in the context of family tribulations:

21st May

> *How truly my beloved Charles does every word of your dear Letter answer every feeling of my heart! Oh God can I ever be sufficiently thankful for possessing such a Brother, such a Friend, on whose kind heart I can rely in every affliction with such full affection; No, my Charles you cannot tell the pleasure your letter has given me, the good it has done me._ not that I have not received kindness from others, but you & you only have enter'd into every feeling of my heart, have felt almost as I do myself for my poor afflicted Anne.[3]_ I cannot thank you my Charles, but how I long to lay my heart on your heart & to read in your dear eyes how you feel for me! ... Adieu my best loved Brother, our dear George is perfectly well & in the most delightful spirits._*

> *Your*

> *Emily Napier[4]*

Emily was the second of the eight children of Lady Sarah (née Lennox) and Colonel George Napier. She had been brought up in Ireland by her aunt Louisa Conolly, whom she grew to love deeply. When Louisa grew frail and elderly Emily took on her care until her death in 1821, and followed this with nine years spent caring for her brother George's children after the death of his wife. Isolated by these circumstances, Emily had no-one outside the family circle with whom she could develop a relationship or to whom she could direct her love. Her brother Charles, the eldest in the family, was the only focus and outlet for her passion, and when he was posted to the Ionian Islands, she was distraught to find that the separation from him was to be long-term.

---

[3] I do not at present know for certain who this 'Anne' is. Emily's brother George had no daughter named Anne. It is possible that it was Anne Louisa, the wife of Richard Napier. They had married in 1817; Anne Louisa, née Stewart, was the widow of William Connolly Staples when she married Richard Napier.

[4] BL Add MS 54529 ff. 20–22. The date on this letter gives no year, but it is filed with letters dated in the year 1814.

Charles, on the other hand, could reasonably have complained that his problem was the opposite of Emily's: he was always with people outside the family in far-away places and longed only to be with his nearest and dearest.

Fig. 1.   **Map showing position of Kefalonia**[5]

A peacetime appointment

Napier first arrived in Corfu, via France, Switzerland and Italy, on 18 July 1819 (see map of Greece with Ionian Islands to the west of the mainland, Fig. 1). He had been appointed an 'inspecting field officer' under Sir Thomas Maitland, the Lord High Commissioner and Governor of the group of seven Ionian Islands.[6] Initially he was detailed to travel through Greece to have a meeting with Ali Pasha with a

---

[5]   Map © FreeWorldMaps.net
[6]   See *The Life and Opinions of General Sir Charles James Napier*, vol. I, pp. 275–285, John Murray, 1857.

view to opening negotiations to secure the independence of Greece from the Ottoman Empire. After two years in the post, Maitland appointed Napier to take over from Colonel Robert Travers as the 'Resident of Cephalonia'[7] in March 1822. Napier preferred the Italian spelling of the island's name, Cefalonia, still in use in Italian in the twenty-first century, and he loved the island so much that he named his younger daughter Emily Cefalonia Napier.

The Ionian Islands had been a British protectorate since the end of the Napoleonic Wars, the French having earlier ended centuries of Venetian rule in the islands.[8] The role of Resident was a military appointment, but although Napier was still responsible to Maitland it gave him considerable autonomy in the running of the island. He was to look back on this period of his life with great fondness: 'They say first love is the truest, and Cephalonia is mine.'[9]

Fig. 2. *Abies cephalonica* on Mount Ainos[10]

Motivated by concern for the welfare of the civilians in his care, he wanted to improve their living conditions and the societal structures. His keen awareness of

---

[7] See **Appendix 1a – A description of Kefalonia in Napier's time** p. 178.
[8] *The Ionian Islands: Aspects of their History and Culture*, edited by Anthony Hirst and Patrick Sammo, Cambridge Scholars Publishing, 2014.
[9] *Revolution and the Napier Brothers 1820–1840*, p. 32, Priscilla Napier, Michael Joseph 1973.
[10] Wikipedia image, https://bit.ly/Ch1MntAinos

the limitations imposed on the people of the island by its physical geography and a very limited road network unleashed new aspects of his leadership qualities.[11]

The island is dominated by a mountain range, of which the highest is the imposing 5,000-foot (1682-metre) Mount Ainos. This and the rest of the mountains in the range feature a species of tree which was originally unique to the island and which was given the botanical name *Abies cephalonica* or Cephalonian fir (Fig. 2). It covers the mountain, giving it a dark aspect, and Ainos was known to the British of the time as the Black Mountain (Fig. 3).

Napier had a heightened sense of justice, and throughout his life intervened on behalf of the powerless in society. Priscilla Napier gave a romanticised account of one such intervention in Kefalonia:

> An old fisherman had brought in a huge fish, and had barely concluded his bargaining with the fishmonger when the agent of one of the island's many feudal chieftains put in an appearance and claimed the great fish as part of his master's feudal due, owing to its unusual size. Voices rose, bystanders joined in, partisan small boys scuffled in the dust, elderly gentlemen arose from under trees and slippered across to have their say. The seller protested, the fisherman despaired, rough hands were laid on his beautiful fish, and the agent's voice rose high in triumph. Suddenly a figure on a white horse was seen to be approaching, elbows working, determined chin thrusting between furry side-whiskers, spectacles gleaming in the bright sun. No further words were needed. The old fisherman pocketed his cash, the fishmonger laid hold of the fish, the feudal agent faded instantly into the landscape. For this was the despot of Cephalonia, the ruthless upholder of justice and of an odd kind of mercy always exercised in the interest of the oppressed, ο Νεπιος,[12] the British Resident; the omnipresence on a white horse, known to family and friends as Charles and Blanco.[13]

---

[11] See **Appendix 1b – Napier's achievements in Kefalonia** p. 180 for a list of Napier's achievements in Kefalonia.
[12] Transliteration 'o Nepios', literal meaning 'the Napier'. In Greek a person's name is preceded by the definite article in both speech and writing.
[13] *Revolution and the Napier Brothers*, p. 13.

Fig. 3. Mount Ainos (the Black Mountain) [14]

Priscilla Napier's is a fanciful account of the story, although to judge from the portrait, Fig. 4, the description of Napier's 'whiskers' is accurate, and in the painting he is holding his spectacles; he was short-sighted from an early age. This portrait, originally a miniature, was painted during his time on the island and shows him to have been quite dapper in his uniform and proudly sporting his military medals.[15]

His training in military engineering with the Royal Staff Corps had given him vital knowledge and practical experience of planning and building the infra-structures necessary for good communications. He began to release what he saw as the grip of Kefalonia's tyrannical tribal leaders; he organised public building works, and over the following few years he accrued a list of achievements of which he was enormously proud.[16] In order to do all this, Napier appointed Captain John Pitt Kennedy[17] to be his 'Secretary and Director of Public Works in the Island of Cephalonia'. Kennedy, fourteen years younger than Napier, had also been trained in the Royal Staff Corps and had previously worked on engineering projects in Malta and the Ionian Islands, so Napier had first-hand knowledge of his work.

---

[14] With thanks to Apostolia of CambridgeGreekCorner: https://bit.ly/Ch1MountAinos
[15] I have been unable to locate the original of this painting.
[16] See **Appendix 1b – Napier's achievements in Kefalonia** p. 180.
[17] For a biography of John Pitt Kennedy see https://bit.ly/Ch1JPK

Fig. 4.   Colonel Charles Napier in his early forties[18]

---

[18] Unknown collection; © A C Cooper (Colour) Ltd; Photograph National Portrait
Gallery, London. Priscilla Napier used this image in her second Napier volume,
Revolution and the Napier Brothers, where it is the frontispiece. She gives the artist as
James Holmes 1777–1860, and annotates it 'From a miniature – Colonel Charles
Napier in his early forties'.

A major area of concern to Napier was the agricultural practice on the island. Finding the traditional Greek farming methods extremely inefficient, he decided the best way to help improve matters would be to demonstrate what could be achieved with more efficient methods of farming. He needed agricultural labourers with experience of this, and fortuitously another British island possession was not too far distant. Malta, a small but strategically vital island had, like Kefalonia, been occupied over the centuries by a parade of nations, and since 1800 it had been in British hands. Kennedy had worked on Malta prior to his posting to Kefalonia, and it may well have been he who suggested to Napier that Maltese agricultural workers would have the knowledge and skills which Napier sought. According to his own account Napier had written to Sir Frederick Adam, his new superior, who had taken over from Maitland as Lord High Commissioner of the Ionian Islands in 1824, outlining his project.[19] Adam had apparently liked the idea, and authorised Napier to instigate negotiations with Malta. Not one for doing things by halves, Napier requested that a large contingent of Maltese with agricultural experience be sent to Kefalonia to set up a farming community.

The site Napier had chosen for his model farm, to be called the 'Maltese Colony', was a beautiful, fertile stretch of land on the east of the island, in an area then called Rakli or Racli, not far from the present-day town of Poros in the district called Pronos. Napier described the location of the colony, giving not only the geographical siting but his colourful theory as to why such good land had become a wilderness:

> I found in Cefalonia, a large and fertile tract of land stretching along part of the eastern shore of the island: this tract was wholly abandoned; and as it contained fine water, and the ruins of the ancient city of Pronos, which commanded a small port, I could not, at first, account for the desolation. I knew that the ancient towns were built in healthy spots; and at Pronos there was no appearance of any neglect, as at Samos: a little inquiry opened my eyes to the real secret, why this tract was abandoned. Between the Black Mountain and the sea, there runs a parallel and lower ridge; and on the sea, or eastern side, of this lower ridge, lies the ground in question. Now the reader must be informed, that the snug little port which I have mentioned, and which is called Poros (or port), is formed by a promontory called, by the inhabitants, the "landing place of the Saracens;" and, on the heights above, among the clouds stands the convent-fortress of Atros, below which is a projecting eminence called

[19] *The Colonies: Treating of Their Value Generally – of the Ionian Islands in Particular*, p. 1. Charles James Napier, Thomas and William Boone, London 1833. The book has been digitised by the British Library and is viewable online: https://bit.ly/Ch1CJNTheColonies

"The look out for the Saracens." Here the inhabitants formerly kept a constant guard, to watch the approach of the infidels. From these two facts, it appeared very evident to me, that, when the ancient city was destroyed, and infidels, and pirates, at pleasure ranged those seas, no man could cultivate ground, or live, in safety, along this tract of coast; the inhabitants therefore, abandoned it, and occupied the valley between this range, and the Black Mountain, keeping a watch for the enemy on the lower range, at the spot above mentioned; on the alarm being given, the women, children, and flocks fled to the fastnesses of the Black Mountain, long before the foe could cross the lower ridge, in ascending the steep, and difficult sides of which he would be encountered by the armed, and resolute mountaineers; therefore, unless the Saracens landed in great force, they dared not attempt to pass this ridge, and the people lived in security on the western side, and even on the more retired parts of it, where it falls back upon the great mountain; but a family venturing to settle on the eastern slope, was liable to be carried away, by any rover of the seas who marked their lonely habitation. Thus were the people driven from this rich piece of ground; and it became so overgrown with arbutus and myrtle, that when I first went there, it was a wilderness, and a very beautiful one. The greatest part of this ground belongs to the convents; and, upon "the landing place of the Saracens," I resolved to plant a colony of their ancient enemies, the Maltese.[20]

Sarakiniko is the Greek for 'place of the Saracens'. The promontory Napier described in the extract above is still called Sarakiniko.

Even with Napier's description of the location, it was difficult to pinpoint where he had sited his farming project. In all my investigations I had to bear in mind that earthquakes were likely to have shifted the terrain somewhat from how it had looked in Napier's time.

The worst earthquake in modern Greek history – known as the Great Ionian Earthquake of 1953 – entailed hundreds of tremors, shocks and aftershocks that struck the region between the islands of Kefalonia and Zakynthos. The most destructive of the quakes measured 7.2 on the richter [sic] scale and actually raised the whole island of Kefalonia 60 centimeters — or almost two feet.[21]

The 1953 earthquake was unusual for its severity but as Kefalonia and Zakynthos are on a major fault line[22] it is unsurprising that there have been and continue to be

---

[20] *The Colonies* pp. 253 ff. C J Napier.
[21] Gregory C Pappas, blog: https://bit.ly/Ch1Earthquake53
[22] See work of Anastasia A Kiratzi and Eleni Louvari, https://bit.ly/Ch1KefTransformFault

many earthquakes in the vicinity.[23] The geology indicators of the area around Poros dictate that the colony was south of the village because from the north there is a dramatic gorge, 80 metres deep, leading into the town, carrying the river Vohynás. On the south side, from the Sarakiniko promontory towards Skala there is a straight stretch of coast. At this point the Poros–Skala road runs along the shoreline, and there is a significant steep escarpment abutting the roadside for the entire stretch. Napier said that he used 'a large and fertile tract of land stretching along part of the eastern shore of the island'. If one removes the road, which would not have been there in Napier's time, the downward slope of the land would continue to the shoreline, and the final slope would have been gentler than it is at present. Edward wrote of how difficult it was to transport goods between the colony and the port of Poros, and one might think that this should have been easy as they were working land which ran all the way to the sea; but as the shoreline water is shallow along that stretch it would have been necessary to take goods by land to the port for loading and onward dispatch to Argostoli.[24]

Fig. 5 shows a map of Pronos, with the Sarakiniko promontory, the village of Agios Nikolaos (St Nicholas), the town of Poros and my theoretical notion of the area known by the British in Napier's time as Rakli highlighted in green.

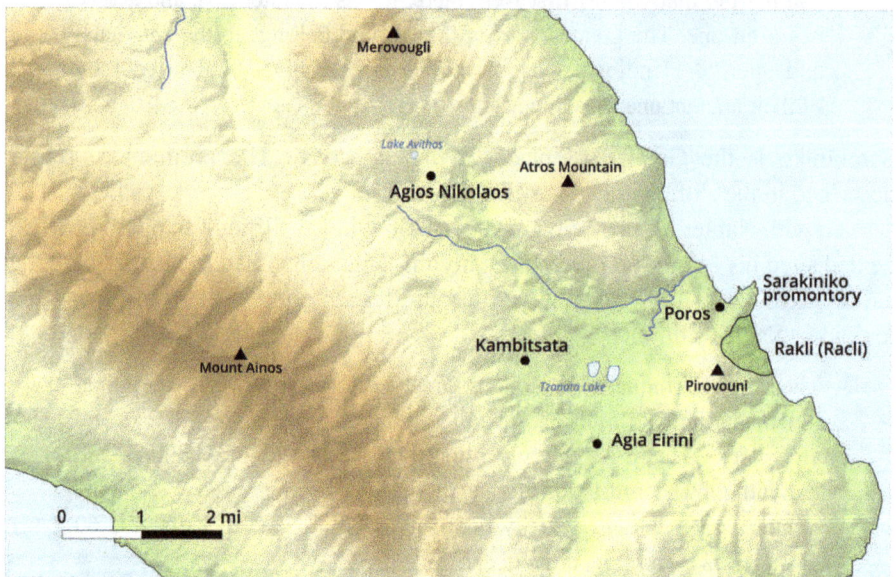

Fig. 5.   Map of present-day Pronos with proposed site of Rakli (Racli)[25]

---

[23] *Odysseus' Ithaca, the Riddle Solved*, Nicholas Enessee, 2001, with thanks to Shirley Ogden for the signposting. In his Appendix II Enessee lists eighty-nine serious earthquakes in the period 1469–1988.

[24] See **Appendix 1c – Nineteenth-century places in Pronos, Kefalonia** p. 181 for background information on the history and geography of the Pronos area.

[25] Map © FreeWorldMaps.net

Demetrio Cambici,[26] a descendant of one of the Venetian families in the elite land-owning aristocracy of the island, lived locally and committed considerable energy, effort and his own funds to help Napier set up the colony. Napier's intention from the outset was to keep to an absolute minimum the cost to the British government of setting up the colony. As he wrote to Sir Frederick Adam:

> I propose getting the Maltese without any cost to the Government of these Islands. I consider the matter as a private arrangement for the benefit of the convents, whose revenues are under my immediate control as your Resident; my own opinion is that the English Government need not interfere, indeed had better not, except in getting the Government of Malta to aid these people in paying their passage to Cefalonia.[27]

He had been told that the Maltese 'knew how to farm'. Each family was to have a small plot of land which they would clear and cultivate. By doing so successfully they would demonstrate better agricultural practice to the Greeks and break the cycle of poverty. This cycle had grown up, because for a long period currants had been grown but their value had depreciated considerably; the currants were exported, along with olives, and had initially brought substantial wealth to the island – but much of the income had to be used to import foodstuffs, particularly corn and meat. Napier was convinced that if the islanders could be persuaded to diversify their cultivation, their economy would blossom. All that was needed was fertile land, and there was plenty of that despite the mountainous nature of much of the terrain.[28]

---

[26] Napier used the Italian version of Cambici's given name. In a letter to Edward not included in this book, written in Italian, the gentleman himself signs himself Demetrio Cambici. Italian was almost certainly Cambici's language of choice. However, his surname was also spelt Cambisi in various other manuscript documents: Kennedy used both spellings at different times in his letters to Napier and Edward Curling.

[27] *The Colonies*, p. 530. C J Napier.

[28] *The Colonies*, pp. 230 ff. C J Napier.

Chapter 2 – First in my heart

At about the same time as Napier was endeavouring to get the Maltese Colony project off the ground, there were two tectonic shifts in his personal life. Firstly, Francis John Kelly died and on 21 May 1826 was buried at Holy Trinity Church, Cookham.[29] At long last Elizabeth Kelly and Charles Napier were free to marry. However, Elizabeth made him wait a further year – partly, no doubt, to leave a decent mourning interval to remember her first husband, but also, as she told Charles, to make certain that it really was his wish to marry an elderly woman of sixty-two while he was still only forty-four.[30]

> "Twenty-three years of great misery has been some trial", Charles admitted, and he told Emily that he was one who could not really do without a home and someone to love; he had really suffered. "I seemed doomed by fate to be a wanderer. Of late years she tried much to persuade me to marry, saying that she could still be my friend and spend part of her time with me and my wife." But he had told Elizabeth "you will always be first in my heart beyond all other things, how can I marry? The only answer she had to make me was, her great age making it ridiculous in me, and that it would be a great happiness to her to see me have children and a home" … "I am not sixteen and do not expect Elysium", but he did expect happiness "with one so very dear to me and so suited to me".[31]
>
> What both had endured in terms of separation and loneliness may be imagined; though Elizabeth had her children, and Charles his devoted family and his casual mistresses.[32]

Napier continued to work in Kefalonia for the time being, knowing that his long-hoped-for union with Elizabeth would take place the following year.

However, four months later came the second, more pressing, eruption in his life. In October 1826, his mother, Lady Sarah Lennox Napier, died. He returned to England as soon as he heard the news. Sarah had been blind for some time, and her memory had faded too, so that her children might well have felt that death was a kindness. Napier visited Elizabeth at Cookham. About this time he wrote to his sister Emily:

> "We all of us have our standards of perfection in this world, and Elizabeth is mine … Each man must be judge in his own case; and as I have no

---

[29] Berkshire Family History Society burial index record.
[30] See *Revolution and the Napier Brothers*, p. 76.
[31] The quotation marks in this extract are Priscilla Napier's.
[32] *Revolution and the Napier Brothers*, pp. 76–77.

particular taste for grey hairs in a wife, it is the opinion that she is superior to all other mortals that causes my marriage. No enjoyment in life is perfect to me without her presence, nothing satisfies me that I do until she approves of it.

Therefore the world may censure and laugh and be damned. ... I do not think you will like Elizabeth much because there is nothing of wit in her style, she is as like William's Caroline in her disposition as can be, without that similarity of habits which Caroline has with you and which affords food for conversation in the absence of wit; but as she is not your wife this don't signify and when we are together I can entertain you!

However, you will like in her a total absence of scandal, a total absence of ill-natured remarks, an absence of all prejudice, and unbounded benevolence and active pursuit of charity both in deed and feeling, and a mind so grateful to the Creator that she never shows a symptom of discontent." Charles thought it took time to appreciate Elizabeth; and he was "not so unreasonable as to expect you to like my wife upon principle and trust". He believed that her goodness and kindness and universal sympathy would do great good in Cephalonia[33]

He was now the senior member of his extended family: his seven brothers and sisters, their spouses and their offspring. This, and the opportunity to spend time with Elizabeth, kept him in England for several months.

News from Kefalonia

In his absence from the Colony, Captain John Pitt Kennedy, whom Napier regarded by that stage as a close friend as well as a colleague, was in charge of Napier's personal as well as his work administration.

On 25 September 1826 the Maltese families arrived in Cefalonia. The national archives in Argostoli holds dated documents listing the names and ages of the arrivals by family.[34]

What might the Maltese families themselves have been expecting on their arrival? The British government in Malta had been experiencing a problem with citizens made homeless for a variety of reasons and, ignoring the stipulation that they send only experienced agricultural workers, had used Napier's request as a way of tidying up its streets. The chosen people had been rounded up and sent, apparently without choice in the matter, on a journey about which they knew very little if anything. They were 'planted', in a manner similar to the Plantation of

---

[33] *Revolution and the Napier Brothers*, pp. 77–80.
[34] I am indebted to historian Angelos Debonos for the transcript of the relevant sections of this list.

Ulster[35] 200 years earlier, on the eastern side of an island which was new to them, in an area of scrub land where they were provided with only basic accommodation. Each 'house' consisted of just two rooms. Napier seems to have neglected to provide tools of any kind, perhaps thinking that genuine farming families would have brought their own or that they would know what was needed and ask for it. Instead 278 souls, many sick and poverty-stricken, disembarked, probably at Poros rather than Argostoli, and seem to have waited passively to discover their fate. Napier was in England, and so was not present to meet them as a group to tell them his plans. In all probability Kennedy and Cambici filled that gap as best they could. A further, and pressing, issue was that the houses being prepared for them were not complete, so Kennedy had to billet the Maltese arrivals in local accommodation, including the convent on Mount Atros.[36]

I wondered why these Maltese people would willingly leave their homes for a destination known only in name to them and with very little idea of what they were going to. For an expansion of this musing see **Appendix 12 – Life in nineteenth-century Malta**, p. 222.

From Kennedy's description of the apathy of the new arrivals, we can guess at the psychological state of the Maltese. Part of their problem must surely have been that they had had very little indication in advance of what they were supposed to be doing in their new roles, let alone how they were to achieve Napier's goals of a smoothly running, efficiently productive community of smallholdings. This sense of being adrift in a new environment without direction would have been compounded by Napier's absence. It would seem that he had neither given much thought in advance to how the Maltese were to be inducted, nor, when it became apparent that there were among them only a very few who were skilled in any form of agriculture, how he was going to remedy the situation. Kennedy did his best, and Cambici did sterling work caring for the Maltese. Napier's original plan was that each family would have a home and individual plot of land. However, even those few of the party who were healthy and agriculturally skilled would not have had experience of working virgin land in Malta. The reluctance which the Maltese showed in knuckling down as expected to work the land, which Kennedy and Napier assumed was a kind of pig-headed idleness, requires some acknowledged mitigation. The Georgians and Victorians seemed sometimes to have no sympathy or empathy for those in their employment, never mind people whom they had

---

[35] 'The Plantation of Ulster began in the seventeenth century when English and Scottish Protestants settled on land confiscated from the Gaelic Irish.' See https://www.bbc.co.uk/history/british/plantation/ for further information. The difference for most of the Maltese who moved to Kefalonia was that they were not given a choice in the matter.

[36] *The Colonies* p. 233, C J Napier.

forcibly removed from one of the British dominions to another. In Napier's case it is quite surprising, as he was very much on the side of the workers in other situations (the Chartists in his later career in England, and in India the native Scindians). The Maltese made it pretty clear from the outset that they did not feel at home in their new environment.

In November 1826 Kennedy wrote to Napier to report on the progress of the new community at Rakli. The Maltese families were not yet living on site: apparently existing buildings were being renovated as well as the new ones being built. Given that 278 people had arrived, the projected accommodation would seem woefully inadequate.

> *I have been frequently at Racli and things go on smoothly but slow in consequence of the weather, It has been one continued torrent of rain the whole of this month, we are just about finishing the third new house, and the roofing and repairing of all the old ones on the shore; These when ready will give cover for the winter to the Maltese, and when I get them once housed in the vicinity of their work I think of suspending building until the spring when we shall be able to carry on the same work at very little more than half the Expence; hitherto our friends have not shown any great signs of Industry since the allotment of their Farms, however their distance from them, added to badness of the weather are sufficient excuses for their Idleness, I hope in the course of a fortnight to get them into their new habitations & then we shall see what they are made of. We are busy getting the valuations of all the private lands lying in the vicinity of the village as well as that of the portions of Convent lands situated in the valley of Racli which are to be given in exchange. Cambici and Karuso are managing this business and I am very desirous of settling it as quickly as possible some of the Proprietors having shown a disinclination to make the exchange ...*[37]

Anastasia

High on the list of Napier's personal concerns was the wellbeing of his current mistress, a fiery-tempered Greek rebel known to us only as Anastasia,[38] who had recently given birth to a baby daughter, Napier's first child, who was given the

---

[37] BL Add MS 54535 ff. 15, 16. The name Karuso only appears once more, much later, when Edward Curling told Napier he was sending Greek exercises to 'Caruso', who was presumably coaching Edward in the language, BL Add MS 54536 ff. 118, 119, quoted on p. 170.

[38] There is no known surname for Anastasia.

name Susan Sarah; Sarah for Napier's mother and Susan possibly for his childhood nurse, Susan Frost. Napier's family knew about Anastasia and the baby.[39]

On 4 December 1826 Kennedy wrote a long letter to Napier, sounding rather fearful of encounters with Anastasia, whom he called variously 'her Majesty', Anastazulla or Stazulla, Greek diminutives of Anastasia. The baby, known as Su, Sue or Susan, was being nursed by a local woman, Nicolachina, who was being browbeaten by Anastasia, although Nicolachina was not without a flaming temper herself. Susan must have been about a year old, as there was a possibility that Anastasia was expecting a second child, although Kennedy reported that it appeared to be what we would now call a phantom pregnancy:

Argostoli Dec 4th 1826

And now I have to give you a piece of news that will surprise you and be welcome; know then that her Majesty's Pregnancy was a false alarm the doctors do not know exactly how to account for it but both she and they think she is not with child she certainly is very much smaller than she was and says that if there be still any doubt on the subject she must at all events have been terribly out in her dates, and that the cause must have produced its effect at a much later period than she at first supposed. I think in my last letter I told you that I feared an explosion between her and Nicolachina; I was not deceived, and a very few days after, it broke out. I arbitrated between them, and bullied Nicolachina with all my might in order to reduce her to obedience, till at length I saw clearly that Nicolachina was not in fault and that Anastazulla was making the house too hot for her. I think with the object of forcing her to resign: I then asked Mum [probably one of the British staff or soldiers] *and several others their opinions as to the Propriety of changing the Nurse & all agreed that such a change must at least be attended with considerable risk to the Child, I saw besides with my own eyes that no creature could be more attentive than Nicolachina and no Child could be going on better than little Su. With these data always before my eyes I determined ... qui conte that Nicolachina must remain until it is time to wean Susan (about two months longer) and screwing my courage to the sticking point I ventured to tell her Majesty so, urging the necessity of her bearing with Nicolachina for her child's sake even admitting her to be the Belzebub described, I told her that I thought her treatment of the nurse was harassing and her displeasure was very great but I*

---

[39]   See George Napier's mention of 'Su' in his letter of 7 April, quoted on p. 28.

stood my ground and after a most diplomatical negotiation which lasted for two days during which I acted the part of a man between an Arbitrator & Dictator & a Tyrant, now arguing, now entreating, now ministering. I succeeded in establishing harmony in the Family. I hope to God I shall be able to make it last for two months, in Short I'm determined it shall, as Susan is going on Capitally, there's not the like of her in all [Ireland] of thrice her age. Decr 28th. I do feel right happy and well satisfied with myself. Ever since my successful negotiation closed Her Majesty's dominions have been in the most full enjoyment of peace and tranquillity and I have had the satisfaction of being received again with her most gracious favour.[40]

As if life were not complex enough in Napier's personal affairs, matters were in need of attention at the Maltese Colony. As mentioned earlier, although those who had been sent there did include a few strong and healthy citizens, single people and families, some with young children, many were unwell or elderly. Kennedy's letter continues:

I have just returned from Racli where Cambici however has ascertained that more than the third part of the Maltese are unfit for farming & both he and Monferato are very desirous to have them wed[41] out that the expence may be avoided of supporting them who are incapable of fulfilling their part of the contract, the fact is Mr. Revacoli[42] acted damned ill in making the Selection he did, and altho' I am not in so great a hurry as Cambici is to get rid of a part of them I still am convinced that we must turn out a few but not until the weather shall have left them at liberty to work and give us the power of gauging correctly as to the merits of each, at all events you need not be uneasy on the Subject, there are amongst them 70 good ... 40 men & 30 Boys who will be perfectly a match for all the land we have got for them, so that there is not the slightest doubt as to the successful result. The exchanges which I told you we were occupied with in my last letter have been nearly all completed, the number of Bacili[43] exchanged is about 300 valued at about $4000 & for which an equivalent has been given in some of the small pieces of Convent

---

[40] BL Add MS 54535 ff. 17, 18.
[41] weeded.
[42] Revacoli was presumably an official in Malta.
[43] Confusingly, 'Bacili' was a term used in the measurement both of volume and land. Measurement and currency were extraordinarily complex in the Ionian Islands at this time. See **Appendix 2 – Castlereagh's Cabinets of Weights** p. 192, which includes contemporaneous information about currencies in use in the Ionian Islands at the time.

*Property scattered about the Island. Cambici calculates that the whole amount of Property united in the vicinity of the village will be about 450 Bacili which 70 hands will be easily able to cultivate. These or other Propietors of land near the village who are anxious to exchange with the Convents; but it will be quite time enough to treat with them after your return as we have got as much as is necessary for the present. The Maltese have all removed down to the village of Pronus_* [44]

Napier later commented:

These people arrived, and … were incapable of fulfilling their agreement. The whole scheme was baffled, by an intrigue at Malta, entered into for the purpose of getting rid of their superannuated paupers and inconvenient characters.[45]

But Napier was not on hand to deal with the problem when the Maltese first arrived. Ten weeks later, Kennedy wrote again, and we learn that contrary to his account in the earlier letter Anastasia was imminently expecting a second child:

Feby. 26 1827 Argostoli

Stazulla and Susan are both as well as can be. Sue has a mouthful of Teeth and lots of tongue. Never cries, and as merry as a Cricket. The hardiest little animal[46] you ever saw, never happy but when out of doors however cold it may be. … Nicolachina still remains and is to remain until after Stazulla's confinement. The whole family goes on as well as possible and Stazulla remarkably correct, all harmony and as easily managed as I could wish.[47]

Napier had not chosen a submissive, ignorant peasant girl for his 'fling'; Anastasia was more than capable of looking after her own interests. The rebellious streak which informed her patriotic calling as a Greek also made her an assertive, almost imperious, character.

---

[44] BL Add MS 54535 ff. 17, 18 – Mr Revacoli must have been the person delegated by the Maltese government to select the people who went from Malta to Kefalonia in 1826. Kennedy may have meant the village of Poros, which is today in the administrative district called Elios Pronos.

[45] *The Colonies*, p. 254, C J Napier

[46] 'little animal' was often used amongst the Napiers as a term of endearment in referring to babies and children, and it would appear from Kennedy's letter that it had a wider use too.

[47] BL Add MS 54535 ff. 27–28.

Chapter 3 – How excellent & how perfect he is

When did Charles tell Elizabeth about his lover Anastasia in Argostoli? Certainly at some point before the marriage he told her that there was in Argostoli a baby girl, called Susan Sarah, who would be aged about a year at the time of his wedding to Elizabeth, and that another child was about to be born. Elizabeth had tried to persuade Napier to marry someone who could give him children, so she may well have been quite sanguine about this. As Priscilla Napier said, the Napiers

> were all Georgians by birth; and Georgian women tended to accept their husbands' illegitimate children rather as they might now accept their Labrador dogs, something bumbly and time-consuming but essentially lovable and part of them … Anastasia had been more than [a casual mistress]. Their love had alternated between ecstasy and tempest: Charles's nearest relations, who are most likely to have heard it from Charles himself and therefore to know, maintain that their love had also been deep and their life together a thing of beauty. Charles was one of those many men who can happily and genuinely love two women at once, specially when one is in Cookham and the other in Cephalonia[48]

In April 1827 the year had almost passed since F J Kelly's decease. Elizabeth wrote to her friends, the Reverend Christopher Packe and his wife Mrs T[49] Packe at Windsor Castle, where Christopher was a 'minor canon' and the vicar of Ruislip Church, to ask if he would be available to officiate at her marriage. We do not have Elizabeth's letter – only the replies she received from both the Reverend and Mrs Packe – but we learn that Elizabeth had told them what a wonderful person Charles Napier is.

The replies are a pair of letters written on a single sheet of paper and on the same day. They are headed with apparently different addresses, but The Cloisters is part of Windsor Castle. We get the impression that Mrs Packe was an old friend of Elizabeth's, possibly even from childhood, as they were both 'maids of Kent', i.e. born in East Kent.

The Cloisters 1st April 1827

My dear Friend

Your letter consoled me too this morning for I feared I should not hear from you again. Forgive me for the fear: I was calculating

---

48 *Revolution and the Napier Brothers*, pp. 76–77.
49 Christopher Packe's wife's full name at marriage was, according to parish records, Tomazine Gentile: FindMyPast parish record, 13 January 1761, St Stephen's Hackington.

whether you had left England or not! & [when Arley] Nims the
postman past the door I was disappointed_ Your long, very
satisfactory Epistle reassured me_ You are certainly going to make a
great change! But if the change is predictive of your happiness it is
for the better If you esteem it such_ & I dare say, as far as it rests
individually, there will be nothing wanting.

The instances you have [given] of Col Napiers extreme generosity,
kindness & consideration are beyond any thing I ever heard_ I cannot
set bounds to my admiration! I never heard of such a disinterested[50]
character.

I had heard you were married, & from that assurance my fears
arose, that I should not hear from you again. It was Mrs Leicesters
news, & came from Mr King._ & now I am upon the subject of that
Lady_ here I will insert her remembrances to Miss Kelly & her sorry
*not to have seen her. I could not let a post pass without telling you_*
And Christopher will be here this evening. I am sure I can answer for
his executing any of your wishes, with double pleasure, if it promotes
your happiness: & feel himself much distinguished by the wish_ but
*he shall answer for himself_*

*Indeed I do feel for Miss Kelly and in her affectionate … to you_*
the witness not only her affection but her duty and [quietness] with
*the filial tenderness, I am sure she would not have been deficient in_*
had you continued together: It is a pity she does not go with you_ she
could have exercised her kindness_ & seen places and Countries;
customs & manners so different, it would have given a […] to her
ideas_ & a fund of information, added to her store of good sense &
sound judgement._ I hope she will be happy._ she is very fond of Miss
Steward and of S...l[51] *& we hope to have the pleasure of seeing her*
at Windsor

But most of ..., too, was not words of course_ but real &
substantial meaning: I must conclude here_ your Books shall be sent
you_ & if I insert all my … & kind wishes to you_ I must copy your
letter_ for you will … a transcript of your own heart_ God bless you

---

[50]   'disinterested' here is used with the nineteenth-century meaning of 'unselfish'. How I
       wish we could have seen Elizabeth's letter to Mrs Packe; it would have told us so
       much about the relationship between her and Napier prior to their marriage.
[51]   This cryptic name substitution probable refers to Elizabeth's son-in-law, Samuel
       Laing.

T Packe

Mes compliments a [sic] *Mons le Colonel*

On the same sheet of paper, the Rev Christopher Packe wrote:

The Castle 1 April 1827

My dear Madam

> *I am most happy to hear not that we shall lose you but of the cause of our loss which is your gain. I shall be most happy to do any thing that may be of service or satisfaction to you: and most willingly offer you M. the use of my little Church and the Church's Rector for the occasion. But I fear that Colonel Napier will find some difficulty in fitting the Licence addressed to me, as I believe it necessary to have resided three weeks [in the] Parish where the marriage is to be performed. If [the difficulty] can be surmounted I will attend at any time you may appoint. You may command my services if you wish them at any Place & I can assure you that it ever makes me happy to confer happiness upon any one, but more especially upon an old Friend. Will you let me hear from you soon?*

> *Most sincerely yours*

C Packe

PS I shall be at Windsor for the whole of this week[52]

The 'Miss Kelly' referred to in Mrs Packe's letter was probably Elizabeth's middle daughter, Mary, who was living with Samuel Laing as governess to his children. From what Mrs Packe says it is clear that Elizabeth had invited Mary to go with her and Napier to Kefalonia but Mary had refused. This outcome was undoubtedly the result of Laing's influence on Mary, and it was to have lasting repercussions on Elizabeth's health.

In the week before the wedding, Elizabeth and Napier were preparing for imminent departure to Kefalonia following the ceremony. Napier received several letters from his regular shipping agent, William Mariner, written from 12½ Capthall Court[53] This letter, written on 9 April 1827, gives a flavour of the preparations:

---

[52] BL Add MS 54541 ff. 15–16.
[53] The house number 12½ is not a typo or printing error. Mr Mariner's handwriting is very clear.

Sir

    *I enclose you a card of the Vessel about to sail in 10 days – She is rather smaller than I supposed. The freight will be 1/6d per cubic foot, & 10 percent primage in the amount of freight_*

    The Insurance not more than £2 percent. The Captn would like to have the Cases, not later than Thursday next._ have the kindness to let me know the name of the person under whose care they remain & his address. I think you have said Brooke's Wharf._ In order to make the required Custom house entry we must know the mark & n^r.[54] of each case & also their separate contents & Value.

    Shall we ship the spinning wheel at same time, or shall we leave it till a more direct opportunity? I suppose the order can at any time be procured by application to Mr Hay of the Colonial Office._

    I am much obliged by your kind inquiries after my health. I regret to say that I am still very lame & weak._

    Your very ob^t /Servt

Wm Mariner

The spinning wheel which William Mariner mentions could have been Elizabeth's; or possibly Napier was taking it with him to show the islanders the British method of spinning. On the third (blank) side of this letter is the following list in pencil, in Napier's hand, of goods he was taking with him to Cefalonia following his marriage:

    Table linen
    Two tables   } *Mahogany*
    A cabinet
    5 Book cases
    800 English & French books
    Table and bed linen
    Pair of Globes
    Plate (English)
    China. English
    Glass. English.
    Iron Mongery
    All English except some of the books and all used by m.[55]

---

[54] The 'n^r' could have stood for 'number' or 'nature'.

[55] Given that Napier's mother had died the previous year, it is possible that 'm' was his mother (whose great-grandmother was the Frenchwoman Louise de Kérouaille,

Letter addressed to:

> Colonel C Napier
> Care of Mrs Kelly
> 21 Sloane Terrace
> Chelsea

Another letter, written on 9 April by Kennedy, would not have reached Napier until after the wedding:

Argostoli April 9 1827

My Dear Colonel,

The day after tomorrow commence a week of holidays & I am going to take the opportunity of running for a few hours to Santa Marena[56] to look at the Church. So as this is likely to be thank God my last letter to you before I see you: hear my confession! Not a single pick has displaced a stone on the Livato Road since you saw it. They have all been working in town on the new Streets; the fact is as the winter set in, I was frightened at the Chaos around me, and fearing that influential visitors might arrive who would perhaps be incapable of supplying from their own heads, all the levels, slopes &c &c which were wanting; to work I went, and the only means I had was the Sappers of Livato which not being able to appear in two places at the same time, your darling Road has been neglected; however as your arrival draws near I begin to get in a hell of a … & after the Festa I intend to put all hands to Livato and work there like a devil till you come back. I know this is the only chance of Salvation I have left. I have begun parapeting the most dangerous places on the Roads near the Town that the Argostoli Cits may be induced to venture out in their one horse Shays [sic: chaises] we have added an eighth wonder to the seven old ones! You'll scarcely believe that we have succeeded in turning a Cologero[57] to account, yet as it is, we drafted two or three from each convent, and sent them together with some of their mules to help in Building the Pronos Village & Cambisi makes them work like men. The first task I gave them was to burn a lime Kiln. Our Roads I think are now sufficiently advanced to allow you to effect your plan of local Constables.[58]

---

mistress of King Charles II) and he was taking books which had been his mother's back to Kefalonia with him. However, it is also likely that some of the listed items belonged to Elizabeth.

[56] This was probably the fortress of Sta Maura on the island of Lefkada.

[57] Cologero or calogero is the Greek word for 'monk'.

[58] BL Add MS 54535 ff. 27–28.

Our 5× great-aunt, Elizabeth Kelly, widow, and Charles James Napier, bachelor, were married at St Luke's Church, Chelsea, on 16 April 1827 and, as promised, Christopher Packe officiated, declaring himself Rector of St Michael Basetlawe.

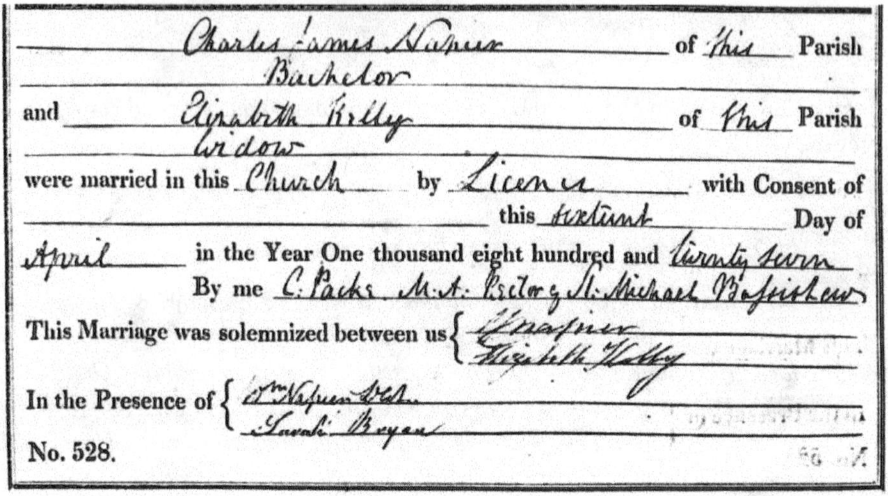
Charles James Napier of this Parish
Bachelor
and Elizabeth Kelly of this Parish
widow
were married in this Church by Licence with Consent of
this sixteenth Day of
April in the Year One thousand eight hundred and twenty seven
By me C. Packe M.A. Rector of St Michael Basetlawe
This Marriage was solemnized between us { C Napier
Elizabeth Kelly
In the Presence of { Wm Napier ...
Sarah Bryan
No. 528.

Fig. 6. Marriage of Elizabeth Kelly, widow and Charles James Napier[59]

Elizabeth celebrated her sixty-second birthday the month after the wedding, and would have been seen by people in all stations of society as an old woman. Napier was forty-four and had many active years ahead of him. For the woman in the couple to be eighteen years older than the man was even more unusual in the nineteenth century than in the twenty-first, when such a marriage would still be quite rare. Nonetheless, the marriage was warmly welcomed by Napier's brother George in this endearing pair of letters:

April 7th

My dearest Charles

Long may you and your Wife enjoy your present happiness and although you are come to years of discretion still I trust in God there are many happy years for you both to enjoy life, & with young Su to educate and bring up you will have plenty of interest & occupation, I only wish you had ten of them, tho they are damned expensive too the Devils. You know it is always usual to make a present to a new married couple, & as you may have the very thing [sic] *trifle I can give I think it better to say as we* [are] *too old friends to mind these*

[59] Image of the marriage record for Elizabeth Kelly and Charles James Napier, from Ancestry.com, with whom the copyright rests.

*little things that I desire you will buy some little thing as my present
to Elizabeth, value 3 guineas and tell her I only wish I was able to
afford to give her something better worth her acceptance. I leave it to
your choice perhaps a fish knife if you are without one but you are to
go to the full value of 3 guineas & I will make Emily pay you at the
same time she settles your coffee pot God bless you my very dear
brother You know how affectionately I love you & how I look to you
as the future guardian and protector of my boys if they lose your
affec^te brother*

Geo Napier

My dear Elizabeth

*Accept my most affectionate congratulations on your marriage
with my brother Charles You have known one another so long that I
need not tell you how excellent & how perfect he is. rather need I say
that I feel much more at rest about him and satisfied that his
happiness as long as you are with him will be complete. I am sorry
you could not come down here because I know how anxious my sister
Emily is to be acquainted with you. However, I trust ere many years
pass away we shall all meet either at home or abroad & believe me
my dear sister yrs affectly*

Geo. Napier[60]

Emily Napier's relationship with Elizabeth was volatile at first. On the one hand
she was overjoyed when Elizabeth wrote to tell her that all was well with Napier.
She realised that Elizabeth could prove to be a reliable commentator on his health
and frame of mind, as she was 'on the spot' in Cefalonia, someone who cared as
much as she did herself about him. From Elizabeth she could get real news instead
of having to rely on deducing his health and state of mind from his shadowplay of
wry wit and evasion in response to her queries. She sounds positively sisterly in
this short note to Elizabeth, written above a longer letter to Napier.

Sept 28th [1827]

*Thank God! the operation is over & our beloved Charles safe; my
dear Sister it is impossible to say what a weight his dear letter of the*

---

[60] BL Add MS 54524 f. 10. These two letters are on the same piece of paper. At that time
a large piece of paper was folded in half for letter writing, and the British Library
counts each leaf of the fold as a single 'folio'. George Napier wrote this pair of letters
before Charles and Elizabeth were married, and he must have allowed nine days for it
to reach them.

25th with your postscript has taken off my heart, for the ...
presentimens [sic] have lain like lead upon my spirits in spite of my
endeavours not even to think upon the subject._ The dear little Susan
too is better & that will help his recovery more than anything except
you being better yourself & I grieve to find how much you suffer from
the heat, I know by experience how completely overpowering it is to
those who do suffer from it not to feel what a terrible ass...ation of
your anxiety & your sickness it must have been, for I trust before this
the rains have come to your relief as your letter did to mine; there
never was anything so unexpected as this dear letter for I had fully
made up my mind to not hearing again for three weeks & had but just
sent my own letter to dearest Charles when they brought me this, I
could hardly believe my eyes or open the seal from anxiety & tho' his
own dear hand writing on the outside assured me he was well, I
dreaded to find it was of some old date which had been delayed. How
I love Sir Frederick for his kindness! And now my dear Sister I will
say good bye to you because I have a political discussion to finish
with Charles for which I had as little heart as ... when I ended my
letter this morning._

your ever affecte sister

Emily Napier

On the other hand, Emily was much more reserved a year later in this letter to Elizabeth, written at the foot of one to her brother.

I think I need hardly assure you my dear Sister that I never thought
of attributing your silence to neglect & if I did not write to you, it was
really as I desired Charles to tell you that I thought you would make
acquaintance with me much better by reading my letters to him than
by any addressed to yourself; & as I suppose that by this time we are
terribly intimate I shall write on without further preface – I can well
understand the weariness both of body and mind you must have felt
for a long time after your arrival at Cefalonia, but if, as I hope, the
climate does not disagree with you I should think judging by myself
that the total change of habits & occupations is more likely to
conduce to your cheerfulness than anything in England could have
done & the usefulness of all that is going on around you will occupy
your mind satisfactorily as well as pleasantly. Your account of my
beloved Charles's spirits & health corroborated as it is by Captain
Kennedy & himself does indeed make me very happy, for you will

*easily believe that I love him with no common affection! From our
earliest infancy he was the chosen favourite of my heart & I can truly
say that my attachment has invariably increased with every
succeeding year of my life._ My poor George's desolate situation at
the time my own bitter affliction ... obliged me to choose a second
home, my promise to his dear wife to take charge of his girls & the
equally sacred promise I had made to take care of Mary & Caroline
Bennet til they married, together with the pain I know it would give
my poor dear Mother if I left England, determined one of the greatest
sacrifices of my life in not accompanying my dearest Charles to
Cefalonia when he so suddenly left us in 1821 & when I parted with
him that melancholy Christmas I felt as if my last chance of happiness
on earth was torn from me! But how differently has the goodness of
God allowed it to turn out! Those dear Children who I then scarcely
loved have become the occupation & delight of my life, & my dear
Charles's solitary circle which used to hang heavy at my heart is now
a happy home with you & his little Susan._ of your kindness to that
Child I need only say it was what I expected from all I had heard of
you & I trust she will reward you for it both by her own conduct to
you & the pleasure it is to her Father to have her brought up in his
house._ I do not mind the violence of character he describes her as
having if it is early corrected, but I do hope he will not let it go on too
long in the idea that it is a mere childish fault which her own sense
will cure._* [61]*

The decidedly prickly tone of the opening sentences of this letter, as well as its
content, illustrate Emily's enduring and passionate love for her brother Charles,
and perhaps reveal the aching jealousy Emily would undoubtedly have felt for
Elizabeth, who would now be living in Charles's home, something Emily had
wished to do since his appointment to Kefalonia. However, Emily recognises that
she must at least treat Elizabeth with respect and observe the niceties of family
etiquette – anything else would have incurred Charles's extreme anger – so she
finishes her letter in a domestically intimate tone, with details of the movements of
the Napiers in her immediate orbit.

[61] This letter is enclosed with one to Charles Napier, and there is no salutation – a detail
which seems to indicate Emily's dissatisfaction with Elizabeth. In square brackets,
there are two separate notes in pencil: [To Elizabeth Napier] and [en. 1st September
1828]. The previous letter in the set, to Charles Napier, is written from Dawlish on that
date.

Chapter 4 – It is wrong, wrong, wrong

Reservations about the marriage were much more strongly expressed by Elizabeth's own family. In particular, her son-in-law, Samuel Laing, widower of Elizabeth's daughter Agnes, felt that the marriage, and indeed the whole relationship, was entirely inappropriate:

> her intimacy too with Colonel Napier during Mr. Kelly's life was not right. I am far from suspecting that there was anything morally wrong in their intimacy, but it was imprudent and therefore wrong. It could only be explained that, from the great disparity in years, it was to be regarded as the intimacy between mother and son. But their marriage soon after the death of Mr Kelly deprived her friends of the benefit of this explanation of the footing they stood on during many of the latter years of his life. It is wrong, wrong, wrong.[62]

Two little items, each given a separate volume number in the British Library's Napier Papers,[63] give the full extent of Laing's disapproval. Each is about the size of an old-fashioned school exercise book, but I think they are both sheaves of letter paper in common use at the time, each with a flimsy cover of trimmed scrap paper. The sheets are neatly hand-sewn together down the centre fold. My theory is that Napier either made them himself or got someone in his household to make them. When he ran out of space in the the first one, another was made; only the first twelve pages of the second have been used. The British Library catalogue description of these two notebooks is helpful:

> Two notebooks containing annotated copies by Napier of correspondence with Samuel Laing of Orkney relating to an attempt by Laing to obtain money from him; 1827–1830. The letters, which include letters of Laing to Napier's first wife, Elizabeth, and one from him to Capt. Lewis Robertson, R.A., are preceded (49133, ff. 1–11) by an introductory note by Napier entitled 'An account of the nefarious attempt made by Samuel Laing of Orkney to swindle me out of a large sum of money' and followed (49134, ff. 11b–12) by a concluding note by Napier, 11 Feb. 1831.[64]

This chapter is largely based on the contents of the two notebooks, but it also includes quotes from Samuel Laing's autobiography and other material. The dispute lasted for over three years, and Napier's account gives full transcripts of his

---

[62] *The Autobiography of Samuel Laing of Papdale*, p. 139, edited and supplemented by further research by R P Fereday, 2000, Bellavista Publications, Kirkwall, Orkneys.

[63] BL Add MS 49133 and 49134.

[64] BL online catalogue page: https://bit.ly/Ch4CJNLaing

own and Laing's letters, totalling 34 double-sided folios,[65] so while there are direct quotations from both Napier's commentary, the correspondence, Laing's autobiography and other sources, most of this account is my summary.

Napier begins with some background information. In the early years of Laing's marriage to Agnes, née Kelly, her father, Captain Francis John Kelly, had been in debt. In fact he was on the point of being arrested for defalcation (defrauding) of the government, and Laing paid his debts in order to avoid, so Napier's account has it, the public humiliation of having his father-in-law go to prison. In 1815 Agnes' brother Henry ran up a gambling debt of £200, which Laing also paid.

Napier was under the impression that Laing was a wealthy man, with an income of between £3,000 and £4,000 per annum. Presumably the foundation for this belief lay in his friendship with Laing while they were students at the Royal Staff Corps barracks in Hythe,[66] and to outward appearances Laing was indeed from a comfortable Scottish family; his father Robert (1722–1803) had been a merchant and sometime provost[67] of Kirkwall, the capital of the Orkney Islands, as in later years was Samuel himself.

Laing's description of his relationship with Elizabeth from the time of his marriage to Agnes is not flattering. He wrote of having to subsidise Elizabeth's lavish expenditure and the expensive accommodation she chose. His autobiography, not originally intended for publication, was addressed to his children.

> I had often, too often, if prudence had governed Mrs Kelly, to make
> remittances, and to a great annual amount, for things which might have
> been dispensed with. To live in houses far beyond her income to live in,
> and in the neighbourhood of London, the most expensive of any county
> neighbourhood, was a ruinous taste … To provide for this thoughtless
> expenditure of your grandmother cost me many sleepless nights, and
> ruined me at that time. I should qualify the term thoughtless expenditure.
> She was astronomical in the way of doing extravagant things. Eco-
> nomical in the detail but extravagant in the object. Thus she would take
> a house of fifty or sixty pounds a year with an income not exceeding a
> hundred and twenty, and would be most economical in her shifts to live

---

[65] In the world of archives, handwritten historical manuscript pages are called folios, see the excellent Wikipedia explanation of their numbering here: https://bit.ly/Ch4Folio It might help to think of the 'front' of a page as the 'recto' and the flip side of that same page as the 'verso'. In detailing locations of quotations from the two volumes of Napier's notes on the case in question, I have given the recto folio number alone, and the verso folio number followed by the letter 'v'. For example f. 10 is the recto and f. 10v is the verso.

[66] *Curling Wisps & Whispers of History*, vol.. 1 p. 30.

[67] A provost in this context was the equivalent of an English mayor, the leader of the local administrative council. It is no longer in use except as an honorary title.

upon the residue. Every year during my marriage she would have us up to England, an annual expense altogether unsuited to our means, but the good sense of Agnes put an end to it. In these matters of self-gratification and whim she was a most inconsiderate woman. Peace be with her. She had much that was good and amiable in her character, mixed with a great deal of imprudence. Peace be over her failings.

She exerted a great influence over my fate. It was to live according to her ideas and wishes, to supply her [so that] year after year I found my means diminishing until at last I had nothing left.[68]

So Laing was blaming Elizabeth for his financial problems. Napier on the other hand records that Laing 'insisted on their having a house Where he and his family could be received,'[69] presumably because he wanted to be able to invite business or personal acquaintances back to a suitably well-appointed property in the London area, so the choice of house might be seen as actually being dictated by Laing's concern to keep up appearances. Each side blamed the other for an excessive awareness of social standing leading to overstretched finances. Napier adds that the assistance Laing gave the Kelly family 'was not without profit to himself; he often gave orders for purchases being made in London And sent to Orkney out of the money given to his family'. Laing was equally vehement about Elizabeth's relationship with Napier, returning to the subject a second time in his journal:

My own grown-up daughter might not approve of it, but there was no room to think ill of the attachment. It was their subsequent marriage, and that within a year of the death of her husband, and what was worse within a few days after receiving the intelligence of the death of Captain Henry Kelly [her] only son at Sierra Leone;[70] it was this which stamped the character and conduct of Mrs Kelly with an evil impression.[71]

Henry Kelly's death was announced in *The Star* newspaper of 12 February 1827, two full months before Elizabeth and Napier married. Under the heading 'Deaths' it simply said 'The 30th of November, Captain Henry Kelly, of the Royal African Corps, aged 29', so there were in fact six months between his death and his mother's marriage to Napier.

Despite Samuel Laing's harsh judgement of her, Elizabeth undoubtedly mourned her only son Henry, and his death must have been a terrible loss. No letters she herself wrote at this time have surfaced, but one written to Napier by her cousin

---

[68] As above, pp. 139–40
[69] BL Add MS 49133, f. 2
[70] See **Appendix 4 – The death of Henry Kelly (1797**–1826) p. 198.
[71] *Autobiography of Samuel Laing*, p. 149.

Anne Mantell, née Oakley, indicates how devastated Elizabeth was by this sad event:

> *My Dear Sir*
>
> *I cannot express to you, how deep the ... is, that I am under for my poor Friend. I know her affectionate heart, and I likewise know, that her expectations have been roused for the future success in life of her dear Henry, consequently another pang is added, the pang of disappointment, to those she is facing as a Mother, for the life of a beloved, and only Son. When you find a proper moment, will you apprise my dear Friend of my sympathy, and of my attachment that can know no end. _ I cannot just now, reply to her long letter, but, to you, I own, that I will hope, that if the bright prospect for her, that is more than hinted at, in the letter, should by this sad event, become overcast, that it will be only for a time.*
>
> *I have addressed you with the familiarity of an old acquaintance, and that because, I have long known you, as having generously interested yourself, in whatever has concerned one, so dear to me as Mrs. Kelly, believe me then my dear Sir, your very faithful friend*
>
> *Anne Mantell 1ˢᵗ 1827. _ [72]*

Dame Anne Mantell was the wife of Sir Thomas Mantell, who had done so much to try and help Thomas Oakley Curling both before he took his family to Van Diemen's Land and, once there, when help was required to progress his application for a land grant.[73] Elizabeth's hint to Anne of 'the bright prospect' was a reference to her forthcoming marriage. There are several letters from Anne to Napier, and others to Elizabeth in the British Library.

That Elizabeth and Napier went ahead with their marriage so soon after hearing of the death of Elizabeth's son Henry can only have been because Elizabeth had by now kept Napier waiting a year after her first husband's death, not to mention the twenty years' wait they had already endured. Her sixty-second birthday fell the month after their marriage. No amount of further waiting would bring Henry back, and if she married Napier she would not be alone while she mourned.

In this period some men were apt to see their womenfolk as commodities or financial assets. When Elizabeth had married Francis John Kelly[74] she would have brought with her a significant dowry. Her father was a successful shipping agent,

---

[72] BL Add MS 54541 f. 5.

[73] See *Curling Wisps & Whispers of History*, vol. 1, p. 202, **Appendix 10b – Commentary on the letter from Van Diemen's Land**.

[74] *Curling Wisps & Whispers of History*, vol. 1, p. 18.

banker and brewer, and he would have sought to ensure his daughter's financial security. But Kelly – who after the wedding had, of course, complete control over the couple's finances – had clearly not used the money wisely: by the time his own daughters were in their teens he was in financial difficulties and he would doubtless have seen that one route to resolving them was for his daughters to make good marriages. This could have been the reason he was so keen to invite the trainee officers of the Royal Staff Corps to his home.[75]

Samuel Laing clearly thought that of the three Kelly daughters, the youngest, Agnes, was the most attractive. His retrospective accounts of her in his autobiography are very romanticised.

> I well remember the last time she was in full health. She had walked to the summit of a hill about a mile from the house and, running down the steep descent, she appeared a bright emanation flying past, her white dress fluttering in the breeze, and the glow of exercise raised her beauty to something angelic …
>
> I never was worthy of Agnes. A being so pure, so single minded, so free from imperfection of temper, so artless, was too good for me, yet she loved me as entirely as I doted upon her.[76]

When he had returned from Spain after the battle of A Coruña in 1809, Laing had visited Francis John Kelly's ancestral home, Kelly House, in the village of Kelly, Devon, where Elizabeth and Agnes were staying. This was surely not a fortuitous coincidence, for F J Kelly had been estranged from his family for many years. Laing describes the inhabitants of Kelly House (still addressing the text to his children):

> The family was extraordinary and old fashioned in every way. Old Arthur Kelly, your grandfather's eldest brother, was the old English foxhunting squire of whom we read in Fielding's novels … He used to weigh himself regularly every day and kept himself closely to his proper weight which was very light, as he was a thin small-made old man … Your grandfather, his second brother was intended for the Church, the living of the Parish being in the gift of the family … Some trifling dispute between the brothers prevented this established arrangement of the second brother getting the Living, and Squire Kelly gave it to a stranger and repented all his life afterwards of having done so. The brothers never met again. Your grandfather went into the Army, married, left the service, and got the appointment of Barracks Master at Hythe, and this visit of your

[75] See *Curling Wisps & Whispers of History*, vol. 1, chapter 3.
[76] *The Autobiography of Samuel Laing of Papdale, 1780–1868*, pp. 136–7, R. P. Fereday, Bellavista Publications, 2000.

grandmother and his daughter to Kelly Hall was the first approach towards a reconciliation between the families.[77]

Francis John Kelly had commenced a university course at Wadham College, Oxford, in 1768[78] but had left without graduating. This could have been the root of the family disagreement. We do not know who engineered the 'reunion' of F J Kelly's family with his brother Arthur in 1809, but it had enabled Laing to assure himself that any claim which Kelly had made about his lineage was accurate. Laing travelled to his own family home in the Orkneys via London and returned a few weeks later.

'Samuel Laing of the City of Edinburgh' married on 21 March 1809 'Agnes Kelly of the parish of Kelly in the County of Devon, a minor' at Kelly parish church.[79] A large part of the reason for the Kelly visitation had clearly been to rebuild the connection with the Kelly ancestral home by an extended stay which would allow Agnes to claim that she was a resident of the village, and so be married there.

After their marriage, Laing had taken his bride to live in Edinburgh – where she died only three years later. Her mother Elizabeth and her eldest sister Eliza went to Edinburgh in the hope of seeing Agnes, but she had died by the time they arrived. Laing returned with Elizabeth and Eliza to their home in Aldborough Hatch, Essex, for a short time, presumably taking his two infant children with him. At some point soon after Agnes's death her sister, Mary Kelly, became a permanent part of the Laing household, taking on the upbringing of Laing's two children, daughter Elizabeth, just under three years old, and son Samuel, less than a year old when their mother died.

Agnes's father, Captain F J Kelly, was still working at this time as barrack master, the family having moved from Hythe to Romford but, judging from what Napier wrote, Kelly's salary was very low, so Laing on his marriage to Agnes became the financial anchor for the Kelly family. Doubtless Kelly had kept his monetary problems secret from Laing until after the marriage, and doubtless too Laing would have deeply regretted his own folly in falling for Kelly's deceit.

He may well have worshipped Agnes – but the powerless position of women in families of the time is brought into sharp relief by Laing's treatment of Elizabeth and her two surviving daughters years later, after her marriage to Napier. Laing would have wanted his sister-in-law Mary to continue to manage his household and to be a suitable companion for his daughter Elizabeth, then aged seventeen. But

[77] *The Autobiography of Samuel Laing*, pp. 134–5
[78] The Registers of Wadham College, Oxford, Part II, 1719–1871, Robert Barlow Gardiner, Bell & Sons, London, available on archive.org: https://bit.ly/Ch3KellyWadham
[79] Parish records of the church of St Mary the Virgin, Kelly, Devon, from FindMyPast online database.

Napier and Elizabeth had invited Mary to go and live with them in Kefalonia. Laing's strategy to prevent this seems to have been to alienate Mary from her mother by casting aspersions on Elizabeth's judgement in marrying a man so much younger than herself. Laing wrote to Mary:

> Mrs Kelly, now turned of three score, is surely entitled to judge herself of the suitable and the ridiculous in any step which she chooses to take in life. I have merely to take care that my children are not mixed up in intimacy with any connection, however near, who is considered by the world to have acted unsuitably or ridiculously. That the world will so judge of a woman past sixty years of age with children and grandchildren grown up marrying not a man of her own age, but a man in the flower of life, young enough to be her son, is unquestionable, and it is equally unquestionable that it is my duty as a parent to take care that my children have no [illegible] connecting them with what the world, perhaps very unjustly, finds unsuitable. ... I do not think it was right of you dear Mary, not to communicate this matter to me, so soon as you were acquainted with and commented upon it. I know it is a subject on which we could not speak without feeling very awkward and confused, but it is a matter which affected my children entering into the world, in as much as the estimation in which their grandmother is held in the world affects them. Elizabeth [Samuel's daughter] thinks that this letter is the first intimation you yourself have received of the matter; if it is, my dear Mary, I must as a parent say that the mother of grown-up daughters, and almost grown-up grandchildren, who is going to change her condition, even if everything is suitable, has no other consultation or announcement of her intention with them than is contained in this letter, shows such an ill-regulated mind, and such a disregard of a correct view of what is due to them, that I do not think it right my daughter and son should imbibe their principles of action, either from precept or example, and I will certainly not allow my daughter to be in communication with her grandmother in any way.[80]

Mary had initially been conciliatory with Napier, writing to him:

> How is it possible not to see some of your kindness to my mother, and not to feel grateful, she expects says [sic] to be happier with you than she has been for the last thirty years ... I am so little able to speak or write about this, but if you do make her happy may God bless you in future and forgive you the unhappiness you have caused her children.

---

[80] *Charles Napier, Friend and Fighter*, pp. 77–78, Rosamonde Lawrence, John Murray, 1952.

But perhaps as a result of Laing's diatribe she became antagonistic:

> It is very likely that seeing my mother with so many luxuries might make it more painful to put up with bare necessities ... I warn you Colonel Napier that I may be led to say and do more than you or my mother may like ... I asked Mr. Bishop [Elizabeth's doctor] if my mother was in a state to be spoken to on business; he was doubtful, and therefore I did not mention Mr Laing's letter ... I am not called on to speak to her and not at all more likely to kill her considering the small quantity of feeling you give [me] credit for perhaps it is necessary to remind you of this ... you may think I threaten, remember, Colonel Napier, you do the same yourself if you can fight I can talk, we may be both unequally unwilling to hurt my mother's feelings. I believe we had both better take the share that falls in the business quietly, you the ridicule, and me the shame.[81]

Two weeks after Elizabeth married Napier, Laing wrote to her with an enquiry concerning her recently deceased son Henry's pension and personal effects. Napier's transcription of what Laing wrote is as follows:

> *Papdale 25 April 1827. Mr. Laing requests to be informed whether it is the intention of M^{rs}. Kelly to claim as mother of the deceased Captain H Kelly the pension Allowed to the mother or sister otherwise unprovided for of an Officer dying on service as Mr. L proposes to Claim it in behalf of Miss Eliza Kelly if M^{rs}. Kelly does not intend to claim it for herself. W. Lockin of the Royal African Corps states that Captain Kelly left a will bequeathing all he was possessed of to his sister Miss E. Kelly so besides his Arrears of pay or allowances and his personal property in Africa Captn. Kelly as heir to his father was owner of what property or furniture plate books or other Articles were in the house at Cookham M^{r}. Laing requests an inventory of such property that he may be enabled to advise his sister in Law Whether to administer or not to the will of her deceased brother."[82]*

Laing presumed that as Henry was heir to his father's possessions everything in the Kelly household at the death of Francis John Kelly would have become Henry's. Because Henry had stipulated that his sister Eliza was to inherit all his possessions Laing seems to have made the further assumption that because he, Laing, was now the senior male member of the Kelly ménage, it was his right to oversee the administration of Henry's affairs. He had already created a rift between Elizabeth and Mary. Now he was attempting a similar strategy to manipulate Elizabeth's

---

[81] *Charles Napier, Friend and Fighter*, p. 78, Rosamonde Lawrence, John Murray, 1952.
[82] BL Add MS 49133, f. 10–f. 10v.

relationship with Eliza in what looks very much like an attempt to claim everything owned by the Kelly family following the death of its only two male members.

Napier wrote

> *as the Villain knew his mother in Law was going to marry me he knew she would be provided for, and consequently* <u>*could not*</u> *apply for a pension _ he also knew she had* <u>*no intention*</u>*. The things at Cookham were* <u>*all mine*</u> *except a few old books and it maybe two or three silver spoons _ now if out of the value of these (at most I should say five pounds) whatever that value was if my wife's due as widow is deducted that is to say* <u>*one third*</u> *and also what she gave Miss E. Kelly on her leaving us, in silver and linen, and also the full value paid [...] for a Gun left by her Brother and which would not bring one third of the sum if sold to any body else if these things are deducted from the value of what was left, this fellow would find the balance not for but against Miss Kelly and in my favour exclusive of a large debt due to me by Captn Kelly for which I have his [receipt] _ the whole letter he knew well enough was nonsense, and it was written entirely to afflict and wound a feeling and bleeding heart alas! It succeeded and he may thank Lord Napier and Sir Alexander Johnston whose cooler heads prevented my making him pay dearly for this letter. It is not impossible he may do so yet curse him. As to the Articles, Miss E. Kelly whose conduct was that of a gentlewoman, might have had them and may still if she and her mother choose to arrange it so _ I don't enter into the case neither shall this rascal.* [83]

By the last phrase Napier meant that the residue of Henry Kelly's will was no business of his, nor of Laing's. What it shows again, too, is the general acceptance at the time of the power men had over women, in that Laing clearly felt he was entitled to make Elizabeth hand over to him the whole of her deceased menfolk's estate. He would then have claimed the authority to manage them on behalf of his dead wife's sisters. We do not know whether Elizabeth replied to Laing's letter. Note that Napier had paid off a large debt for F J Kelly, who, as mentioned earlier, was clearly not capable of managing his financial affairs, having been similarly bailed out by his son-in-law Laing in earlier years.

In contrast to any scheming which had underlain the Kelly marriages, Napier's marriage to Elizabeth appears to have been entirely a love match. It could be said that as Elizabeth would have been in financial straits had he not married her he could just have been 'being kind', or she might have been seen to be ensnaring him;

---

[83]   BL Add MS 49133, f. 10v–f. 11.

but later correspondence with friends and family as well as the one letter we have from him to her indicate that he loved her very much. We do not know what Elizabeth's response to Laing's enquiry about her son's pension and personal effects was, but Laing's next gambit was on a much larger scale.

Three years after his marriage Napier received from Laing the first of no less than eleven letters claiming that Napier owed him all the money which he, Laing, had expended on keeping the Kelly family, from the time of his marriage to Agnes in 1809 until the Napier marriage: seventeen years in total. Napier, incandescent with rage, wanted to challenge Laing to a duel. He asked Sir Alexander Johnston to be his second, but Johnston, together with his (Johnston's) grandfather, Lord Napier, managed to discourage Napier from that course of action. Ultimately Napier recorded his gratitude to them, declaring them to have been right in their advice, for Elizabeth's and his daughters' sakes.

In 1829–30 Laing, with his daughter Elizabeth and son, young Samuel now both in their mid-teens, accompanied by Elizabeth Napier's daughter, Mary, were staying in Tours for an extended period. In conjunction with his harassment of Napier, Laing expressly forbade Elizabeth from making any contact with her grand-children; in a letter written from Tours, dated 1 November 1829, he wrote

> M*r*. Laing [*presents*] *compliments to Colonel Napier _ M*rs*. Napier intimates in a letter to Miss Mary Kelly that she intends coming to Tours in spring in Order to be near her and her Grand Children _For obvious reasons M*r*. Laing cannot permit his Children to have any communication or intercourse with M*rs* Napier _ if M*rs* Napier therefore had any intention of coming to Tours next spring M*r*. Laing must be under the necessity of removing his daughter during the Winter which her health and Other circumstances would make Extremely inconvenient at that season.* [84]

Napier's opinion of Laing was derogatory in the extreme. His commentary on Laing's letters is peppered with epithets such as 'villain', 'liar', 'scoundrel', 'blackguard'. About this letter he wrote

> This infamous letter I received at Cefalonia the 11 Dec*r*. 1829 While my poor wife was lying at the point of death as I thought at the time _ I had no answer to give but trying to shoot the villain if ever I came to England I therefore gave no ans*r*. [85]

It was perhaps unwise of Napier not to have sent a written reply to Laing at this point, but given that he was busy in his role as Resident of Kefalonia as well as

---

[84]   BL Add MS 49133 f. 11v.
[85]   BL Add MS 49133 f. 12v.

caring for his ill wife, he could be forgiven for finding silence the easiest way to deal with Laing's preposterous missive.

In his fifth letter Laing tells Napier that he has written to two of Elizabeth's relatives: Captain Lewis Robertson, a nephew of Kelly's; and Elizabeth's cousin, Anne Mantell née Oakley. Laing sent Napier a copy of the letter he had sent to Robertson, apparently doing this in order to indicate to Napier that he could make his accusations public if he so chose, thereby putting further pressure on Napier to pay up. The version of the saga which he sent Robertson differed significantly, though, from his own accounts to Napier. This is what he wrote to Robertson:

> *Colonel and M^rs. Napier on their marriage thought proper to break off and renounce all connection with my family. They neither intimated that this marriage was to take place nor communicated this marriage when it had taken place, and it is in fact only from public report that I understand my mother in Law is again married.* [86]

Laing acknowledged later in this letter that Robertson had already declined to get involved, but in any case, as Napier pointed out in his commentary:

> *The lying scoundrel wrote Mary Kelly then living with her mother and <u>before my marriage</u> that he would break off all connections with his Mother in law and tells her to tell us so and he himself says so see Letter No. 2.*

Attempting to be objective in my presentation of this saga, I have tried to see it from Laing's point of view. He might be said to have had a case in claiming that Napier's long-term association with Elizabeth, and its ultimate outcome of marriage, should have meant that Napier took on the responsibility for her finances over that period. However, whatever the ostensible dependence of Elizabeth on Laing, we know that it was Napier who had set the Kelly family up in Stone House in Cookham in 1819. This is corroborated by an item at the London Metropolitan Archives dated 1828, showing that the house insurance was paid by the owner, Edward Imber,[87] naming as a recent tenant Charles James Napier. In any case, Francis John Kelly was still alive, and although he had retired from service as a barrack master in 1817, he had an army pension, and ultimately it was he who was responsible for the upkeep of his household. Napier had, as he wrote in his commentary above, also paid off a debt of Kelly's, for which he had a receipt. Napier would not have wanted to embarrass Elizabeth by telling anyone about his generosity, although we know that Elizabeth had told her friends the Reverend and

---

[86] BL Add MS 49133 f. 16–f. 16v.
[87] LMA MS 11936/514/1082194 Records of the Sun Fire Office.

Mrs Packe something of it in their correspondence immediately prior to the wedding.[88]

The conclusion one is tempted to arrive at is that Laing firstly saw Napier's marriage to Elizabeth as a threat to his (Laing's) hold over the Kelly family finances, so at the very least he heavily influenced Mary and to a lesser extent her sister Eliza in how they should react to it; and secondly he saw it as an opportunity to deal with his own financial difficulties. Just as F J Kelly must have been secretive about his financial situation in 1760 when asking Thomas Oakley for Elizabeth's hand in marriage, Laing would have been careful to keep from Napier the fact that he was struggling financially.

R. P. Fereday, in his excellent commentary on Laing's autobiography, writes of the outcome of Laing's earlier financial ventures, highlighting not only his financial incompetence but also his tendency to blame other people for his losses:

> It is characteristic of Samuel Laing that, having pondered on the question whether he might have been rash in his business speculations, he decides that he was blameless. Instead he finds fault with his brother Gilbert, who had financed Samuel Laing's ventures not with a gift of capital but by arranging a bank loan. Malcolm, James and Gilbert took a more critical view of their younger brother's business exploits and the resulting debts for which Gilbert was guarantor. In the Laing Mss there is a letter from Malcolm to James, dated 7th August 1818, regretting the "rigid economy" which Gilbert had been forced to pursue after "the wild waste that has been made of his fortune during his short absence on the continent. So much is the loss sustained from a brother's commercial gambling or speculation in trade." Malcolm arranged the sale of Gilbert and Samuel's lands in Orkney, which raised £8,000. Even then Gilbert still had to raise a further £16,000 to cover losses incurred by Samuel's rashness, with little prospect of Samuel ever recompensing him.[89]

The stress which Laing's letters must have engendered in Elizabeth cannot but have had a profound effect on her health. She was already frail, and the mental distress on top of the major move to Kefalonia would have inevitably set her on the downward spiral from which her health never properly recovered. For Elizabeth and Napier, having waited so very long to marry, their joy must have been greatly marred by this tribulation.

On 15 February 1830, Laing, now in London, wrote to suggest that he and Napier meet for arbitration with Sir Ronald Ferguson and Sir Howard Elphinstone, both men retired from military service and who, as Laing said, 'stand High in Colonel

---

[88] See Mrs Packe's letter of 1 April 1827 to Elizabeth, BL Add MS 54541 ff. 15–16, p. 23.
[89] *The Autobiography of Samuel Laing*, p. 191, note 176.

Napier's own profession'.[90] Napier had initially agreed to attend this meeting, but then discovered that 'these two officers [had] electioneering connections with Laing's family!' Both Laing's nominated arbitrators were, said Napier, 'depending on [Laing] for a vote when Elections were rife!' Napier continued:

> *However it signified nothing as one don't refer to arbitration the attempt of an imbecile swindler to extort money*

and gave his reason for initially agreeing to the meeting:

> *indeed my having any correspondence with this fellow arose from Sir Alexander Johnston thinking it better to show him I was quite ready to let my conduct be known to any one Laing chose _ Alexander was right.[91]*

But Napier's withdrawal from the meeting annoyed Laing and drew a tirade from him, dated 6 November 1830, Here is a flavour:

> I defy you to find a man of honor or of Common sense who will say upon reading my letter of 20 October and your letter of 24th that it is not a proposal of a reference on my part and an acceptance of it on your part. If this was not your meaning what was your meaning? Was it that there should be a reference on my part but not on yours? that the reciprocity should be all on one side? Are you afraid to put your honor or your purse in the hands of such men as Sir Ronald Ferguson and Sir Howard Elphinston? What is it you would be at? ... I cannot for a moment suppose that you are seeking to avoid a fair reference of a claim of honor to Gentlemen of the highest professional and private Character still less can I suppose that you are attempting to sneak out of a reference you had accepted of by endeavouring to twist your acceptance into something which you Cannot give a meaning to yourself.[92]

Napier wrote four formal responses to Laing's first nine letters. The opening of the fourth, dated 8 November 1830, began:

> *The very near connection which subsists between your family and mine in consequence of my being married to your mother in Law, has made me hitherto, as you must have seen, most anxiously abstain (in hopes of inducing you to do the same towards me) from using towards you any expression which could in any way either wound or irritate your feelings.*

---

[90] BL Add MS 49133, f. 18v.
[91] BL Add MS 49134, f. 1v
[92] BL Add MS 49134, f. 8–8v.

and ended:

> *I am at last compelled by a respect for my own Character to desire that all farther [sic] correspondence between you and me, on this subject, shall cease and that you will, if you really believe that you Have any pecuniary claim against me seek for <u>such redress as you may think proper</u>. C Napier*

In other words Napier called Laing's bluff. By the phrase 'seek such redress as you may think proper' Napier probably meant 'either take me to court or meet me in a duel'. Napier must have been pretty certain that Laing would not wish to do either: the first would have involved substantial financial outlay on Laing's part, and in the second he would probably have come off worst and might even have lost his life.

Still, however, Laing persisted. Lord Napier and his grandson Sir Alexander Johnston had kept a close eye on the progress of the dispute over the three years it lasted. Napier wound up the saga thus:

> *After this letter the fellow sent two more by the same post which, in Lord Napier's presence, I returned in an Envelope with the following letter written from his Lordship's dictation being myself too angry to write without letting some offensive expression escape, which my friends Lord Napier & Sir Alexander Johnston said ought not to be.*
>
> London 11 Novr. 1830
>
> Sir
>
> *I refer you to my last letter to show you that I have already declined all farther correspondence. I therefore beg leave to return your two letters (which I received this morning) <u>unopened.</u>*
>
> C Napier

In Napier's introduction to his record of the dispute he had written

> *I have made this sketch of the dishonest conduct of M^r. Laing (Why I call a fellow M^r. who has neither the honesty of a man nor the manners of a Gentleman I know not.) in Great haste while people are talking so that it is without Arrangement and merely a jumble of facts to keep a memorial that at some future period I shall put in order And if the ruffian gives me any more trouble I will publish, and oblige him*

to hide his head in his nest in the Orkneys which I suppose contains society of the <u>same stamp</u> or he can find but few to speak to.[93]

Contrary to Napier's supposition Laing was in fact an influential character in the Orkneys, remembered for significant contributions to the Kirkwall communities, including improvements to the administration of agriculture, increase in production of kelp and the foundation of a herring business. He had clearly had sufficient wealth at some point to purchase the island of Eday to add to the Laing estate, 'He later claimed, very optimistically, that by owning the whole of Eday and managing it more efficiently he raised the total rental of his Orkney property to £950 a year.'[94]

Napier's final comment spells out why the dispute had worried him so much:

11 Feb[ry] 1831 London

Here closes my hurried record of this nefarious attempt of Samuel Laing to rob me of my property (for his Claim amounted to all I possess!) it was also an attempt to harass my wife to death, and as in the first instance she was necessarily spoken to, to know if she had given Bond for money and how the matter stood, it nearly succeeded damn him I leave the rest of this matter now with him _ he of course does not mean to risk his carcass in a duel after a lapse of 3 months so I conclude that the Affair is at rest while <u>I live</u>. at my death the villain will try some horrible trick Against his Mother or if she is dead against my Children which I trust this statement will assist in baffling _[95]

After Samuel's eldest brother Gilbert's death the next Laing brother, Malcolm, had taken over the business. He in turn had died, in 1818, and as their brother James was engaged in business with the West Indies that left Samuel to take over the family businesses in Scotland. This included, as well as the lead mines and sheep farming, a kelp enterprise and a herring factory which James had encouraged Samuel to set up with the intention of supplying trade to the West Indies. However, he did not thrive as a businessman, and in 1834 he decided to sell much of his Scottish holdings:

On the Drontheim Fiord [Trondheimsfijord], Norway – 4th October 1834 – This a new scene in my life. Finding it impossible to keep my estate together, the interest of the debts accumulating and a sale of the whole or of the greater part of it necessary, I went up to Edinburgh after my

---

[93] BL Add MS 49133, f. 8–f. 8v.
[94] *Samuel Laing of Papdale, Orkney, a Kelp-Laird's Political Ambitions*, 1824–1834, R P Fereday, https://bit.ly/Ch3LaingFereday
[95] BL Add MS 49134 ff. 11–12.

daughter's marriage, settled with my agents that they should have full powers to sell under the superintendence of Mr. Cunningham, Advocate, and of my son, without any interference, providing they pay me £240 a year until the estate is sold. I have taken my £60 per quarter of a year, and in order to be out of the way of any interference with their operations, I came over to Norway in June.[96]

To outward appearances, both at the time and in the longer view of present-day historians, Samuel Laing was a person of standing in the Orkney community, having been provost of Kirkwall and having, as mentioned above, introduced improvements in the local economy which provided lasting benefits. Despite the upheavals which his personal interactions caused in his private life, Laing is well remembered in Orkney.

But from the time of his daughter Elizabeth's marriage in 1834, when he was himself aged fifty four, his career took a completely different turn. He became a successful travel writer, based mostly in Norway.

Samuel Laing is remarkable for two very different careers: first he was a liberally-minded, public-spirited and popular provost of Kirkwall whose innovations in farming and fishing did much to lay the foundations for 19th century economic prosperity in Orkney. His own success in financial terms was less secure, and when his landed estate ran into difficulties, Laing left Orkney to follow a quite separate second career as a traveller, writer and translator of Norse sagas.

His agricultural experiments were among the earliest in Orkney. At Stove in Sanday he removed cottars from the land of the main farm as a preliminary to growing new crops and introducing improved breeds of cattle and sheep. The displaced cottars were resettled on self-contained crofts adjacent to the farm. His scheme was widely copied, and large farms with peripheral crofting communities became a common pattern of settlement throughout the islands. The attempt to introduce Merino sheep to Stove was less successful.

Laing is also remembered as the founder of the herring fishing in Stronsay. [97]

---

[96] *The Autobiography of Samuel Laing*, p. 162.
[97] As above, p. 1, Foreword by W P L Thomson. Orkney historian.

Chapter 5 – Your little chicks

As for Anastasia and her daughters, according to Priscilla Napier and Rosamond Lawrence[98] Charles's original intention was that the girls should stay with their mother after his marriage; but Anastasia had other ideas. Both Priscilla Napier and Rosamond Lawrence were connected to the Napier family, the one by marriage and the other by descent, and they both relay a story, but differing on the detail of when it happened. According to the story, Napier was on board a vessel taking him away from the island when Anastasia is reputed to have put her two offspring into a boat and pushed it out towards the passing ship. She herself disappeared, whether back to the mountain recesses of the island or further afield is not known.[99] Charles and Elizabeth had no alternative but to take on the care of the girls, and they became utterly devoted parents. It is possible Anastasia realised that her daughters would have far better lives with the Napiers than she could provide; however, she must also have felt that to stay in Argostoli with her daughters, once Elizabeth arrived with Napier and they were living in his Argostoli house, would have been emotional gymnastics she could not tolerate.

Elizabeth was won over sooner or later to having Napier's two daughters, Susan Sarah and Emily Cefalonia, as part of the family. In fact it is more than likely, once it was apparent that the girls' birth mother refused to take responsibility for them, that Elizabeth would have needed no persuasion; Napier had already told his sister Emily that Elizabeth had tried persistently in earlier years to persuade him to marry someone younger so that he could have children, and the precedent of Napier's sister Emily's experience showed that when a mother, for whatever reason, was unable to cope, a child could be successfully brought up by a loving relative. However, Elizabeth was not a young woman and had always been of frail constitution. So it was a tall order to expect her to take on the upbringing of Susan

---

[98] *Charles Napier, Friend and Fighter*, Rosamonde Lawrence, John Murray, 1952. Charlie Napier, Secretary of the Clan Napier, writes that Lady Rosamond Lawrence's 'full maiden name was Jane Rosamond Napier, the daughter of Colonel Edward Napier and Martha Louisa Buddicom. She was born on 19 July 1879 and died on 16 February 1976. [She] was married to Sir Henry Lawrence, a member of the Indian Civil Service. She married him in 1914 and lived in India and wrote a journal called "Indian Embers" which gives her genealogy.' Rosamond was descended in the direct line from William, 7th Lord Napier, who was the half-brother of George Napier, father of Charles James Napier: 'so Rosamond was a distant cousin of CJN and when she lived in India, she actually lived in the house that CJN built when he was out there. She was apparently very proud of her connections to CJN, hence the book she wrote.'

[99] Priscilla Napier writes extensively about Napier's relationship with Anastasia in *Revolution and the Napier Brothers 1820–1840*, pub. Michael Joseph, 1973; see her index for nine separate references.

Sarah (scarcely a toddler when Elizabeth arrived in Kefalonia) and a newborn babe, Emily Cefalonia.

The solution was radical: the children would be sent to a boarding school. Napier, a passionate believer in education for all, girls as well as boys, was anxious to make long-term educational provision for them, and he did this by setting up a girls' school. He would certainly have consulted Elizabeth for advice on how to do this. Having researched possibilities, he received the following letter from a Quaker, William Allen, who ran a teacher training programme in Lindfield, Sussex.[100] Allen used the Quaker conventions, addressing Napier as 'Friend', not using the 'pagan' names of months, and eschewing the use of 'you' and 'yours' in favour of the older 'thee', 'thou' and 'thine'.

Near London 16 of 8 month 1827 [101]

My dear Friend

*I have great pleasure in recommending to thy kind notice & patronage ---- Dickon [sic] & Henrietta his wife who I think are calculated to be eminently useful to thee in the formation of Schools they have learned our system at the Borough Road and Henrietta is ready to establish a Girls School immediately under thy patronage two years ago Lord Bathurst sent out at my request to Corfu 125 copies of Scripture Lessons in modern Greek in large sheets & 500 of a smaller edition. Sir Frederick Adam could supply thee with them I am most desirous that their contents should be riveted in the minds of the young Greeks, as the most precious Lessons of Religion & morals that this world ever saw_*

I wish you could have Schools of Industry like mine at Lindfield I enclose a prospectus and also a copy of my Colonies at Home printed at the Press of my School of Industry. Pray read it attentively and say whether some modification of the plan of a 3 acre farm in page 22 might not be useful in Cephalonia_ would it be too much trouble to send me information on the following points

---

[100] *William Allen Quaker Friend of Lindfield 1770–1843*, Margaret Nicolle, smallprint, Haywards Heath, West Sussex, 2001. See also William Allen's publication *Colonies at Home* ... https://bit.ly/Ch15WlmAllenColoniesbk

[101] 16 August 1827. Quakers at this period did not use the names of months because of their connection with ancient gods. Some present-day Quakers still prefer the numbers to the names. 'Friend' was, and occasionally still is, the formal mode of address for Quakers to people whom they do not know, as well as in more informal settings between themselves.

*What kind of food do the poor live upon and what weight of it does
each Person consume on an average day*

*Are the articles mentioned in my "Colonies etc" grown in the
Island or could they be made to grow*

Would Cows, sheep Goats or Pigs thrive

Would the cultivation of Cotton be profitable

Are there any who understand spinning & weaving

*What weight is afforded by any given number of square yards in
the articles employed by the natives as food*

What is the nature of the soil

Is land cheap or dear

*Would it be possible to find a liberal native who would purchase
an Estate of 150 acres & establish a village of 50 three acre Farms
as described on page 22 of Colonies at Home[102] in such a village the
all important points of a moral & virtuous education might be secured*

*I do hope that thou wilt try to find time to reply to this Letter. I
send the Reports of our School Society & of our Prison Discipline
Society and beg thy acceptance of the following Tracts as Specimens
of the work in my Schools of Industry viz*

Dialogues in Infant Schools do pray establish one

Christs Spirit a Christians Strength

Sabbath Reading No. 1

Gleanings No. 1

*I purpose to send out by Dickson a number of Greek Testaments
for the use of the Schools*

I remain with cordial attachment

Thine sincerely

Wm Allen

Napier annotated this letter, '*From William Allen the Quaker, 16 August 1827*'.

Mr George Dickson and his wife Harriet were duly appointed teachers at Napier's new school, and arrived the following spring.

Towards the end of the year 1827, Napier still had a lot of faith in the potential of the Maltese Colony project:

---

[102] *Colonies at Home*, William Allen, printer Charles Greene, Schools of Industry, Lindhurst, Sussex, available free on Google books: https://bit.ly/Ch3ColoniesatHome

I feel proud of this Colony: it is being of use to our kind to have taken three hundred starving people, fed them, and made them turn a desert into a garden. Napier to his sister Louisa_ 24th Sept. 1827 [103]

As we know from Elizabeth's letter to her sister-in-law Emily, dated 8 September 1827, Napier had been very unwell at this period and even had to submit to surgery; but as ever he overcame the illness and thought only of his work projects.

Napier's relationship with his mistress Anastasia has been mulled over by a succession of biographers, particularly her abandonment of her two daughters when Susan was only a year old and her sister a matter of months. The story that Anastasia put them in a boat and pushed them out to sea to intercept the vessel on which Napier was aboard is highly dubious. Two letters from Emily Napier to her brother shed a little light:

Dawlish 18th Nov^r [1827]

... by the way Anastasula's patriarchal ideas have brought about "a consumation devoutly to be wished" & I am delighted to think you have your chicks all to yourself for I hope my little namesake will soon make herself sufficiently agreable to be admitted into company with her sister._ You may guess how provoking your caution on public affairs is to us who already know the upshot or rather down-shot of the Armistice & are dying with impatience to know the probable consequence of our glorious victory at Navarino! People are much divided here in their sentiments. [104]

Emily offers a little straw of insight into Anastasia's thinking. But what was meant by the phrase, 'patriarchal ideas'? Anything which Anastasia said to Napier by way of explanation or excuse for abandoning her children has to be seen, however, in the context of her chosen path as a Greek rebel. She would have realised that with Napier and his new wife her daughters were bound to have all the advantages of a British colonial family's upbringing: greater stability, better education, the protection of a distinguished military family.

Fought in the Bay of Navarino, in the Ionian Sea, in October 1827, the major naval battle between on the one side the allied forces of Britain, France and Russia and on the other the Ottoman and Egyptian forces was a turning point in the effort to ensure Greek independence from the Ottoman Empire. The British squadron was

---

[103] Quoted in an unpublished thesis submitted for an MA degree by Audrey Harrison Heron, 1952 *The Administration of Col. Charles James Napier in the Island of Cefalonia. 1822–1830*, Institute of Historical Research, University of London, Senate House. No reference given.

[104] BL Add MS 54529 ff. 7–11.

led by Vice-Admiral Sir Edward Codrington. 'It was the last major naval battle in history to be fought entirely with sailing ships, although most ships fought at anchor. The Allies' victory was achieved through superior firepower and gunnery.'[105] If you look again at the map of Greece, Fig. 1, p. 7, you will see how close Navarino (now called Pylos) is to the Ionian Islands. In fact the smallest of the Ionian Islands, Kythira, is 75 nautical miles south-east from Pylos. The battle would have been the talk of the islands for many days afterwards. There are several paintings of the battle, done by British, French and Russian artists. Fig. 7 was executed by George Philip Reinagle, who accompanied Admiral Codrington's British squadron through the Mediterranean and was an eye-witness at the battle.

Fig. 7.   The Battle of Navarino, 20 October 1827 [106]

---

[105] https://en.wikipedia.org/wiki/Battle_of_Navarino
[106] Image from https://www.wikiart.org/en/george-philip-reinagle – see also https://collections.rmg.co.uk/collections/objects/12115.html

Chapter 6 – Selling boys like a flock of sheep

Back in England, after the failed adventure to Van Diemen's Land, Jane Rowcroft, formerly the widow Jane Curling, and her second husband, Charles Rowcroft, were trying to re-establish themselves in their home country. In September 1827, eighteen months after their repeat marriage[107] in Surrey, they bought from a Mr Wall a boarding school in Streatham, together with the existing pupil list. No doubt Charles and Jane had discussed ways of educating the younger Curling children while also making a living which would support the family, and it appears that they had arrived at the idea of buying a school to finance the project. In addition to any monies remaining from the sale of Rockthorpe in Van Diemen's Land, funds were available from Jane's mother, who had died in 1822, bequeathing her daughter Jane £1,000. Rowcroft was a named beneficiary in his father Thomas Rowcroft's will of 1826, but the will was not proved until 1835,[108] so the couple were wholly reliant on Jane's financial reserves. The reason Thomas Rowcroft's will took so long to prove was almost certainly a consequence of the unusual circumstances of his death. He was a colourful character in his own right, and his story adds significant background to his son Charles's saga:

> Thomas Rowcroft (1768?–1824) ... was educated in France and had been in the three great oceans' before he was twenty-one, seeing Ascension, the Cape, Madagascar, Mauritius, Bourbon, India, and Sumatra. He was involved in Young's abortive New Holland scheme and in an unsuccessful trading venture in the far east. (He claimed to have lost £48,000.) On his return to England in the 1780s, he joined the family business, and advanced himself in the City. He was elected Alderman for Walbrook in December 1802, held the office until 1808, and worked actively for public charities during this time.
>
> Rowcroft's business was based largely on the naval stores trade with Russia, and in 1810 he suffered a great reverse when, furthering Napoleon's continental blockade, the Russian Government impounded British ships and cargoes. He strove unsuccessfully for the next six years to obtain compensation for himself and fellow merchants for this action, and he claimed to have lost some £300,000 as a result of it.
>
> With his business failed, and disappointed at not having been chosen either Lord Mayor or M.P. for the City, Rowcroft sought a diplomatic post. He asked the 2nd Earl Liverpool for the Consulship at Constantinople in October 1817, who replied that this was not in his gift;

---

[107] For details of Charles Rowcroft's original marriage to Jane. See *Curling Wisps & Whispers of History*, vol. 1, p. 122–123.

[108] TNA PROB 11/1711/475 Probate copy of the will of Thomas Rowcroft.

and in February 1819 he offered himself for service in Sierra Leone. In the end, the Government sent him as Consul to Peru, where he died on 11 December 1824 after being shot by a sentry in Bolivar's army whose challenge he ignored.[109]

From the above quotation we can deduce that there was probably very little, if any, estate for Thomas Rowcroft's executors to distribute to his beneficiaries when the will was eventually proved.

Now we come to an episode with distinctly Dickensian overtones. A Mr Evans had placed his six-year-old son Robert in the Streatham school while Mr Wall still owned it. Mr Evans had then set out for Calcutta, leaving his former landlord, solicitor Mr Thomas Carter, as his agent. Rowcroft, in two letters, written 6 and 17 September, asked Mr Carter to visit little Robert. But Carter replied that Messrs Wall and Rowcroft had misunderstood his position regarding Mr Evans: while Evans had given Carter power of attorney over a sum of money which Evans would send to Carter on his arrival in India, which was to be used to pay Evans' various creditors, including the school fees owed to Mr Wall, Carter saw his arrangement with Mr Evans as restricted to the administration of financial matters and not extending to taking an interest in Robert.

Rowcroft was naturally anxious about payment of Robert's school fees. Mr Carter assured him in a letter of 19 September that he had every expectation that payment would be forthcoming from Evans, as he, Carter, had 'the fullest reliance on his honour and respectability'. Carter said he had 'no funds or securities in my hands to enable me to make any advance, or to take any responsibility on myself'.

The story was followed in various newspapers between 22 and 30 December, and Rowcroft himself ensured publication on 27 December 1827 in the *Morning Chronicle* of correspondence on which he based his case. [110]

> On receiving this letter from Mr Carter, I wrote to him the following letter:-

[109] *Thomas Rowcroft's Testimony and the 'Botany Bay' Debate*, Alan Frost, journal article, *Labour History* No. 37 (Nov 1979) pp. 101–7, pub. Liverpool University Press. A footnote to this article says 'I have taken these details from the Rowcroft letters cited in the following notes. Miss Betty Masters, Deputy Keeper of the Corporation of London Records, has kindly supplied some information. https://www.jstor.org/stable/27508387

[110] All of the quotations in this chapter from this point are taken from a lengthy article which Charles Rowcroft succeeded in getting published in the London *Evening Standard* of Friday 28 December 1827.

"Sir_ I have received with very great surprise, and pain, your letter of the 19th inst.; and I lose no time in communicating to you, as a friend of Mr. Evans, the position of his son. It is impossible for me to provide board, education, clothes, and all other necessaries for the son of a gentleman who is a total stranger to me, and who is now on his way to a distant part of the globe, without having some responsible agent to refer to. Neither will my means allow me to incur such risk, nor can I be expected thus to add the total charge of another member to my family. Under these circumstances, painful as the decision is, I beg leave to acquaint you that I cannot provide for Mr. Evans's son: I should be happy to receive any information which your kindness to Mr. Evans, or to his child, may prompt you to give, which might justify me in taking charge of him.

I am, sir, your obedient humble servant,

CHARLES ROWCROFT

To this letter I received no reply until the 4th of October. In the mean time I made inquiries of all whom I supposed to have any knowledge of the child or his parents. From a lady whose name I do not like unnecessarily to obtrude on public attention, I received the following account of Mr. Evans, the father of the child; namely – that the child was an illegitimate child of this Mr. Evans; that she was present in the house when Mr. Evans brought the child to place him under the care of Mr. Wall and Mr. Chervet (Mr. Chervet being at the time, or about to be, a partner of Mr. Wall's); that she, knowing Mr. Evans, called Mr. Chervet aside, and represented to him the imprudence of taking charge of this child, as she could assure him there was no chance of receiving payment.[111]

Mr Wall told Rowcroft that 'A Mr Gatfield of Snowhill, who deals in Leghorn hats, and a Mr. Walker of Broad Street, a ship-broker, are related to [Robert Evans] by marriage'. So Rowcroft wrote to Mr Gatfield, from whom he received the following reply:[112]

"London, Oct.3, 1827

"Sir,_ In reply to yours, you may act according to your own discretion, as regards Robert Evans; neither father or child have any claim upon me, but quite the reverse. How Mr Evans could leave England with a child

---

[111] *Morning Chronicle*, 27 December 1827, p. 3.

[112] The quotation marks at the beginning of first lines of paragraphs are Rowcroft's own, and indicate that he was quoting from original documents.

apparently so destitute, I cannot imagine; but if it be any encouragement, I do believe that eventually the child's expenses would be defrayed; but, observe, I undertake no responsibility. I reply to yours as a matter of courtesy, otherwise I would not have answered the letter.

"I am, sir, yours obediently

"CHARLES GATFIELD, Jun.[113]

Rowcroft became increasingly alarmed. It looked as though he had been saddled with a boy abandoned by his parents, with no-one in England who was willing to take responsibility for him or to pay his school fees. On 5 October Rowcroft received a reply from Carter, who on the one hand said that the boy's father owed him £200 and on the other assured Rowcroft again,

'I have a firm reliance upon his honour, and feel assured, if the remittance which his mother promised to send to England does not arrive before he gets to India, that he will promptly [send it] himself. I assure you I feel no anxiety for fear of losing my money, and you may feel equally satisfied, in my opinion.'

Mentioning Robert's mother, and implying that she was already in India, must have confused Rowcroft, given the earlier information that the boy was illegitimate.

From our vantage point 200 years later, it would seem that Carter and Wall were both either exceptionally naïve in taking Evans' word that he would remit payment on arrival in India, or they were exceptionally devious in attempting to persuade Rowcroft that he was unreasonable not to trust the word of a man whom they told him was 'honorable' – and by implication not to trust them. Carter wrote: '

My advice is, for you to wait till Mr. Evans has an opportunity of remitting from India; it cannot add much to your debt; and I think, under the circumstances, you should do so, and not place the child in a situation which may attach disgrace to him through his life, and misery to his parents.'

Rowcroft could have been waiting for payment for as much as a year had he followed Wall's and Carter's advice and waited for Robert Evans' school fees payment to arrive. First, 'The voyage from England to India via the Cape of Good Hope took six months at least, and you might have another three or four months of traveling to do before reaching your final destination.'[114] Then on his arrival in India Mr Evans would have had to request his bank in India to transfer funds to England, which would have necessitated awaiting the journey of a letter of

---

[113] *Morning Chronicle*, 27 December 1827, p. 3.
[114] *Passage East*, p. 1, Ian Marshall and John Maxtone-Graham, Howell Press, 1998.

authority from India to England. Did Wall and Carter really assume that Rowcroft would have the resources to take on a debt of 30 guineas[115] for as much as a year? Both of them said they would fund the child themselves but were not in a position to do so; Carter gave his own large family as his reason, but did not consider the possibility that Rowcroft might be in a similar position. From a twenty-first-century viewpoint, it seems ridiculous that Rowcroft, or Wall before him, could have thought it sensible to run a business such as a private boarding school without making advance payment for its pupils a requirement, and I am further astonished that Rowcroft could have taken on the business without reviewing thoroughly, in advance of his purchase, the accounts of the seller, Mr Wall.

Rowcroft's response to Carter's letter graphically illustrates his dilemma and reveals new levels of concern, naming a family of four further children whose fees like Evans's were unpaid:

Streatham, Oct 5, 1827.

Sir,_ I received your letter of the 4th instant this morning. I assure you I feel bitterly the state in which the improvident neglect of his parents has left little Evans; and I regret to state that there are four other children in this house (the Fitzpatricks) in a precisely similar state of destitution. I have nine children of my own family to support; and I leave it to the consideration of any reasonable man, whether I can be expected to add the burthen of the entire support, of clothing, subsisting, and providing for five individuals who have no claim on me. For the last five weeks I have endeavoured to find out the relations and connexions of the parents of this poor little boy; I have provided food and shelter for him, as a duty, during this period; but the same duty irresistibly impels me to regard the welfare of my own family. If my means would permit, I would willingly continue to contribute to his support; but I am not able to do so. I do not wish to make a profit from this child in distress; if my bare expenses, my mere outlay of money, were secured to me, I would willingly wait for six months, rather than place him in the hands of the parish. This I would do with pleasure, but more is not in my power._

I am, sir, your obedient humble servant

CHAS. ROWCROFT

To T. W. Carter, Esq., Maidstone, Kent.[116]

Seven weeks later, having received no reply, Rowcroft wrote again to Carter:

---

[115] Today's equivalent, given on the Bank of England Calculator site, would be £2681.74.
[116] *Morning Chronicle*, 27 December 1827, p. 3.

Sir_ I am so reluctant to place little Robert Evans in the hands of the parish officers, that I write again to you as the agent of Mr. Evans, on this painful subject. I have refrained thus long from taking this step, in the hope that something might transpire to prevent its necessity, and I write to you now to give the poor little boy the last chance in his favour. Already I have had, within three months, five failures in my school; this child makes the sixth; I have nine children of my own family to provide for; to provide for more is not a question for consideration; it is impossible for me to do so; and I cannot refrain from expressing my surprise that you should expect me to incur a debt for the support of a man's child of whom I know nothing, and whom I never saw, when I can hardly support my own. I am sorry to trouble you thus often on so painful a subject, but I feel that it would be a neglect of duty were I not to write to you, as the agent of Mr Evans, relative to his child. And I earnestly hope that you may feel yourself justified in preventing this sad calamity to the son of your friend.

I am, sir, your obedient servant,

CHARLES ROWCROFT.

P.S._ Can you inform me where the mother of this child resides? or can you give me the address of any person who, knowing Mr Evans, would take any interest in his child?[117]

Again, Rowcroft received no reply. In the course of his enquiries he had discovered that the child had lived for a time at Shorne, so he wrote to the minister of the parish church, outlining the problem. He said that if he could not find someone to take responsibility for the child he would be forced to hand the boy over to the parish workhouse and asked if the vicar knew of any of the boy's relatives living in Shorne. The Reverend Staines, replied:

Rochester, Dec. 11, 1827.

Sir_ The boy, respecting whom you have kindly interested yourself, we can only learn was born at an inn in Rochester, then taken to London by the mother and afterwards placed as a nurse-child with a poor person at Shorne, whose name is Eastdown, who says he knows nothing of the mother, except her bringing the child to them, and taking him away.

Eastdown complains that the parents are indebted to him 3L., which they promised should be sent from India. We cannot find that the boy has

---

[117] As above.

any relations in Shorne, nor have we been able to obtain any information which can lead to the parents.

    I am your obedient servant,

W. T. STAINES.[118]

Rowcroft concluded that if Mr Evans was not even prepared to pay the wet-nurse for her care of his son it was unlikely that he would pay the school fees. He then had to decide whether he could commit himself to taking the boy into his family. He decided that he could not, because

> after many waverings, after many times speaking to the assistant overseer (Mr Whithall) of this parish, I was obliged to submit to the hard law of necessity, and to place in the hands of the parish officers a child whom my straitened means would not allow me to support, I gave the letter from the Rev. Staines to Mr. Whithall, to show to Mr Laing, the magistrate of this parish: Mr. Whithall reported to me that Mr Laing thought I should return the child to Mr Wall from whom I had received him.

Rowcroft did as he was advised, sending the boy to Mr Wall in the care of two of his school ushers, Mr Curling[119] and Mr Dobson.

  On Friday 21 December 1827 a newspaper article reported that Mr Wall went to Marylebone police office, taking the boy with him:

> On Friday week [Friday 21 December], Mr Wall, of Cirencester-place, Fitzroy-square, appeared at this office with a boy about six years old, and stated that he had formerly kept a boarding-school at Streatham, but had sold the establishment with the pupils four months ago, to a Mr. Rowcroft.[120]

Over the following thirteen days newspapers around the kingdom syndicated reports of the case, heard in 'Marylebone Police Office'.[121] Wall had resorted to official complaint, but without reference to Rowcroft, so when Wall first brought it to public notice he did so without Rowcroft's knowledge.

  The *Belfast Commercial Chronicle* reported that the magistrate, Mr Rawlinson,

---

[118] As above.

[119] This could have been Edward (aged 20 at the time), Henry (18) or Charles (17). Schools were usually run on a system of senior pupils becoming assistant teachers, known as 'monitors' 'ushers' or 'masters'. We learn from later letters that Edward was working as an attorney's clerk in 1828 and he may have been working there in 1827 too which would indicate that the 'usher' was one of his brothers.

[120] *Kentish Weekly Post* or *Canterbury Journal* – Tuesday 1 January 1828.

[121] Buildings called Magistrates' Courts were being introduced in this period, but generally magistrates heard cases either in their own homes or in local police offices.

understood what it was to sell the good-will of a school; but having never heard before of selling boys like a flock of sheep asked if a list of them was given to Mr Rowcroft when the bargain was made. Mr. Wall said 'Their names were all enumerated including this boy (Robert Evans)'.[122]

From those newspaper reports we see that Robert Evans had been placed with Mr Wall six months previously, confirming that he had joined the school in June 1827, long before the Rowcrofts took over. Mr Wall relates that not one of the people who might reasonably have been expected to take an interest in little Robert – his father's agent, Mr Carter, and the two family relatives, Messrs Gatfield and Walker – was prepared to do so. Mr Wall therefore 'had no alternative but to place the child in the workhouse, where, with proper information, the parish officers were willing to receive him'.

The magistrate, Mr Rawlinson,

> considering it a very unfit situation for the child, and that the parish ought not to receive such a burden, desired Mr. Wall to bring the child near the Bench, that he might ask him some questions.
>
> The poor little fellow, who is but six years old, had listened attentively to what was said. As his case appeared to become more unfavourable, his tears increased, and when Mr. Rawlinson asked him, "Why my good little boy, don't you spend your holidays at Streatham?" he could [barely] say in answer "Because Mr. Rowcroft said I must go to Mr. Wall's". He said that Mr. Curling and Mr. Dobson, two of the ushers, brought him to town; Mr Dobson waited at the corner of the street, Mr. Curling pushing him and his bundle into the house, and he saw him run away.
>
> Mr Rawlinson remarked that the conduct of the parties towards the little creature had been very cruel and improper. He desired Mr Wall and the officer to take him back immediately in a hackney coach to Streatham, and tell Mr Rowcroft, if he did not receive him, measures would be taken to compel him, and in the meantime to treat the child with the greatest kindness, and by no means as a pauper. [123]

Rowcroft felt aggrieved that he had not been called on to present his side of the story, and attended the court himself the following day, carrying documents (presumably the correspondence he had had with various parties concerned). He asked to speak to Mr Rawlinson, who said that if Rowcroft waited until the previous

---

[122] *Belfast Commercial Chronicle*, Wednesday 26 December 1827.
[123] As above.

night's cases were dealt with he would speak with him then. Rowcroft waited all day and eventually tried again to speak to Rawlinson, who was disinclined to listen.

Rowcroft accused the magistrate, Rawlinson, of damaging his good name by relying for his judgement, in Rowcroft's absence, on a biased account of events given by Rowcroft's accuser, Mr Wall. Rawlinson said 'The child is in the hands of Mr. Yates, who has very liberally undertaken the charge of him for 12 months, and I am very glad of it', and effectively claimed to have no responsibility to Rowcroft, who eventually said that he would seek redress elsewhere.[124][125]

Rowcroft then did two things. Firstly, he wrote a letter addressed to the Right Hon. the Marquess of Lansdowne, Secretary of State for the Home Department:

Streatham, Dec. 27, 1827.

My Lord_ I beg leave to call your Lordship's attention to the subject of the Police Report of the Office of Mary-la-Bonne, as it appears in The Chronicle of this day. ...

... That your Lordship should sanction by the authority of your silence, the monstrous principle, that a stipendiary Magistrate might pronounce at hazard, an opinion on an ex-parte statement_ that he might blast with the breath of his official authority the character of an Individual, I cannot for a moment suppose.

I can imagine, that in Turkey or Morocco, a barbarian Magistrate might sport with impunity with the feelings and with the characters of his slaves; but in England_ from an English seat of justice!_ to hear a Magistrate, with reckless disregard to the miseries he inflicts, pronounce an opinion on an ex-parte statement, is as disgusting to the feelings of civilized men, as it is alarming to the liberty of the subject.

No man's character would be safe, were a Magistrate permitted to pronounce an official opinion in the absence of the party accused, and before he had heard his defence. By what statute of Parliament did Mr. Rawlinson pronounce that this child ought to be supported by me? By what law of humanity?_ Did Mr Rawlinson, when he pronounced his opinion, know whether I was able to support this child? Did he know whether I was able to give food to my own? Did he know whether I was actually living or dead? Did he know, in short, anything about the matter, except what the party evidently interested and desirous to get rid of the child chose to tell him?

But might he not have known all this? Ought he not to have inquired, before he pronounced his opinion? Did not common sense suggest to him, that possibly the statement made before him was false? Did not

---

[124] *Morning Advertiser*, Thursday 27 December 1827.
[125] *London Evening Standard*, Thursday 27 December 1827.

gentlemanly feeling suggest to him, that it was due to a gentleman of respectable family, not hastily to pronounce an opinion injurious to his reputation? And did not a sense of justice suggest to him, that it was contrary to his duty, contrary to practice, and contrary to law, to decide on a case before he had heard both sides of the question?

... My Lord, my sufferings as a private individual are but as dust in the balance, compared with the importance of this question to the interests of the public.

As an injured man I complain, and I call for redress ...
I have the honour to be, my Lord,
Your Lordship's most obedient
And very humble servant,

CHAS. ROWCROFT.[126]

Rowcroft was asking Lord Lansdowne to intervene on his behalf and ensure that the magistrate listened to his side of the story.

The second action Rowcroft took, the same day, was to publish copies of all his correspondence, in chronological order, including the letter to Lansdowne, in the *Morning Chronicle* of 28 December. He linked the letter sequence by narrating his other efforts at each stage of the story.

While Rowcroft, from his published account of the affair, clearly had a justified grievance, he could at the very least be accused of reckless imprudence in not having researched the finances of the establishment he was buying. It would appear that he had not investigated either the administration of boarding schools in general or of Mr Wall's establishment in particular before purchasing the school. As we would see it from our twenty-first-century viewpoint, before he agreed the purchase he should at least have asked Mr Wall how fees were paid, ensured that he saw the accounts and receipts, and asked for bank references; but perhaps things were not done like that in 1828: perhaps the contention was that a gentleman's word was good enough.

The magistrate told Rowcroft that little Robert Evans was to be looked after for a year by a Mr Yates who was the Vestry clerk at Streatham. This presumably meant that Mr Yates would pay his school fees for the academic year, during which time everyone hoped that Mr Evans' payment would arrive. This, in turn, meant that Rowcroft had no further worries for that year with regard to Robert being included in his school. However, we do not know what happened to the four Fitzpatricks whom Rowcroft mentioned being in the same predicament as Robert. Also, the arrangement with Yates did nothing to exonerate Charles Rowcroft of the

---

[126] *Morning Chronicle*, Friday 28 December 1827.

accusation of neglect of his duties as a school proprietor, which the former school owner, Mr Wall, clearly implied in his own widely published account of the dispute. There is no known response from the Marquess of Lansdowne, nor have I been able to find any published repudiation of this 'accusation' in newspapers of the following months. In any case, this unsatisfactory result does not seem to have prevented the Rowcrofts from continuing to run the school in the immediate aftermath of the court case.

Chapter 7 – Great interest

At some point in the first months of 1828, things went very wrong at the Maltese Colony, and Napier was afraid it would fold before it was properly off the ground:

> After trying in vain, for two years, to make them cultivate the ground, the local government of Cefalonia was obliged to stop the issue of rations to these people, which it was bound to make for only six months; and, instantly, the Maltese spread over the island, begging for food. It was necessary to relieve them, and I had no time to lose, for they were in want of sustenance.[127]

We can imagine Elizabeth and Charles sitting at supper one evening in the Resident's house in Argostoli, Charles bemoaning the state of affairs at the colony. Elizabeth might have received a letter from Edward that morning, updating her on the parlous state of the Curling family's situation. With a keen interest in her new surroundings and in helping her husband, might she and Napier, mulling over two disparate and distant problems, have found a wonderfully creative solution to both?

It is more than likely that prior to her second marriage Elizabeth had kept in touch with Thomas Oakley Curling's family, both when they were in Van Diemen's Land and after their return. We know that, as 'Aunt Kelly', she had received news of the Oakley Curlings through her sister Catharine,[128] when Edward was still at boarding school in Ramsgate, and while we do not have any of Elizabeth's letters to them we can be certain that she did keep in touch with them, particularly after the death of their grandmother, her much-loved sister. She knew her great-nephew Edward to be a hard-working, intelligent young man with plenty of farming experience both in England and on the virgin territory in Van Diemen's Land. With such a long-standing knowledge of his character and abilities, it would have been natural for Elizabeth to ask her new husband to consider inviting Edward Curling to Kefalonia so that Napier could assess the young man and see whether he would be a suitable candidate to work with Napier in developing the agricultural practice on the island.

Circumstances had placed Edward Curling outside the usual career path for his station. His father, Thomas Oakley Curling (Thomas II), had, by taking his family to Van Diemen's Land, disrupted a Curling tradition going back to the mid-fifteenth century: over at least nine preceding generations[129] Edward's ancestors had been yeomen farmers and mariners, their roots on the Isle of Thanet, and gradually

---

[127] *The Colonies* p. 255, C J Napier.

[128] See *Curling Wisps & Whispers of History*, vol. 1, pp. 182 and 197, Catherine's letters to Thomas Curling III dated September and October 1819, transcripts kindly provided by Carey Bayliss.

[129] See the family history website, www.curlingofthanet.wordpress.com, Clive Boyce and LucyAnn Curling, begun in 2015.

spreading from there only a few miles further afield into east Kent. As the post Napoleonic War agricultural depression became more protracted, Thomas II had been unable to see a way of ensuring that his six younger boys could continue in this tradition, but he saw an opening for farmers in the colonies and hoped it would be the solution. As we know, this did not work out.[130]

Edward, now back in England, downhearted at the loss of his father and the failure of the dream, was unable to see a way to reinstate himself and his family in the agricultural yeomanry of Kent. To become a tenant farmer he needed funds for the rent and rates. In that era a network of contacts was essential to make any headway on a career ladder in any field of work, and the more influential the contacts the better one's career opportunities. This network was referred to as 'interest', implying that a more influential person had taken an interest in the prospective worker. Now, in the twenty-first century, professional careers advice at secondary school and careful choice of tertiary education are what channel young people towards their chosen career, with networking, often through professional contacts rather than family, as an additional tool to finding the ideal first job. But in Edward's time, when stepping away from the family's traditional work roles, it was almost always essential, even for educated men, to negotiate their life's work through contacts in their family circle. But no-one in the group of influential Kent men who had signed his father's testimonial seems to have been able, or possibly willing, to help … or perhaps he was too proud to ask.

Edward, at the age of twenty-one, would have wished to obtain a job worthy of his intelligence and which also used his considerable experience on the land. However, he was obliged to take on the role of eldest son, as his brother Thomas III, a newly qualified apothecary,[131] had refused to help the family on their return from Van Diemen's Land. The Rowcrofts' school was in difficulty from the outset. Edward therefore felt he could not afford to wait for the perfect agricultural opportunity to present itself but saw the necessity of taking any job he could obtain. With his mother and seven dependent siblings relying on any extra income which could be found, he started work as an attorney's clerk in an unknown location, although we know that his employer's name was Delmar.[132] This Delmar was probably either Charles Delmar or a relative of his. Charles Delmar owned Upper Goldstone Farm in the parish of Ash-next-Sandwich, the home of Edward's uncle,

---

[130] See *Curling Wisps & Whispers of History*, vol. 1, p. 114, **Chapter 11 – Universally Respected by All**.

[131] Thomas Curling III sat and passed his oral examination at the Apothecaries Hall on 5 May 1827, on the premises of the Worshipful Society of Apothecaries, whose archives hold records of all certified apothecaries from 1815 to 1858. Thomas Curling's record is catalogue reference WSAA MS 8241/4. See http://www.apothecaries.org/ for further information about the present-day WSA.

[132] See Edward's letter BL Add MS 54536 f.106, p. 134.

Michael Becker III.[133] Delmar had married Michael's sister Mary, Edward's aunt, in 1823. He was the son of a Canterbury brewer, a freeman of the city of Canterbury,[134] and lived at Elmstone Court, three miles from Goldstone.[135] He was the grandson of smuggler William Baldock, reputed to have had an estate worth more than £1 million at the time of his death.[136] Baldock was the owner of both 'Elmstone Court' and Upper Goldstone Farm at the time of his death in 1812 and bequeathed them to Charles Delmar senior, on condition that he produced a male heir.[137] (If he had not done so the property would have reverted to Baldock's nephew, W H Baldock.) With such a financially weighty family contact one might have thought Edward, his mother and family would have received greater assistance than a referral to a clerking job.

A farmer to the marrow, Edward found office work irksome. In May 1828 he was staying with his uncle when he received a letter from Napier. He sat down to write this reply:

Goldstone May 29th 1828

Sir

> *I duly received your letter, and cannot help taking the opportunity of expressing my most grateful thanks for the interest you have so kindly taken in my welfare, and also for the £25 you had the goodness to remit_ I immediately decided on accepting your offer and am now taking leave of my friends in Kent, and shall take my passage for Cephalonia as soon as I possibly can after my return to town_ The difficulty of procuring any respectable situation in England without great interest, particularly for young men who like me have no profession or trade to recommend them and the many thousand competitors to cope with, most of them perhaps possessing more advantages than myself had long ago convinced me that I had but little chance of advancement here, and had determined me to take advantage of the first opportunity that presented itself of trying my fortune in another country. You may easily imagine therefore the pleasure your letter gave me not only by advising me of a situation*

---

[133] See *Curling Wisps & Whispers of History*, vol. 1, p. 165 ff., **Appendix 4a – The Becker-Solley family of Kent**.

[134] UK Poll Books and Electoral Registers for the county of Kent, 1830, p. 84, ancestry.com.

[135] Kent Tithe Award Schedule 1842.

[136] See *Curling Wisps & Whispers of History*, vol. 1, p. 51.

[137] *Blue Anchor Corner*, a blog about a smuggling 'company', called the Seasalter Company: https://bit.ly/App5aDelmarBaldock

exactly suited to my inclinations but also by enabling me to leave a miserable dependent employment where I received a salary scarcely sufficient for subsistence, and where from the confinement I was completely ruining my constitution.

*As I shall I trust be with you soon after the arrival of this letter I shall not enter into any detail of events, which would perhaps be interesting to Mrs Napier, but reserve all news til I have the pleasure of seeing her_ I have just parted with Miss Kelly [138] who appears to be in excellent health_ she writes I believe by the same post by which I send this_*

> *With kind regards to Mrs Napier*
> *Believe me*
> *Your ever grateful*
> *And very humble serᵗ*

Edw Curling [139]

The letter was addressed thus:

> *Via .....*
> *Col Napier CB*
> *Cephalonia*
> *Corfu*

The letter is annotated in Napier's own handwriting:

A good letter from Mr Edward Curling, my wife's nephew 1828.

Here was an extraordinary opportunity that might lift Edward and his family out of their misery. The vista of hope which Napier's invitation opened up must have seemed almost unreal. Even though Edward was still aged only twenty-one there had been so many disasters in his life: the failure of the family farm in Thanet; the protracted anxieties that he, his mother and siblings had endured while their father

---

[138] Eliza Kelly was Elizabeth Napier's eldest child by her first husband. Eliza is recorded in the 1841 census as aged 50 and employed by the Delmar family at Guilton Rectory, Wingham, as a governess. A decade later her 1851 census entry records her at Guilton Rectory as a 'visitor', and her age at that time was given as 68. A letter written to Napier in April 1853 from Guilton Rectory, Wingham in Kent, is signed Eliza Kelly, and it is apparent that she lives at the rectory. There was a strong link between the Delmar family and Jane Rowcroft's family, the Beckers: Charles Delmar had acted as guarantor for her father, Michael Becker, when he had bought the lease of the rectory in 1795.

[139] BL Add MS 54536 f. 102.

negotiated a possible route out of destitution; the hardships of a long-distance voyage by sea; the trek up country to the new farm in Van Diemen's Land; helping his father to build a rudimentary home from scratch, then clearing the land around it to begin farming only to have it all slip through their fingers when his father died; and since their return to England, the Rowcrofts' boarding school initiative, which seemed to be on very shaky ground.

But Napier needed someone to take the colony in hand. A miraculous synchronicity had brought together this need and Edward's search for a more fulfilling way of life. From this time onward, Charles James Napier acted in every way in the role of father to the Curling siblings. The unfailing care and practical help he gave them was inspired by his love for Elizabeth, and he held fast to their welfare right up until his death.

Edward accepted the invitation with alacrity. He sounds very excited, eager and grateful; his life experiences were finally coming into their own, and his migration with his father to Van Diemen's Land held him in good stead on a less obvious front, too, giving him a more open mind on working elsewhere in the Empire than in England.

There must have been great excitement in Michael Becker's house at Goldstone when Colonel Napier's invitation arrived for his nephew Edward. In all likelihood, no-one in the house or in the village knew the location of Kefalonia; a world map might have been consulted to see where Edward's journey would take him.[140]

Edward's mode of address in his letters to Napier was always formal, and in this first letter he extends the same courtesy to his aunt, Mrs Napier. In later letters he refers to 'my aunt', but never uses her first name.

According to Napier's official account of the Maltese Colony, he did not initially tell Edward about the possibility of a permanent post in Kefalonia, nor invite Edward to Kefalonia specifically to resuscitate the Colony. In his published version, Napier's invitation was for Edward to visit Kefalonia to learn the local languages.

> Mr. Curling … came to the islands by my advice, to learn the modern Greek, and Italian languages, and with very different views from that of being employed by the Ionian Government.[141]

However, Edward's letter above implies otherwise. A post 'exactly suited to my inclinations' could only have been one connected with agriculture and an active outdoor life. Napier was anxious not to be seen to be practising nepotism, but in the case of Edward and later his siblings such an accusation might have been a

---

[140] For a contemporaneous description of the island of Kefalonia see **Appendix 1a – A description of Kefalonia in Napier's time** p. 178.

[141] *The Colonies* p. 255, C J Napier.

reasonable one, although the Curling men always strove assiduously to justify his faith in them.

Sometime in the next month or two, Edward arrived in Argostoli. The phrase 'take my passage' in his letter indicated that he was going to be travelling by sea, probably on board the English Packet[142] to Corfu and onward in a local boat from there to Kefalonia. He would then have had to endure up to twenty-five days' quarantine in the lazaretto:[143] there had been an outbreak of the plague in the Ionian Islands in 1815–16,[144] so awareness of the potential for a pandemic travelling through the British Empire was heightened. No doubt he used the time well, Napier lending him language text books on Italian, Greek and Maltese.

When Edward was eventually released, Elizabeth Napier would surely have been beside herself with delight to welcome her sister's grandson to live in their house, a lively and energetic young man with whom she might have felt her husband would bond; Edward would have had a wonderful family welcome.

After more than three weeks incarcerated with his books in the lazaretto, Edward would have had a good idea of the linguistic challenges he had taken on. Having learnt French at school, he might not have found Italian, another Romance language, particularly difficult; and even Greek, while requiring the assimilation of a completely new alphabet, has many words with parallels in English; but Maltese (which Edward would need for his work at the Maltese Colony) was another matter. Although it uses the Roman alphabet its roots are in the Middle East, having much in common with Arabic. Malta, like the Ionian Islands, had suffered the ravages of centuries of invasions, including Italian, French and Arabic as well as English. Her inhabitants had assimilated the languages of the invaders so it is likely that some of the new arrivals to the farming colony would have spoken at least some English and Italian, but Maltese was their mother tongue.

Sadly, because of the 1953 earthquake, no trace of Napier's original house in Argostoli exists. However, in a remarkable book, a photographic record of pre-earthquake Kefalonia,[145] there is an image of an old photograph of it on the sea front of what used to be Maitland Square, now called Rizo Spaston:

---

[142] See **Appendix 7a – Packet ships** p. 200.

[143] Napier had had the lazaretto built as one of his first projects when he took up the Cephalonia Residency in 1822. The word 'lazaretto' was widely applied to buildings used for quarantine, and is still in use in a few places, see https://en.wikipedia.org/wiki/Lazaretto. See **Appendix 7b – Quarantine in Kefalonia in 1828** p. 204 for a journal account of quarantine as it was conducted at Kefalonia in 1828 only three or four months before Edward Curling's arrival on the island.

[144] *From observatory to dominion geopolitics, colonial knowledge and the origins of the British Protectorate of the Ionian Islands, 1797–1822*, Evangolos Zarokostas, PhD thesis, University of Bristol 2018, available online: https://bit.ly/388NjwQ

[145] *Cephalonia of Old Volume I, Argostoli*, p. 74, collated and published by the Corgialanios Foundation.

Fig. 8.   Napier's house on Maitland Square[146]

In the book, the images are linked by the cycle ride of a fictitious little girl, Christina, around the town of Argostoli the day before the 1953 earthquake. The caption which accompanies the above image says 'Look Christina, the best friend of Cephalonia lived in this house, Charles James Napier'. The little girl in the photograph standing as though talking to someone through the window adds to the story and there is a man up a ladder making repairs to the front of the house.

In his first months on the island Edward lived with Colonel and Mrs Napier for a period of acclimatization while Napier was assessing him with the expectation that he might be the right person to revive the hopes of the Maltese Colony. As well as improving his language skills, Edward's priority list would have included accompanying Napier or his staff around the island to familiarise himself with the geography and to understand the problems and limitations of the setting. Napier would certainly have taken him to the south-east of the island to introduce him to Demetrio Cambici and show him the dilapidated state of the colony.

Napier and Cambici, together with Kennedy, had spent much time planning the colony. These three men came to know each other very well, united by their vision for the development of the island, and although Edward was very much their junior he became the fourth member of an exclusive team, included in many of the discussions about decisions and later regarded as a friend by the older men, with whom he kept in touch until their deaths.

Napier would have introduced Edward to many other people in all ranks of society with whom Edward would have to work. He would have developed Edward's understanding of the Maltese Colony project, with its aims and the diffi-

---

[146] I am grateful to Elaine Valianou, who researched this detail for me.

culties encountered, and might well have arranged for Edward to shadow the relevant officials. The progress not only of the colony but of all his plans would have been constant topics of conversation at mealtimes, whether with guests or in the privacy of the Napiers' homely domesticity. It was an induction period full of exciting change.

Although Napier professed to have invited Edward to the island purely to improve his language skills, it is extremely unlikely that the idea of asking Edward to take on the rejuvenation of the colony was *not* in the back of his mind all along. He may not have voiced it as a proposal publicly until he had had a chance to assess the young man. However, when the Ionian government withdrew food from the Maltese and they scattered across the island, Napier had to act quickly:

> I had no time to lose, for they were in want of sustenance. Not one Greek in the island, and only one Englishman (a Mr. Curling) knew any thing of agriculture, beyond the cultivation of vines, and currant bushes. Mr. Curling possessed talents, activity and a good knowledge of agriculture, both practically, and as a science.[147]

Napier implies that Edward had career plans other than being employed by the Ionian government

> which his being so employed put an end to. I did not, therefore, wish to employ Mr. Curling; but I saw that either I must do so, or that the colony was lost; and I, consequently, gave him the charge of it.[148]

Although none of them were aware of it at the time, Elizabeth's marriage had given Edward and his siblings the only 'interest' they would ever need.

---

[147] *The Colonies,* p. 254, C J Napier.
[148] As above.

Chapter 8 – Maltese Colony I:
Everything appeared most confused

Now came the great day when Napier gave Edward a final briefing on his duties at the Maltese Colony and Edward set out from Argostoli, in its magnificent west coast harbour, to the austerities of the undeveloped district of Pronos on the east coast of Kefalonia. He had as yet no horse of his own, so he probably did the journey on one of the regular sailings of coastal boats. Having lived in comfort for three months with his great-aunt Elizabeth and her husband Charles Napier, he was about to revert to the harsh conditions of life as a settler.

In Argostoli, the capital of the island, there was a cosmopolitan gentility that had been nurtured through the centuries by the administrations of different conquering powers,[149] and was currently in the hands of British officers and their families. The enormous U-shaped natural harbour, whose shores included not only Argostoli but Lixouri, another significant town across the bay, was perfect for visiting vessels of all sizes. Amongst other public buildings, Napier had built the lazaretto, where disembarking visitors to the island were quarantined. Napier's own house in Maitland Square was a stylish one (see Fig 6, p. 28). But Pronos, the area on the east coast where Edward was to be based, had comparatively few habitations, and the accommodation to which he was going was the most basic possible, a two-room cabin with an earth floor. However, in Van Diemen's Land with his parents, he had experienced life first with no solid shelter at all, and then a 'house divided into one room'[150] which he had had to share with his parents and seven siblings; so he was well prepared for the rigours of Pronos.

From very early times in temperate Europe the agricultural administrative year has followed the seasons. In the nineteenth century, Michaelmas (29 September), still marked the half-year, with agricultural accounts for the past six months due on 30 September. So 1 October was often used to begin a new employment, which is why we find Edward arriving at the colony to begin this exciting stage in his career on that date. In the next three chapters we follow him through two full farming years and into the third. The material is taken almost entirely from *The Journal of the Maltese Colony in Cephalonia*,[151] a work journal which he commenced on his first day, no doubt at Napier's request. These chapters are roughly divided into agricultural years, but because they are largely an overview of Edward's life and

---

[149] Social history exhibits at the Corgialenios Museum in Argostoli support this. There is an excellent set of photographs on this TripAdvisor page: https://bit.ly/Ch6CorgMus

[150] Description of the Curling family's home on the Lake River, Van Diemen's Land, *The Diaries of John Helder Wedge 1824–1835*, eds Crawford, Ellis & Stancombe. Royal Society 1962.

[151] BL Add MS 49114 ff. 1–22b.

working practices in the colony, there are inevitably overlaps. I have tried to keep any correspondence from the period in its chronological place. As mentioned earlier, all quotations from Edward's journal are in italics, and I have included the shorter quotations in the body text in order to help the flow of the narrative.

By the time Edward arrived at the colony, almost all of Napier's plans for it had dissipated, not least because many of the Maltese had dispersed across the island. The idea of allocating each family a smallholding had gone, and it became apparent that the whole plot of land would have to be turned into one large farm. Not only that: Edward would have to educate his community in proper land management from first principles – and before that, he had to revive the spirits of this group of people who would by now have been feeling, with some justification, hopeless and abandoned.

Edward saw that with the reduced numbers of Maltese he would have to enlist Greek labour too. This could be turned to advantage, because he planned to lease the land to Greek farmers on the understanding that they would follow his instructions on how to use it. As they saw the improvements in their income and standard of living, word would spread and gradually better farming methods would take root.

Fig. 9.   Watercolour sketch 'Cambici's House Racli Cefalonia'[152]

---

[152] BL Add MS 49147 f. 20, Napier's sketchbook.

On the evening of 1 October 1828 Edward arrived at Rakli *too late to do any thing with regard to the Maltese*. He stayed that first night with Cambici, see Napier's Watercolour sketch 'Cambici's House Racli Cefalonia' Fig. 9. Cambici would have told Edward how the colony had progressed thus far, what he saw the problems to be, and what the urgent necessities were. Cambici owned an estate adjacent to the colony, and Napier wrote of him in the highest terms in later years, as did Edward himself. In Napier's British Library sketchbook I found a wonderful watercolour sketch that he did of Cambici's house. Napier's pencilled title is almost indistinguishable, but peering at it through a magnifying glass you can just see that it says 'Cambici's house Racli Cefalonia'.

Numbers in the colony were much reduced by the time Edward arrived. He was taking over supervision of the colony from a Mr Baynes, who stayed for a few days after Edward's arrival. On his first morning, Edward went to the colony, where

> *every thing appeared [most] confused the Maltese nearly all sick_*
> *Mr Baynes and I got some mixed corn ground and served out the flour*
> *as rations to the sick and sold it to the labourers_ employed those*
> *who were able to work in cleaning out the houses and making a drain*
> *behind them as the dampness of the floors was evidently a great cause*
> *of the sickness_ stayed this night in Mr Bayne's house but was unable*
> *to sleep on account of the myriads of fleas I had collected in going*
> *around the houses of the Maltese_ could not pay the workmen having*
> *no small money_*

There may well have been some murmurings about this among the people who had been put under his supervision, but on the following day Edward received money from town and was able to pay everyone.

The house that was to be Edward's had been occupied by Baynes. We are not told what Baynes' precise role was, but it is clear from what Edward later wrote about the many ways in which Cambici actively supported the project that Baynes was simply a basic overseer.

Eleven days after his arrival Edward received a letter from Napier saying he had ordered Baynes' removal. At the time 'removal' in this context would have meant what we mean today when we say we have 'moved house' permanently to another location. The house was one of the cabins which Kennedy had built for the Maltese. It was British government property, and Baynes was not forcibly removed, just asked to leave so that Edward could take over the job.[153] The next day, 12 October,

---

[153] See other letters in the collection for similar uses of the word: E C to C J N, for example, 11th November 1830: '*Capt Kennedy removed to the mountain immediately you were gone and the change of air did him a great deal of good*'; and also Catherine

Mr Baynes left for Argostoli and Edward moved into the house permanently. Baynes may have resented Edward's appointment, particularly as it would have meant that he, Baynes, was no longer receiving payment for his role in the colony.

The majority of entries in Edward's journal are very brief – a phrase, a sentence or two on the day's activities, showing the development of tasks, which fall into two groups:

The necessities of developing the land and buildings

    i.   making the labourers' houses habitable by digging water channels, cleaning the rooms thoroughly and whitewashing them

    ii.   making the ground usable by removing stones which were subsequently used to build walls, uprooting tree stumps (used to make charcoal) and finally ploughing the land

    iii.   improving drainage and terracing the steeper slopes

    iv.   specific farming developments such as enclosing land for a farmyard and farm garden, making a threshing floor or constructing a hen coop.

The farming routines of each season

    v.   ploughing and re-ploughing the land to bring it to a fine tilth

    vi.   sowing and planting

    vii.   weeding

    viii.   harvesting

    ix.   burning charcoal

    x.   storing harvested produce

    xi.   sending produce to market in Argostoli.

Manuring – building a fertile soil through a strong supply of animal manure – was one of Edward's primary aims, but until he had sufficient livestock to provide this, he used a variety of soil enhancers.

Although the colony had been established for two years prior to Edward's arrival, it is clear that any original motivational impetus had been lost. Judging from the amount of foundation work which Edward had to oversee, there had been very little management of the farm, with no overview, direction or aim apart from Napier's original one of showing the local farmers that (a) much greater diversity of land use and (b) far better crops, were more possible than they had hitherto realised.

Three hundred Maltese had arrived in Kefalonia in late 1826. We don't know exactly how many of them were still in the colony when Edward commenced work

---

Curling to Edward's brother Thomas Curling 4 September 1819: '*we removed from thence on 17th inst to this place, where we are settled in a very pretty convenient house*' (see *Curling Wisps & Whispers of History*, vol. 1, p. 181).

in October 1828, because in the intervening two years many of them had dispersed round the island. Poor health was the overriding concern initially. In his first week he *sent 23 sick to town.* This reduced his numbers still further, and we do not know how long they were away. Throughout the journal there are references to workers from outside the colony whom he called either *calogers* or *Greeks*. 'Caloger' is the Greek word for 'monk',[154] so Edward was certainly employing extra hands from the monasteries. What is not clear is whether all of these men were monks and he is therefore just alternating labels for the same group of men, or whether in fact there were two groups of Greeks – monks and laymen – working at the colony. But as Edward had a lot of business with local monasteries it is possible that all his Greek workers were also monks.

There would have been considerable hostility to the colony amongst ordinary Greek farmers. Whereas Cambici was unusual amongst his fellow countrymen in seeing the advantages of Edward's scientific approach to improving the productivity and diversity of agricultural work, most local Greek farmers would naturally have felt affronted by a young British man telling them they did not know how to farm their own land. The Orthodox monks may have felt it their Christian duty to work amongst the Maltese, or more mundanely they were probably in need of the wages. These monks, and indeed the majority of the island's population, were Greek Orthodox, whereas the Maltese were Roman Catholic, in recognition of which they had been allowed to bring their own priest to the colony. Edward and Cambici initially had confrontations with both the Catholic priest and his Maltese congregation about their not working on feast days, but as the Maltese and Greek Orthodox feast days often fell on different days, Edward was usually able to have some kind of work force in spite of the saints.

Making the houses habitable was the priority, so on his first day in the colony, while the men dug a drain to take water away from behind the houses, the women and children carried out the rubbish.

In the days following Baynes' departure, when rain prevented outdoor work Edward had the men cleaning the houses. Initially they piled dirt and rubbish outside each house, but he organised them to take as much as possible in baskets to distribute it over the land. It is apparent, from the basic nature of the tasks he had to organise them to do, that the majority were very dispirited by the time he arrived, with no drive or sense of initiative, and of course many of them had been ill when they had originally disembarked on their arrival from Malta. As mentioned earlier, they had been transplanted from Malta and were not at all the agricultural workers for which Napier had asked; many who came were destitute, with no previous experience of working on the land. The Maltese were so dispirited that they had

---

[154] I am grateful to Alison and Costas Scourti for assistance with Greek language and other research queries.

even lost interest in personal hygiene – he visited the convalescents on 14 October and *insisted that the sick should wash themselves every morning, and also the labourers.*

Nevertheless, by 7 October – only six days after his arrival – all available Maltese were working on the land whenever the weather allowed. He had two Greek ploughs worked by two men, and the rest of his workers were hoeing the land *with their heavy hoes* to break it up in preparation for sowing potatoes. He had chosen these as his first planting because he had been told by locals that it was a good season to do it. The women and children were set to carrying out manure; Edward expected children to work alongside the women in what was often heavy manual labour.

For the first three months Edward does not record the weather in any systematic way, although he often writes notes such as *Heavy rain, Rained hard all day* or *Fine weather.* The weather affected three things: the health of the Maltese, the tasks which could be completed, and the growth of the crops.

On 13 October he had

> *two ploughs at work but were obliged to leave off on account of the heavy rain which came on about 11 o'clock_ As many of the houses had a good heap of dirt and rubbish before their doors, I employed the men between the showers to carry as much as possible out on the land in baskets*

and on 16 October 1828 it was *Too wet to begin planting potatoes.* Over three days in early November rain severely impeded progress, but by the middle of the week he was making headway in water management:

> *3rd November Heavy rain without interruption the whole day_*

> *4th November Heavy showers_ In the intervals [attempted] to build walls &c*

> *5th November Showery weather_ all Maltese and also Greeks hoeing in wheat_ my waterfurrows having effectually preserved the land against the heavy rains I took care to make plenty of them to day*

On Catholic feast days the Maltese labourers downed tools at their priest's command, and Edward's efforts to persuade them otherwise were initially to no avail. On 11 October he

> *offered the men pay if they would work and explained to them that being Saturday they would be two days without food if they did not, in fact I tried every thing to persuade them, but all to no purpose as*

the parson was against me_ the two ploughs and the Greeks were of course at work.

As roads on the island were still in the early stages of development, the principal means of bringing large loads of any kind to the colony was by sea. On 13 October *a boat arrived with 3000 lbs of potatoes and 30 bushels*[155] *of wheat for seed*. The same day *other steers*[156] *arrived from the convent* [157] and Edward gave to Greeks the work of breaking them in. Less than a week after stepping into his new role, Edward had the *convalescents cutting potatoes for planting*. Three thousand pounds of potatoes seems an enormous quantity, however it may have been that they were not all to be planted but some used for food for the Maltese until the farm began to be productive; six months later, at the end of March, Edward had almost his whole workforce planting potatoes because it was late in the season, so he must have created a store of them when they first arrived. A traditional way of doing this is to 'clamp' them, a technique which requires no building.[158] The Maltese had brought their own Maltese hoes, and Edward got them using these to plant the potatoes in rows, a man using the hoe to make a hole and a boy following after him putting a potato in each one.

It took quite some time for those who had been unwell when Edward arrived to recover – he was still recording provision for them on 25 October: *women cleaning wheat for the sick, the others with convalescents cutting the potatoes which arrived yesterday*. In fact, it was not until December 1828 that he wrote *decreased our sick list to day, probably occasioned by the two or three fine days we have had*.

Roll call was introduced by Edward, and he imposed the sanction of docked pay for non-attendance. His only previous experience of people management would have been watching how his father did it, first in Kent and then in Van Diemen's Land, where farmers were entitled to employ trusted convicts as extra labour. He was still a very young man[159] and at the beginning he had difficulty asserting his authority with some of the workers. On 16 October, he *stopped the pay of several*

---

[155] See **Appendix 2 – Castlereagh's Cabinets of Weights** p. 192, on weights and measures in Kefalonia of this era. At this time, each of the Ionian Islands had variations in their weights, measures and currency.

[156] 'steer' in this context means cattle. They were probably draft oxen, for pulling ploughs.

[157] Brought up in the Roman Catholic faith, I had always understood the places where monks live to be 'monasteries' and those where nuns live to be 'convents', but Edward always calls them convents even though he never mentions nuns, only the 'calogeri' or monks. On a visit to the present-day monastery at Agios Andreas I saw both monks and nuns.

[158] Clamping requires the potatoes to be put in a mound and covered with soil. See *Self Sufficiency*, John Seymour, p. 182, Corgi paperback edition.

[159] Date of birth 6 February 1807 (Mildenhall Document), making Edward 21 years old when he started work with Napier.

labourers for not coming in time for roll call. Initially at least, Edward seems to have favoured physical chastisement, but he learnt a lesson in staff management on 24 October. He found his Greeks had *all left me in consequence of my having given each a splat on the head for refusing to cover in a little clover seed after they had done ploughing.* He set the Maltese to work with the ploughs and noted grumpily that *they plough better than the Greeks.* He also reported that he *sowed the wheat myself_ reploughed about ¾ of an acre which had been well manured and sowed some swede turnips as a trial.* Edward frequently reported that he had land reploughed once it had been manured, and then ploughed a third time before sowing the crop.

This is the only entry where he clearly indicates that he himself was working in the field, sowing wheat. His journal entries were generally made in note form rather than full sentences, so that when he recorded activities it is unclear whether he himself was engaged in the task or he was delegating it. It is more than likely that his was a very hands-on style of management, not least because he loved the outdoor life and the work of farming itself.

As the health of the sick improved, Edward employed them in light work such as cutting seed potatoes ready for planting. On days when it rained without inter-mission some at least of the men were employed indoors, cleaning out the rooms of their houses and whitewashing them. However,

> *some of the houses were in a sad state with the rain and I do not see how we can remedy it without a great deal of labour as the earth which is constantly washed down behind them is above the level of the floors_ we cannot spare the time now.*

On the 15th there was a sudden hurricane which blew a ship to shore where it *was lost, but the crew got on shore safe.* Edward and his workers would have had a clear view of the wreck, as their homes were built on a slight elevation behind the coast-line.

There were difficulties, too, with the Greek ploughs which Edward complained of several times, on the 18th saying:

> *as on account of the miserable construction of the Greek plough I was not able to make furrows for the potatoes I had them planted with the Maltese hoes_ viz one man made a hole with his hoe and a boy attended him to drop in the potato the moment the hole was ready and by putting up sticks I managed to get the rows tolerably straight and at equal distances.*

Again, on 23rd he wrote:

*the ploughs are the most miserable instruments I ever saw_ they have no mould board and consequently do not turn the land over but merely root it up like the snout of a pig and by the beam being fastened to the yoke of the bullocks the ploughman can only regulate the depth by standing with one foot on the rest thus hopping along at a great inconvenience_ there is only one handle and the shead is about 3 inches wide_*

The Greek ploughs were probably 'ard' or 'scratch' ploughs[160] which do not have mouldboards. Fig. 10 shows an example, labelled the Hesiod plough, from the website of the Kotsanas Museum, the Peloponnese branch of the 'Museum of Ancient Greek Technology':[161] This is a photograph of a reconstruction of the plough.

Fig. 10. The Hesiod Plough

The text from the museum's web page states

It was an ancient tool for the cultivation of land that continued almost identically to be used until recently. It consisted of the metal ploughshare, the heavy oak share-beam, the handle which was held by the ploughman, the curved plough-tail and the long pole that had the yoke which was tied to the animals of tillage. In the "light" plough the share-beam, the plough-tail and the pole were of the same piece of timber.[162]

---

[160] https://bit.ly/ArdScratchPlough
[161] http://kotsanas.com/gb/index.php. Hesiod was a poet of ancient Greece, one of whose poems, *Works and Days*, describes the farming practices of his day: https://en.wikipedia.org/wiki/Hesiod
[162] See this page of the museum website: https://bit.ly/HesiodPlough

Such ploughs had been in use around the world since ancient times and are still, even in the twenty-first century, used in some countries. A mouldboard plough is much more complex – and crucially it turns upside down the sod it lifts.[163] In the nineteenth century there were several different designs of turn-wrest ploughs in use in England. The term 'turn-wrest' is defined as follows: 'This is a dialect term used in Kent and Sussex and widely adopted in the nineteenth century by plough manufacturers for most types of one way plough. It is the traditional type of Kent and Sussex wheeled and swing ploughs on which the mouldboard (wrest) is actually removed from one side to the other side of the plough to change the direction in which the furrow is thrown'[164] Fig. 11 is a drawing of the Kentish plough which would probably have been the type of plough Edward knew from his childhood in Kent.

Fig. 11. Kentish turn-wrest plough[165]

A detailed description of the merits of the Kentish plough is given in The Domestic Encyclopedia of 1802, the expansive entry being justified thus:

> We have been induced to give this description of the Kentish Plough, because it is an instrument of great strength, and eminently calculated for rocky and hilly countries, as it turns the soil to a considerable depth, laying it perfectly level, without making any furrow, or opening; a circumstance of equal advantage and importance, in dry situations.—The

---

[163] Search for 'mouldboard' here: https://www.bbc.co.uk/news/business-41903076
[164] Museum of English Rural Life web page:
https://www.reading.ac.uk/Instits/im/the_collections/the_museum/ploughs.html
[165] From *A Rudimentary Treatise on Agricultural Engineering*,1852. G H Andrews, CE, John Weale, High Holburn, p. 40. Alamy stock photo.

price of the whole, with its tackle complete for drawing, is computed to be about five guineas.[166]

We can understand why Edward might have wished he could obtain a better plough for the colony, where the terrain exactly matched the above outline.

After the land had been ploughed, Edward wrote that he *Commenced putting in wheat with the ploughs*. This seems a bit strange considering his derogatory views on the primitive nature of the ploughs available. One would have thought the furrows these ploughs created would have been too deep and wide for wheat. Jethro Tull's horse-drawn seed drill, invented in 1700, sowed seeds in neat rows, but Edward whould surely have mentioned it if he had had access to such a machine. Perhaps, he used the Greek ploughs to scratch shallow drills for the wheat seed and then broadcast it by hand. Meanwhile the Maltese continued to plant potatoes and prepared two empty houses *for the expected reinforcement from Argostoli*. He also planted some cabbages.

Twenty-five Maltese arrived, as expected, from Argostoli on the evening of 25 October. They may have been those who had previously left the colony when funds were stopped prior to Edward's tenure and among them may have been people whom he had sent to the hospital when he first arrived.

The potato planting was finished on 23 October – not bad going considering they had taken delivery of the 3,000 lbs of seed potatoes only ten days previously.

At the end of Edward's first month in post, a distinguished group visited the colony: Sir Frederick Adam, Lord High Commissioner for the Ionian Islands; Colonel Charles Napier, Resident for the Island of Cefalonia; and Captain Kennedy, Director of Public Works. Edward does not comment on their reactions to what they saw at the colony, but ten days later he *received a letter from Colonel Napier dated Nov[r] 2 informing me of my appointment to be Director of the Colony*. A moment of excitement and quiet satisfaction for Edward that he had official recognition from local government of his progress in the initial stages of his work – independent, too, of Napier, who was 'family'.

Again at the beginning of December *Col[l]. Napier visited the colony and it was settled that the garden, farm yard &c should be at St Nicolo close under a beautiful fountain of water.*[167] Edward must have had his eye on this spot for a while; he used the word 'garden' in the old sense of a Kentish market garden, where a wide variety of crops – particularly vegetables for human consumption – were grown on a smaller scale than the area needed for field crops such as grain, Indian corn and potatoes, with a quick succession, where possible, to make the best use of the land. He also conducted seed trials in the garden. Writing about cattle management, he

---

[166] *Domestic Encyclopaedia*, vol. 3, p. 402, 1802 https://bit.ly/Ch6KentishTWPlough
[167] See **Appendix 1c – Nineteenth-century places in Pronos, Kefalonia**, p.181.

yarded them at St Nicholas, indicating that the space he called the yard was for livestock management, and specifically on that occasion to keep them out of the garden. The garden wall would also shelter young plants from prevailing winds, and he found space for a hotbed and a cold frame in which to bring on tender seedlings.

On 12 December Edward was

> *Clearing ground with Maltese_ Calugeri with mules bringing grain*
> *for consumption_ 2 men making walls behind the houses 4 others*
> *making the walls of the garden at St Nicolo_ commenced making a*
> *chimney to my house_*

The 12th, too, saw a showdown with the priest, as Edward wrote

> *Festa to day with Maltese but by dint of argument I induced them all*
> *to work except two families who were still too much priest ridden!!!*

The underlining and the three exclamations marks are original, and betray Edward's triumph at the victory. His confrontations with the Maltese priest and his frustrations that he could not get the Maltese to work on feast days were to an extent mitigated, as mentioned earlier, by the fact that the two churches, Roman Catholic and Greek Orthodox, did not share many feast days; for example while 13 November was a *festa* for the Maltese, the calogers were at work putting in tares[168] at St Nicolo.

Finding enough jobs to keep all the Maltese occupied could sometimes be difficult: there was always work for the men, but women and children received pay and were expected to work too. On 1 December 1828:

> *the women and children are most of them now employed piling*
> *together the roots and stones and clearing away the brush wood as*
> *the men work with their pickaxes_ less than half would suffice for this*
> *but I have no other work to set them about, and therefore they are a*
> *useless expence to us.*

However, Edward usually managed to find tasks for them, sometimes indoors, depending on the weather. On 16 October 1828 it was *Too wet to begin planting potatoes,* but he still had *all Maltese and three ploughs and Greeks, hoeing and ploughing in tares on dry land,* and indoors the women and children were *making a new floor in one of the houses that are empty.* This would have been an earth floor, because the women and children would probably not have had the skills or strength required to make a flag or board floor.

---

[168] 'Tares' is another name for vetch, which is a green manure crop also used by Edward as a fodder crop.

Rather than merely employing only adult male labourers Napier had planned the colony as a proper village community with family groups, perhaps a little like the model which the Quaker William Allen had recommended in his letter about teachers.[169] But this model presented tensions between the British government's responsibility to the Maltese employees, the purpose of the colony (to educate the Greeks in British farming methods) and the efficiencies necessary to run a business which was required to make a profit. Despite the fact that women and children regularly worked in the fields, Edward appeared to be complaining that he had to sustain too a large number of 'employees', women, children or invalids, who were inadequate for the work, and yet he had a duty of care to them. A further hindrance was the severe limitations of available equipment: the Greek hoes appear to have been inadequate, but he found the ones brought by the Maltese were satisfactory. He also commissioned new ones to be made, writing on 22 January 1829: *began weeding Swede turnips with hoes I have had made in town.* Maybe the several different tasks for which he used them required different kinds of hoes.

Edward was constantly aware of cost efficiency in deploying his workforce; for example, the 28th saw beans being sown, and the following day Edward detailed how he did this, putting them in rows to enable *after cultivation, but as the men can only use their hoes at this work I am afraid they will not pay for so much trouble.* He also wondered whether this was the right time to sow them, although he had been told it was. These little musings remind us that Edward was not only managing the creation of a new farm on virgin territory but doing so in a climate which was entirely unfamiliar to him.

Balancing the need to build a family-based community against running the colony profitably was a difficult conundrum. Not surprisingly, some of the Maltese found the life too demanding, and on 20 December, another festa, Edward

> *received a letter from Capt Kennedy instructing me to get ready the women and children that wished to return to Malta to go tomorrow in the gun boat to Xante.*[170] *47 chose to go and signed the Release that I had received*

and the following day

> *The boat having arrived embarked the 47 Maltese gave them three cheers as they went off_ there is a little chance now of the Colony paying its expences.*

---

[169] See William Allen's letter, p. 49.
[170] The Ionian island known to the British at that time as Xante or Zante is now called Zakynthos.

With fewer 'dependants' to feed and clothe there was now a possibility, remote though it might be, of putting the Maltese Colony project on a sound financial footing.

The departure of this group signalled a refocusing away from attempting to embed a community of agricultural families in a village setting, although about seven women and eleven children remained.[171] *Terracing the newly cleared land ready for currants or cutting the natural grass with which the Colony abounds* was sometimes done by women and children. Many repetitive tasks were assigned to them, and much of their work was merely carrying materials from one part of the farm to another. Having in the early days carried out rubbish and manure from the houses, later they carried stones for walls – and even carried *a wall composed of small stones intended for the farm yard,* presumably carrying the stones in containers. When the mason began building a barn, the women and children spent weeks carrying stones for it. They carried grain crops to be stored and green manure which they spread across the land. In October 1829 the women, without the children, were cleaning barley for seed, spreading seaweed on the land and *clearing cotton,* and in January 1831 *Boys [were] as usual with stock, except two who were constantly employed with the mules and donkeys carrying out manure.*

1 November was the Festa di San Gerasimo. As it was a Greek feast day honouring the patron saint of the island, none of the Greek labourers was available, but there was no problem in getting the Maltese, who owed no allegiance to the saint, to work.

> They *made drains slanting down the hills on steep wheat land* ... *in hopes these will be a protection against the rains by carrying off the water before it has time to form a current strong enough to carry away the soil.*

The first crop of wheat was just showing above ground.

The next few days were very wet. In the intervals between showers wall-building was in progress. Edward, pleased with the effectiveness of his *water furrows,* quickly made plenty more.

As already mentioned, Napier had written to Edward on 2 November, confirming his appointment. Much more ebullient than Edward's restrained journal of 7 November formally recording the appointment, Edward's second letter was written the day he received Napier's. It continues the emphatic acknowledgement declared in the first letter, written from Goldstone, of his indebtedness to Napier and tells us how much he delights in the work he has been given to do.

---

[171] See Fig. 29, p. 128.

Dear Colonel

Notwithstanding your assertion that I am under no obligation for the appointment your letter informed me of, I must express my gratitude both to you and my Aunt for having placed me in an independent situation, with a salary much more than sufficient to provide me with everything I can wish for and where it depends on my own exertions and good conduct alone to ensure a continuance of it. Not only do I thank you most heartily for this, but also for the many acts of, I may say, parental kindness and attention I have received since the day I first landed in Cephalonia. Had it not been for you I should still in all probability have been in some Lawyers or other office deprived of air, exercise, and every comfort of life, despised, neglected and almost insulted by every one. Now I shall lead what of all others I most delight in, a Farmers life, shall have plenty of every thing, and enjoy a high and honorable situation under Government. I will say no more, let my actions as far as industry, zeal & integrity can do so, testify whether or not I am sensible of all you have done for me, and whether in these respects, I am not worthy the opinion you have formed from my past conduct and exertions

With best wishes and prayers for the health and happiness of my Aunt and yourself,

I am
Your obliged and faithful
humble ser^t

Ed^w Curling

Edward was now, still at the comparatively young age of 21, isolated in his new home, away from any other native English speakers. In a solitary role of authority among those with whom he was living, he might have had periods of psychological stress. However, a couple of times he mentions help in the colony from army personnel, and there may have been a small detachment of soldiers detailed to patrol the Pronos area. Personal entries in his journal are sparse. Fortunately, Cambici lived less than a mile away, at a place now called Kabitsata, Kapitsata or Kambitsata.[172] As well as knowing the background of the colony, Cambici was a

---

[172] The word 'Kambitsata' means 'Kambitsi's place'. It embodies a little etymological history of its own: the Venetian family name Cambici, spelt the Italian way despite centuries of the family's habitation on Kefalonia, was pronounced in Greek

keen farmer, and he and Edward struck up a firm friendship, exchanging agricultural expertise and ideas for improving land use. Cambici was a generous host, and Edward's Italian doubtless improved quickly in his company. Having taken a keen interest in the success of the colony since its inception, long before Edward's arrival, and indeed taken upon himself the welfare of the Maltese when they first arrived, Cambici would have had many insights to share. Edward dined with him twice before the end of the year, on Sundays 9 November and 14 December.

He left the Pronos district for the first time on 10 November: *I went into Argostoli_ Labourers putting in vetches and barley making floors &c –*

On the 15th two ploughs were putting in tares, *the other two preparing some ground for lucern* [173] so now there were four ploughs. In fact it may be that the colony had as many as six ploughs, because on 23 October he wrote *6 Maltese with the ploughs*, and while it is not clear that there were six machines it seems unlikely that Edward would have had the men sharing the work, because that did not happen in any other entries on ploughing.

Caterpillars were a problem. On 17th *earthed up cabbage plants_ the caterpillars have nearly left them_ the other day the leaves were covered with them* but he does not record whether he had a remedy.

The following day Edward received a harrow from town and tried it out, but the land *is too steep to allow of it being used in many places to advantage as it will slide down the hills too much_*

Ploughing and hoeing-in wheat, tares and vetches continued. Olives were gathered on 24 November. On that day, too, Edward began to organise the clearing of new land, but on the 28th he noted *the men get on uncommonly slow with the new land on account of the number and size of the roots_ they work it chiefly with pickaxes and turn it now about 2ft deep_*

'Cambitsi'. Edward Curling spelt it Cambisi, whereas Cambici himself used the 'c' in his signature on a letter he wrote to Edward in 1831 – and the Italian pronunciation of that, transliterated into English, would be 'Cambichi'.

It is clear from the names of villages on present-day Kefalonia that several of them have their origins in the Venetian and Greek family names of the estate owners who lived there; for example, Tzanata, Mavrata, Lourdata and Troianata are all villages on Kefalonia. In Greek, Kambitsata is written Καμπιτσατα. The letter 'μ', called 'mi', makes the 'm' sound, and 'π', pi, makes the 'p' sound, but when these two letters are written together in Greek they are pronounced 'b'. ''The Greek 'β', Beta, actually makes a 'v' sound and is pronounced 'veta', which is why Greek people call Lord Byron, who was and is a hero in Greece, what sounds in English like 'Lord Viron'. This orthographic convention and its transliteration have produced firstly the Greek pronunciation and transliteration of the Italian Camb- as Kab- so Kabitsata, and secondly the English transliteration of the place name on maps as Kabitsata.

[173] Another leguminous vetch-type crop.

Even though Napier had made sure that language-learning was top of Edward's priorities in his first few months in Kefalonia, it was still a relatively short time in which to gain sufficient command of one language, never mind three, to be able to speak with authority to his workers and other contacts.

The beginning of December 1828 was very wet. Between showers the labourers cleared more ground. On the 4th, a wet and very cold morning with snow on the mountains, the Maltese were once again clearing ground, and Edward recorded that *all the Calogeri except 8 and the bullocks except two left the Colony for their respective convents.*

Some of the land for the colony was leased from the convents. Edward hired bullocks for ploughing from them, and from this and other entries we see that monks from the convents were employed on the farm.

Ploughing had finished for the year by 6 December, so Edward *employed the Calogeri that remained carrying out dung and clearing land*, along with the Maltese men. On that day too, a mason arrived on the scene, repairing houses while the women cleaned them. Clearing ground continued for much of the winter.

Edward *shot a tolerable number of woodcocks* on the 7th. He had to feed himself, and any animal which he could kill for his own consumption saved him money.

Fig. 12. Woodcock, Francis Orpen Morris (1810–1893)

A dog would have made hunting for food much easier for Edward but he never mentions owning one. Throughout his life Edward was frugal in his habits, sometimes from necessity and otherwise from force of habit and upbringing. At that time too, there was much more of a culture of productivity, and even the British soldiers had a garden, from which Edward received some white turnip seedlings on the 13th.

Fig. 13. Woodcock Shooting, William Heath, 1795–1840 [174]

Charcoal burning commenced on 8 December, using the roots cleared from the land. This was a craft widely practised in earlier centuries in England. Fig. 14 and its accompanying text from the *Illustrated London News* show how it was done in 1879.

> Some tracts of woodland in the Epping and Hainault Forest districts of West Essex, not above fifteen miles from the heart of busy London, are devoted specially to the growth of the hornbeam, a tree which is scarcely known in many other parts of England. Its wood is the best material for charcoal, and the commercial value of that substance makes it well worth cultivation. The process of burning, which is

[174] William Heath, 1795–1849, British Woodcock Shooting, undated. Yale Center for British Art, Paul Mellon Collection, B2001.2.881.

performed on the spot, or near it, when the trees have been cut down, is a peculiar branch of rustic industry, and those employed in this business, often dwelling through a long summer time in simple huts or booths, where they lie in readiness to tend the fires beneath the heaped masses of wood covered with pieces of turf, have their characteristic features and ways. It is a work requiring great experience, as well as incessant vigilance during many days and nights, before the perfect charcoal can be extracted and deposited in the bags, to be carried away and ground. The appearance of a burning heap, with jets of flame and puffs of smoke issuing from many crevices in its sides, cannot easily be forgotten by those who have seen it at night.[175]

CHARCOAL BURNERS IN EPPING FOREST.—SEE PAGE 440.

Fig. 14. Charcoal Burners in Epping Forest[176]

On 12 December Edward had *the calogeri with mules bringing grain for consumption*. Having been in post less than three months, Edward had not yet been able to grow grain to feed the workers and had ordered some from the nearest convent, getting some of the calogeri who lived there to bring it. The colony's crop

---

[175] *Illustrated London News*, 8 November 1879, with thanks to John Weedy. See
 Appendix 8 – Charcoal burning p. 208 for a review of the processes involved.
[176] As above.

of olives was sent to the mill on the 22nd, and Edward noted that *they produced 112 lbs of oil*. It seems strange to measure oil in lbs, but that is how he did it.

In mid-December Edward let slip his frustration with the workers' lack of expertise:

> *Men employed ... making charcoal ... It appears to me that they cannot understand the art of making this as more than half the wood is wasted. Had we any means of carrying the wood to the sea shore I think it would sell for more than the charcoal it makes_*

To reinforce his water defences, on the 11th Edward had had two men building walls *to prevent water from coming down the creek behind the houses*. He also started work on the farm, *marking out the walls of the garden at St Nicolo*, following the colonel's instructions. Wall-building became a significant activity from that point on, with these two men still working on their walls the following day while *four more are making the walls of the garden at St Nicolo*. Another building activity which started on the 12th was a chimney for his house. Six men were at work on the 19th, dismantling walls to *make them level*.

On Cambici's advice Edward *put some walnuts and almonds in the ground in a basket of manure_ Cambisi tells me they will be ready to plant out in March_* He also *fitted up a hen roost* on 23rd, *for the 36 fowls I had bought for the colony*. Christmas, as we know it on 25 December, seems to have been completely ignored. It fell on Thursday. Edward's only entry was: *23 to 25 Cloudy_ men at the same work. it is astonishing how things have grown in the last three days the potatoes begin to look tolerably and the Swede turnips better_*Perhaps the absence of Christmas festivities highlights the fact that it was the Victorians who created the Christmas we know and although Edward did live the latter half of his life under Queen Victoria, in 1828 he was still a 'Georgian'.

Three days later, he *finished the hen roost and removed the fowls to St. Nicolo*. Heavy rain that night necessitated clearing up the following morning. After that, Edward rounded up all the pickaxes of the colony and sent them to be forged, probably because they had become blunt from so much use on the hard, stony ground.

Even on his single day off each week, Edward was thinking about his work. On Sunday 28 December he *went round several villages to see the sows previously to them being bought for the Colony*, noting that he would really like to have *some of our English breed before long*. He also went to the convent of Pirge, and *brought away the best poney they had for my use*. Prior to this he would have had to walk everywhere in the vicinity or rely on sea transport.

Early on the morning of 29th, Edward went to St Nicolo and surprised

a Greek lying in ambush within a few yards of the hen roost_ As I had
no proof that he intended to steal the fowls so as to be able to proceed
against him, I only gave him a sound thrashing and let him go.

A note in the margin explains that the Greek had no business there except to rob.

So the calendar year ends on a low-key note, but in his first three months Edward had pulled the colony off its knees, got the labourers fit, improved their living quarters, started improving drainage, commenced building work on the farmyard, including renovating and improving his own house, and had begun planting in a systematic way.

Chapter 9 – Maltese Colony II:
As good land as I have met with

There were many infrastructure projects requiring Edward's attention, but he had nothing approaching the technological advances available in England at the time, let alone those we take for granted in the twenty-first century. The mountainous nature of the inland border of the colony meant that rain or snow run-off was a permanent winter feature, and Edward saw that it was washing away what good topsoil there was. He had two solutions to this: drainage and terracing. The drain to take water away from behind the houses was the first of many. Then any stone cleared from land was used to build walls, making enclosures for livestock, creating field enclosures and supporting terraces – but all of this had to be done one shovel-ful of soil or one stone at a time by his workers; there were no mechanical diggers, no concrete mixers, nothing except shovels, picks and muscle. As we have seen in the last chapter, he resorted to ancient crafts like charcoal burning, in use since the iron age, and, for barriers and even buildings, cob walls.[177] Terracing steep hillsides is another ancient skill, practised the world over, to make the best use of steep-sided hill and mountain land which would otherwise be much more limited in its agricultural use.

Fig. 15. A view of terracing in the Arakli valley, Kefalonia

The garden and farmyard walls were important in different ways, and from January 1829 Edward dedicated many of his workers' hours to building them. Together the

---

[177] Cob, also known as cobb, is a building material that comprises subsoil, straw (or another fibrous organic material), water, and occasionally lime … traditional English cob, which was used up until the 1800s when it began to be replaced by more modern construction methods, was a mixture of clay-based subsoil, sand, straw and water.' From Designing Buildings wiki, https://bit.ly/CobWalls

garden and farmyard would transform the tasks of growing plants and managing the animals. On 27 September 1829, Edward reported good news, *Men employed making cob wall_ this being finished high enough to keep bullocks in I yarded them for the first time this morning_* but he was frustrated because

> *if it had been finished a week ago, we should have saved all the damage which some old wild cows, which we had from the convents to fatten, have done the young plantation of currants_ All the men in the colony were unable to put these in the small place made for our working bullocks, & we were obliged to leave them out; in the night they entered the plantation and have done damage enough to make one mad_ the farm yard will save this in future_*

Water needed careful management throughout the year. Even though rainfall in Kefalonia was and is high compared to that of mainland Greece, it drops close to zero in June, July and August.[178] As well as drains taking water away in the winter, watercourses channelled it to the fields in the hot months, and Edward had his workers developing this drainage system at intervals for many months. He commends the irrigation system of his friend and advisor, Cambici, on which Edward may have modelled his own.

Making sure the floors remained dry was essential to improving the health of everyone living in the colony; flooring appears over a dozen times as a task in the journal. On 9 November 1829 he *began new flooring [for] one of the houses.* This work continues through to the end of the month: 30 November *making new floor in one of the houses_* and 9 December *Rain all the morning_ Mason new flooring house.* Edward was employing the mason to make a new floor: this surely meant that the mason was installing hard floors. If Edward had wanted the earth floors renewed he would have got the women and children onto the task again, as mentioned earlier. But the mason was a skilled man who would have commanded a higher wage, and he was probably putting down flagstones. Edward never indicates that he was reflooring all the houses, but the number of times he assigns the task over many months would indicate that that was exactly what he was doing.

Whitewashing was another ongoing task. Often, when the weather was wet, Edward had the Maltese whitewashing their houses. Although he does not specifically say the interiors are being painted as well as the exteriors, the task crops up so often that he must have been getting them to paint the inside as well as the

---

[178] See web page 'Greece Weather, Climate and geography' on the website Travelguide.net: https://bit.ly/Ch9IonianClimate which says 'November to March is the rainy season, most notably on the Ionian Islands'. See also **Appendix 9a – Temperature tables, April–October 1829** p. 211–212 created from Edward's records in 1829.

outside – and he would not in any case have assigned exterior painting during heavy rain, as the paint would have been washed away. In mid-January 1829, Edward recorded *Heavy showers_ flooring and whitewashing houses_ clearing land.* Edward kept a close eye on the way the colonists were looking after themselves, and whitewashing was a significant part of this. Only a month later, when there had been *Rain all the morning*, Edward again made Maltese whitewash their houses. We might wonder why he repeated this process so frequently. The clue is in the properties of the paint recipe, the mixture traditionally used for whitewash:

> a low-cost type of paint made from slaked lime (calcium hydroxide, $Ca(OH)_2$) and chalk (calcium carbonate, ($CaCO_3$), … is usually applied to exteriors; however, it is traditionally used for interiors in food preparation areas, particularly rural dairies, for its mildly antibacterial properties.[179]

Whitewashing appears again in July. Edward clearly considers frequent repainting an essential part of house maintenance. He may have known of the hygiene property of the paint, but it might also have been in his mind that clean, brightly painted homes would be good for morale.

The majority of the outdoor work in January was land clearing and making walls, two linked activities. Clearing land involved removing stones, and these were used for building projects. *Making protecting walls* – farmyard walls, field walls or the banking for terraces – was a regular activity. Land clearing and making walls continued into March, but Edward had more than one technique for wall-building. On 30 April, *commenced making a cob wall for the farm yard at St Nicolo which I think will answer very well.* This is puzzling, as he had also mentioned beginning building work in the farmyard at the end of December. Perhaps there were sheds to shelter livestock.

Turnips were an essential fodder crop, but Edward's initial sowing ran to seed too quickly. He transplanted some of them as a source of seed – and probably fed the rest, small though they might have been, to livestock. Despite this initial hiccup, turnips were a favourite crop, Edward writing on 11 May 1829 *My Swede turnips look very well, though there has been scarcely any rain since I sowed them* and on 16 June, *My Swede turnips look beautiful, they were sown about the right time for a Spring crop, I shall give them another deep hoeing in a day or two.*

An important project was begun on 28 May 1829: *Mason digging foundations for a barn_ I want to get the foundation wall built to be able to make a floor for thrashing.* 10 June: *getting on as fast as possible with the barn foundation that I*

---

[179] https://en.wikipedia.org/wiki/Whitewash

*may make the threshing floor_*, 11 June: *I put the corn in stacks till the threshing floor is ready* and by 12 June: *Mason & assistant cutting stones for the barn.*[180]

Fig. 16. A barn at Agios Nikolaos, Kefalonia[181]

The barn and its threshing floor were essential to the long-term success of the colony. Much stone-carrying ensued, again done by the women and boys, throughout the rest of June. Edward was very anxious to get the threshing floor ready in time for his grain harvest. He manufactured this from scratch, detailing the recipe in his entry for 15–16 July:

> *All getting stones down for the barn and farm yard_ Mason laying the floor for thrashing_ It is composed of the following materials 6 boxes of lime 6 of sand and 1 of iron filings_ the receipt[182] said blood was required but I had none_*

Edward did not say where he had read the recipe, possibly in his *Agricultural Dictionary*, mentioned earlier in the journal. Despite being short of the one

---

[180] Edward's two different spellings, 'thrashing' and 'threshing', illustrate nicely the fluidity of spelling at this time.

[181] Jeff Morgan, 2006, Alamy stock photo This barn looks as though it is built of stone. It is unlikely that this is Edward's barn because he probably built his near the colony. If this one predates the 1953 earthquake, it is remarkable in an area of Kefalonia which was otherwise devastated.

[182] Recipe.

ingredient, the floor, finished on 23 July, was *as hard as stone*. Once the foundations were laid and the floor usable, the mason progressed to the walls, working with an assistant to cut the stone. As time was pressing and the urgent necessity of harvesting loomed, almost all the colony workers – men, women and children – were involved in the final push to carry enough stone for its walls. The masons meanwhile were *cutting stone for the barn* and then, with the foundations finished, building the walls began on 22 July.

There were – and still are – several steps involved in taking wheat from a plant growing in the ground to flour ready to be used for baking. Reaping was the first task, cutting the wheat stalks low to the ground with a scythe and bundling it into sheaves or stooks. It had to be left to dry in the sun and, when it was ready, carried to the threshing floor. The outer hard inedible husk had to be separated from the edible kernel. From ancient times this was done by hand, although from the eighteenth century onwards machinery was being developed to speed up this and other harvesting processes. But Edward, as yet, had no machinery, and his workers used a rudimentary tool, a flail, two lengths of wood joined by a chain link. The worker held one length in his hand and swung the other down on the grain.

Fig. 17. Threshing of corn on a threshing floor[183]

---

[183] Universal History Archive/UIG /Bridgeman Images.

Flails were new to the Maltese. In June 1829

> it is ridiculous to see the Maltese thrash with the flail, they never saw
> such things before_ they are accustomed to tread out the corn with
> horses a bit like the old testament oxen.[184]

However, five weeks later

> the Maltese learn thrashing tolerably quick and would now beat the
> Greeks hollow_ on account of the superiority of our flails, the Greek
> flails being so heavy that one can hardly lift them and the thong that
> ties the swingle to the handstaff is about 2 ft long+ [sic].

The final process in extracting the grain was winnowing it. From the threshing, the husks and kernels of wheat would have been mixed together on the floor. As the husks are much lighter than the grain, from ancient times separating kernels and husks was achieved by allowing the air to carry them away. It was not a task requiring great skill, as the two little girls in Fig. 18 demonstrate:

Fig. 18. Winnowing corn in Brittany, France[185]

---

[184] 'You must not muzzle an ox when it is treading out the corn.' Deuteronomy 25:4, Jerusalem Bible 1974 edition.
[185] Frederick Goodall, 1822–1904. Museums Sheffield.

Edward wrote:

> As we have no wheat in the village began thrashing some on one of
> the old Greek floors_ this as a matter of course fills it with dirt and
> small stones_ we are obliged to clean it with the wind but this will
> soon be remedied as I have ordered a winnowing machine to be made
> which I expect in a few days.

Relying on the wind was of course a risky business as there could be too much wind
or too little. This was another biblical technique and one which Edward quickly
replaced with a machine something like the one in Fig. 19.

Fig. 19. A German winnowing machine, 1839 [186]

Although there were several *beautiful days* in January 1829, Edward also recorded
on the 26th

> the rain and cold weather keep back the crops very much I cannot yet
> earth up the potatoes those that were above ground have been cut
> down by the frost_ the others are coming up.

---

[186] 'Duitse handwanmolen uit 1839' by Rasbak from https://bit.ly/Ch9Winnower, licensed
under CC BY-SA 3.0

The health of the Maltese workers was always worse in cold wet weather. On 29 January 1829 Edward recorded *a great addition to our sick list to day_ I do not know the reason*. In the second week of February there were two more sickness records: *9ᵗʰ–11th 'this cold weather makes many of the Maltese sick* and again *12ᵗʰ–14ᵗʰ very few of the Maltese worked_ the others chose to remain in their houses not being able to bear the excessive cold*.

The chill of the winter air was a real problem for the Maltese. Edward's attempt to solve this problem was to order warm outdoor attire, and on 11 January (a Sunday) he *Received 50 great coats for the Maltese*, and six days later he took delivery of 33 more. Edward was not inconsiderate in deploying his workers, and would alternate outdoor and indoor tasks when it was showery, for example *Constant heavy showers_ in the intervals clearing land close to houses* and *The weather was so cold that the Maltese could not be put out of their houses_ a few however worked some in the garden, others planting Carubi trees*.

But with fine weather Edward's workforce could make great headway, as on 16–17 February:

> *Fine days_ clearing, making walls, working the earth round the currants and grapes, carrying out manure &c_ commenced the walls of the farm yard at St Nicolo_ Calogeri ploughing.*

In recording the weather, Edward occasionally gives us glimpses of the landscape, the setting of the colony and its fauna:

> *February 6ᵗʰ Showers of rain and hail all day_ much snow on the mountains lots of woodcocks*
>
> *9–11 Feb showers and cold weather*
>
> *15ᵗʰ, Sunday, Beautiful day_ the snow on the mountains drove the hares down_ shot two.*

In the spring there were far fewer on the sick list, although in April *on the 15ᵗʰ four men fell ill while at work*. However, by 24 April Edward reported that *the Maltese were never in a better state of health than at present, we have not one sick every one works except 2 old women and the infants*. The weather had been fine and warm for some time, and this was surely the main reason for the improvement in the health of the workers – but spring was not exclusively balmy and settled. On 1 May there was a *Tremendous gale of wind all night and day from the north_* but he still had *men at work as yesterday* and next day *Wind still very strong_ Thermʳ 58*. In August *3 men fell ill with fever on the 17ᵗʰ this is the first sickness we have had for a long time indeed*. Between 2 and 7 of September, *7 cases of fever 3 very bad ones,* and on 8 *Sent in the sick Maltese to the hospital,* but by the 15th *Maltese nearly all returned from hospital well.* Edward himself was very rarely ill, but on

> 20th–24th October [1829] *Went into town owing to illness_ Labourers under the care of Sergeant McGuaire* [sic] *putting in barley_ bought 3 more bullocks and 2 cows for 84 dollars.*

Edward was working in an isolated area and alone, so that visiting the doctor was a significant expedition. But he cannot have been seriously ill, as he would have had to travel to town either on horseback across country or by boat from Poros, and moreover he was well enough on the same visit to go to market and buy cattle. Although the model farm was the brainchild of Colonel Napier, it was an officially sanctioned project financed by the British government of the Ionian Islands, with the consequent advantage of support from the local garrison in Argostoli. This support enabled Edward to leave his post for the four days during which he would have seen the doctor, and stayed with Napier and his wife.

Fig. 20. Cattle in Kefalonia[187]

As well as having an initially unskilled and demoralised workforce, Edward was working land that had been abandoned so long by the Greeks prior to the colony's commencement that it was effectively virgin.[188] Some of the stones were so large that he wrote on a couple of occasions that stone had to be blasted, probably with gunpowder obtained from the barracks in Argostoli.

> Large boulders in the field that were too large to be dug out and drawn off presented a special challenge to farmers. They basically had three options: (1) dig a deep hole next to the boulder and tip into it, (2) split the boulder into smaller pieces, or (3) leave it in the field. All three approaches were used. Given the difficulties of removing these boulders a number of detailed explanations for splitting them were published. One advantage of splitting the boulders was it provided pieces of stones with

---

[187] With many thanks to Cecilia Jenkins for use of the photograph.
[188] *The Colonies*, p. 233 ff. C J Napier.

one or more flat faces suitable for building projects. The boulders could be split using the fire method, hammering wedges into existing cracks, quarrying the boulder, or blasting. Blasting by far was the most discussed method in the literature … The blasting method was introduced into Great Britain in the 1670s from Germany.[189]

Scrub and rocks had to be cleared, but the urgent follow-on task was to build up the quality of the soil, whose preparation was crucial to satisfactory harvests. Soil improvement required a battery of techniques: it had to be cleared of scrub and stones, then ploughed and reploughed to bring it to a fine tilth, and above all improved with fertiliser to provide nutrients for the growing plants. The various fertilisers and soil improvers which he used were crops in themselves.

The best fertiliser was animal manure, preferably from cattle. In Edward's experience, livestock should be husbanded in the English way, keeping cattle in enclosed land and saving both cow and horse dung for use on the land. If a herd was successfully developed it would build up two other sources of income, dairy and meat. He had started his dairy herd six months after taking over the colony, but with an extremely limited budget he could increase it only gradually. There was the added problem that cattle manure needs to be well rotted before use, otherwise it is too acidic for seeds and young plants. So, knowing that it would be a long time before he would have an adequate supply of manure, he turned to other soil nutrient sources. The next best fertiliser came from leguminous crops.[190] There are many forms of leguminous crops, and they have the added benefit of being useful either as fodder for cattle and other farm animals (tares/vetch, clover/trefoil, lucern) or as food for human consumption (peas, beans and chickpeas).

There are several different species of tares, some with long thin spikes of small blueish-violet flowers, others like one I saw growing in the verge as I was walking along the road from Poros to Sami one day, a dramatic spike of red (Fig. 21) which I fancifully imagined to be a descendant of Edward's plantings. The flowers of all these vetches have the characteristic 'sweet pea' shape, although much smaller than the ornamental garden flower.

---

[189] *Field Clearing: Stone Removal and Disposal Practices in Agriculture & Farming*, James E Gage, *ASC Bulletin* 76, 2014, pp. 33–75 https://bit.ly/Ch9blasting

[190] A plant family which includes peas, beans, clover, vetches, lucern. This group of plants has the valuable property of fixing nitrogen in the soil, which is then available to other plant groups. Nitrogen is a component of chlorophyll and therefore essential for photosynthesis. Lucern is also known as alfalfa. https://bit.ly/Ch9leguminousPlants

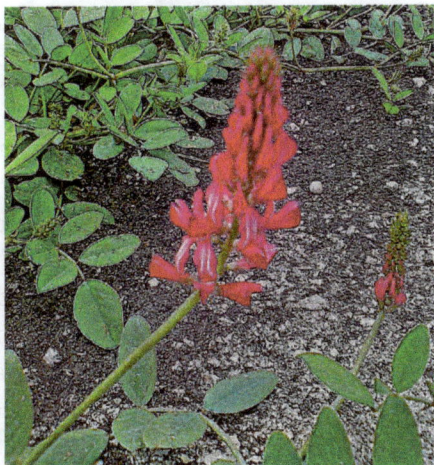

Fig. 21. Red Crown Vetch or sainfoin (holy hay) LAC[191]

Only two weeks after his arrival in September 1828, Edward had organised sowings of tares,[192] and a week later had put in clover. Of all the crops tares proved to be the most successful, but Edward was disappointed that the cattle did not fatten up on them in the first year, and concluded that the crop needed grinding at the mill before feeding to the cattle because they found it difficult to digest. Another marginal leguminous crop was lentils, but Edward only mentions it once. The carob tree is also leguminous.

Two other fertilizing materials he used were seaweed and heath, both of which were freely available and only required collecting. Towards the end of July 1829 Edward had men *carrying up seaweed for manure* and a couple of weeks later, *Women spreading seaweed over the land.* The same month he wrote

> *Our straw owing to the heat is very brittle I have sold it for 6 dollars*
> *a thousand_ we must set to work as soon as we can to collect together*
> *all the heath possible to supply the place of it for manure*

and later in the year both men and women were *gathering heath for manure.*

His care for stock, principally ensuring a good mixed diet for them, was, Edward implied in his first year-end report of September 1829, a new idea he had introduced on the island:

> *I see no reason why bullocks should not be fattened in this country_*
> *the good this will do Cefalonia by preventing so much money from*
> *being sent out of it I leave more competent judges to determine_ if it*

---

[191] Photograph taken near Poros, Kefalonia, LAC.
[192] Which he also called 'vetches'.

answers with us the Greeks will soon commence at it, and thus a new
field of rendering themselves independant [sic] *will be opened to them*
*which now they have not the least idea of_*

Prior to the arrival of the British, the Greeks did have cattle, and they also kept pigs, although probably only one or two per family. Horses – or more likely ponies, mules or donkeys – might have been used as pack animals between the villages, especially before Napier improved and increased the road network. No doubt domestic fowl would have been kept by the Greeks, too, so Edward did not have to introduce them. It was his management of livestock which was new to the islanders. He had quickly been able to ensure a proper supply of eggs and chicken meat for the table by setting up his hen coop, and he would do the same with other animals.

As soon as the cattle joined the colony, feeding them generated several tasks. The animals could, of course, be put to pasture to graze and in doing so they began the manuring process – but if they were to fatten well and produce strong, healthy calves they needed much more concentrated nourishment than that provided by the largely uncultivated rough pasture of the valley and hillsides.

Barley was primarily a fodder crop, although it may also have been available as food to the farm workers. Thirty bushels of barley seed had arrived at the same time as the seed potatoes, but Edward waited until November to sow it. This might have been partly because the ground required a lot of preparation to bring it to a fine tilth, or he could just have been waiting for the due season. At this time, too, he commenced sowing wheat. He used different techniques to accomplish the sowing of grain crops, with the *Maltese hoeing in wheat* [*and*] *ploughs putting in barley*, and presumably assigning the Greeks to the ploughs. The barley may have been fed to the cattle and he certainly used it to fatten hogs, but the wheat was for human consumption. We do not have many records of individual Maltese families, but we know that the Mallia family were the colony's bakers.[193] Surprisingly, Edward did not cultivate oats, although his journal records several times that the island abounded with wild oats and that they grew very well, in one instance being *full 7 feet high*.

On 15 March 1829 *Mr Lusi a farmer of Cefalonia went over all the land with me, he agrees that it is very good.* A couple of days later, Edward recalled

> *Mr Lusi says he has seen* [*currants*] *planted in Italy in rows 8 yards*
> *apart with mulberry trees at short distances to support them_ I will*
> *try some in this way with pear and apple trees which he says will not*
> *injure the currants, but which I doubt very much.*

---

[193] See later in the story.

Disatisfaction amongst the workers surfaced on 23 March, when Edward *found that eleven of the Maltese had absented themselves for the purpose of soliciting more pay_ I went off to town after them the remainder of the men planting potatoes_*

Things were not looking entirely rosy for the colony. On 26 March 1829 in an extended journal entry Edward wrote angrily:

> *the Colonel tells me that it is reported to the Maltese Government that the land of the colony which was assigned to the Maltese and which we are now working, is worth nothing and that no cultivation can make it produce a good crop_ whoever has reported this would have shown much more sense had he not made so unfounded an assertion, which not only shows him to know nothing of Agriculture, but also to be a downright fool, not only is our land equal to all and superior to most parts of Cefalonia which I have seen, but as good land as I have met with in any part of the world_ without manure, and with scarcely any cultivation we shall I hope, even this year have an average crop of corn, though in many places I have sown wheat after wheat_ Every one who has seen the Colony since I have been here has concurred with me in thinking our land is of the finest quality_ this is sufficient proof I think therefore that the person who has reported this and who I understand is the quondam Doctor of the Colony, knows no more on the subject on which he has written than any cockney that has never left the streets of London.*

It was probably no coincidence that the following month *Sir F Adam visited the Colony.*

On 6 April, some more special visitors: *Colonel Napier, Capt & Mrs Napier & Capt Kennedy visited the colony_ the Colonel determined in order to induce the Maltese to stay, to allow more pay to those that deserved it_ viz 9d instead of 6d a day.* The visit of the eleven Maltese to Argostoli had proved fruitful.

Captain and Mrs Napier were Charles Napier's brother Henry and his wife, who spent an extended period on the island in 1829. There is a wonderful account of their visit to the Pronos area, including their stay with Cambici, and concluding with Henry's early morning walk with Edward Curling. The original record is from Henry Napier, but is relayed by Priscilla Napier in her book *Revolution and the Napier Brothers*:

> Signor Cambici receiving them "en prince; and after a good substantial supper Al Greco, that is to say a whole lamb roasted; plenty of fowls; bread piled up on shining silver plates, and plenty of excellent wine with divers patriotic songs by our host, we were not sorry to go to our beds, tired from a ride of near thirty miles in the heat of the day.

Cambici is a patriot, zealous, sincere, and enthusiastically attached to the cause of Grecian Liberty; he is rich too and maintained a hundred men commanded by his brother but all paid by him, at the siege of Missolonghi." His wife was handsome, but more dame de ménage than lady of the house. "She did not sing, but the patriotic airs were sufficiently interesting from the touching beauty of their music alone, independent of the place and the person who sung them. The struggle was not ended, the hearts of all were in it, and it was in itself glorious. Could we have understood the words we should of course have felt them more, but there was no lack of sentiment even in the sound, and assuredly none in our feelings. ...

Little Hanmer Bunbury[194] who was of our party, having lost his arm by a Turkish shot at the Battle of Navarino became an object of strong interest, as well as of curiosity and respect, not alone to Cambici and his household, but to the Papa or Priest and many of the neighbouring people of every rank as soon as the fact became known. The fact of an English child losing his arm in defence of the [Greek] cause excited deep interest and many a shaggy head peeped in at the door or window to see the young hero."[195]

Henry Napier recorded that the conversation they had that evening with Cambici centred on farming and in particular varieties of grass. He included a rare insight into Elizabeth Napier's kitchen management in Kefalonia:

Cambici had introduced Lucerne into Cephalonia, and Charles [Napier] had brought Guinea grass: Cambici showed them also a kind of couch grass which was native, "larger, stronger, and fully as difficult to eradicate as couch grass", which might do, as it did in Naples, as "a most nutritive food for cattle ... We entered on this with great eagerness." ... "There seems no reason why there should not be as fine beef, mutton, butter, milk and cheese, not only on the Colony but all over Cephalonia as in England; at all events for a great portion of the year. Mrs Napier has

---

[194] Richard Hanmer Bunbury (1813–1857) https://bit.ly/HanmerBunburyLetters 'He learnt to paint with his left hand and his ink and watercolours are held in the National Gallery of Victoria, Melbourne. Sketcher, naval officer, civil officer and pastoralist, he was born in Mildenhall, Suffolk, in December 1813, fourth son of Sir Henry Bunbury and his first wife, Louisa Emilia, née Fox. One of his elder brothers was Henry William St Pierre Bunbury. Richard was midshipman in the navy when, aged about fourteen, he lost his right arm at the Battle of Navarino in 1827.' https://bit.ly/Ch7Hanmer. At the time of this extract from Henry Napier's journal Hanmer Bunbury was aged about sixteen. Hanmer continued his career in the navy until, in 1840, he left the navy and emigrated with his wife Sarah Susannah Sconce to Australia.

[195] *Revolution and the Napier Brothers*, Priscilla Napier, Michael Joseph, 1973. p. 99.

already made at Argostoli incomparable butter, cream so thick that I mistook it for clotted cream, excellent cream cheese; veal of the first quality and admirable bacon, put on the table, all charges included, for twopence halfpenny a pound! This astonished her Greek and most of her English neighbours, but there was nothing to prevent their doing the same but indolence."[196]

Henry Napier and Edward Curling were

up at four next morning for a good close look at the ruins of Pronos, "for I had not seen half enough of the latter the evening before. Its excessive and peculiarly romantic beauty still hung about my mind like a first love, so that I could not rest without a second sight of it". Henry was on foot, but [Edward][197] Curling had trusted himself to a local pony, "nearer the size of a Dog than a Horse, and more like a Bear than either ... my guess would be that Ulysses' old dog Argus fell in love with Penelope's donkey and hence the Cephalonian Shelties", Henry speculated. They climbed steadily, with Henry splashing in and out of the mountain streams and envying Curling his local sandals, so much better adapted for rock climbing than his own heavy boots which allowed no play to the toes. Henry made two sketches, and they were on the way down when Curling jarred his feelings by shooting a heron, "noble, stately, bold and proud, just alighted in the marsh ... I have often marvelled at the recklessness with which really excellent and even tender-hearted men, when once the gun is in their hand, shoot right and left, and kill merely for the pleasure of killing. Nay, I have done so myself, but always with a dash of remorse, and hope never more to do so, for there is something so repulsive in the dying struggles of any animal as to paralyse all previous pleasure." He hoped a further step in civilization would "in time confine shooting to animals which serve for food, but there it must stop, unless we turn Pythagoreans or Hindoos ... Why is man incited as it were to bloodshed even by the very construction of his frame and juices ..."

Up on Pronos, as Henry and Curling were standing among its gigantic tumbled stones, gazing at the distant coast of Greece, a huge eagle appeared overhead, "now sailing to and fro with a sort of disturbed dignity, now again bearing down on us like a three-decker ... there is something peculiarly fine in the measured vibrations of an Eagle's wing

---

[196] *Revolution and the Napier Brothers*, pp. 99–100.

[197] Priscilla Napier initially referenced Edward as 'Edward Curling', but a confusion developed in part of her account, and in this passage she names him 'Charles Curling'. A visit by Edward's brother Charles to Kefalonia is not mentioned in any primary sources and Priscilla Napier's mention of a 'Charles Curling' is the only one in this period of the story.

… Cambici told us that there are many of them among these hills, and that he has known them, when people were near and seeking for their nests, clutch up a large stone in their talons and then hovering over their adversary endeavour to crush him by dropping it on his head." The soaring eagle in its strength, the high air of Pronos, so serene and beautiful, made Henry feel that the archaic men who made it their dwelling must at any rate have been extremely healthy, "running up and down these rocks like goats". Time was when he could have been as swift, but now Curling had the legs of him.[198]

The same month, Edward bought five cows from the local convent, and five months later he bought more:

> *five old bullocks and three cows having landed from the Morea[199] and being cheap I bought them for fattening and working_ As I could do nothing with the Convent cows which were as wild as hares I sent them all away_ When these cows that I have bought calve we may hope to commense the formation of a dairy I have desired Cambisi to write for three more_*

On 18 April Edward *went up to the Convent of Pirgi and brought away 5 cows_*
Ten days later he reported on their progress: *my cows begin to be tolerably quiet but give scarcely any milk_ I believe from not being accustomed to be milked they will not give their milk*, but good news on 11 May: *one of the cows calved_*
At the other end of the livestock scale, bees were his smallest charges, and he *hived a swarm of bees at St Nicolo_* on 10 August 1829. We don't hear about them again until August, when the Maltese

> *took our honey to day_ the Maltese have an excellent method of doing this without destroying or injuring the bees_ the hives are built generally with 6 square flat stones with tiles on the roof to keep off the rain_ the stone at the back is not fixed to the hive_ the Maltese opens this and cuts away as much honey as he thinks proper, merely defending himself from the bees by a sack over his head and keeping*

---

[198] *Revolution and the Napier Brothers*, pp. 100–101. Henry Napier, 1789–1853, had a distinguished naval career. His chief interest was history, and he wrote *Florentine History from the earliest Authentic Records to the Accession of Ferdinand the Third, Grandduke of Tuscany,* in six volumes, published in 1846–47. He was aged 40 at the time of his visit to Kefalonia. https://en.wikipedia.org/wiki/Henry_Edward_Napier

[199] The Morea was the name for a large area of south-western mainland Greece whose western border was the Ionian Sea, making it the part of the mainland closest to Kefalonia. See Wikipedia https://en.wikipedia.org/wiki/Morea

a little fire of cow dung on a tile close to him, the smoke of which
*prevents the bees from going near him_*

So even if the Maltese were as ignorant of farming ways as the writings of Napier and Edward give us to understand, some of them at least had knowledge that stood the community in good stead.[200]

More building was happening at St Nicolo – on 3 August, *three masons at work at the farm yard wall_ many of the Maltese assisting them.* While keeping an eye on structural maintenance, Edward was also *filling up the watercourse behind the houses* in June and July 1829. This was possibly a development of the drain which Edward had had dug on his first day at the colony. In his end-of-year report he mentions Cambici's excellence in irrigating his crops, and he himself knew how vital was a summer supply of water. In his March report Edward wrote extensively about the critical contribution which rain makes to the state of the land. Reading his journal, it is apparent that for Edward, it was essential to look for solutions to problems thrown up by the terrain and climate, and that was no more than any good farmer would do; it was ingrained in him by his experience with his father.

At the end of September, twelve months since he had first taken over the colony, Edward wrote a comprehensive and lengthy report in his journal, on the developments to date. He was objective about recording the difficulties and setbacks as well as clear progress.

---

[200] See **Appendix 9b – Beekeeping** p. 213 for further information and images of stone beehives.

Chapter 10 – Change of air and scene

In the first two weeks of October 1829, as Edward began his second farming year, there was an air of settled purpose about the colony, a succession of autumnal tasks being carried on without incident: ploughing, harrowing and 'hoeing in' wheat and barley. He also had the *Mason plastering a wall, 2 Greek labourers burning gypsum and women spreading seaweed over the land.*

Gypsum has many industrial uses in the twenty-first century, but this mineral is most commonly used in making plasters of various kinds including what we commonly call 'plaster of Paris' for setting fractures in human and animal bones; its other major use is in wall plaster. Edward must have used it in making such a building plaster for finishing walls: in the same entry he has the mason plastering a wall.

Seaweed was collected from the beaches in Kent when Edward lived there as a boy. R K I Quested writes 'Sea-weed was much collected, mixed with earth and dung in the manure heaps.'[201] It is still widely used in the twenty-first century as an organic fertilizer, available now in liquid form.

In the third week of October he *bought 3 more bullocks and 2 cows for 84 dollars_* Still anxious about the quantity of fertilizing material required for the colony, in November 1829 Edward had the workers *carrying into farm yard all the grass possible for manure.*

His hogs having been shut up for fattening in August 1829, they were finally ready for slaughter in October. On the 16th, he *killed one of [his] fattened pigs, it weighed 132 lbs_ put it all in pickle for hams and bacon_* and on 28 November, *Sent in 160 lbs of bacon_* 9 Dec 1829 *killed a pig and sold all to the Maltese except the hams,* evidence that the colony might eventually become self-sufficient in food.

On 21 Dec 1829 Edward

> sent in two bullocks 2 days ago_ they were not very fat owing to their not digesting the tares ... and my not having other food to give them_ they weighed 695 lbs and with the heads and offal sold for £11_5_9_ They cost us £7_16 and they have eaten about 5000 lbs of vetches which at 4$ a thousand is £4_6_8_[202] making together £12_2_8_ thus the balance is rather against us_ I expected that we should have had

---

[201] *The Isle of Thanet Farming Community*, R K I Quested, self-published, updated edition 2001.

[202] Edward often shifts between the dollar and the British pound, but this is the only time he mixes them in the same sentence. (The dollar was used in most parts of Greece at that time, as the phoenix, introduced after independence in early 1829, wasn't readily accepted. Eventually, in 1832, the drachma was introduced instead. See Wikipedia https://bit.ly/Ch8Phoenix)

*the balance on the other side of the account, but the fact is we have not got proper food to give them_ however, this itself is sufficient to make us go on with them on account of the quantity of manure which is thus collected_*

He had a scientifically objective and financially aware approach, monitoring the work constantly and recording in his journal improvements to be made in the future. However, to the watching administrations, both British and Greek, this openness might have been seen as an admission of failure.

The building work brought a different set of snags. On 21 January 1830 Edward had *men terracing land and bringing stone down for farm yard wall where the cob wall has fallen down.* Either the original cob work was not well done or the wall could not withstand the weather. Or both. It is possible that heavy winter rain had undermined the wall. Edward waited until April and got the mason to rebuild the wall, using stone. Terracing had become a regular feature of the labourers' work.

It was not until March 1830 that he followed Mr Lusi's suggestion of the previous year: *Went to Samos and brought away 250 Mulberry trees and planted them in the lines of the young currants.* A fortnight later he *Ingrafted a number of Mulberrys* [sic] *on Plane trees.*

At the end of March 1830, Edward wrote a half-yearly report. This was not as detailed as the yearly reports which he submitted at the end of September. In it he recorded a conversation with Mr Lusi:

As currants have fallen so much in price I am preparing to follow the system which Mr Lusi tells me is practised in Italy_ viz. leaving the rows of vines about a rod and a half apart, and in the rows planting mulberry or any other sort of tree thought most profitable over which the vines are allowed to extend themselves_ he [Mr Lusi] *contends that we might have the same quality of currants in this way as in the mode now practised, that we could have also the profits of the trees, and be enabled to have a crop of anything we liked between the rows_ I have already planted some mulberry trees in every third row in my young plantation ....*

The concepts of inter-cropping and companion cropping were not new ones. The two ideas are not dissimilar, although the first is more concerned with making the best use of space, while a good simple definition of the second is 'two plants that help each other to grow'. Careful choice of companion plants is essential to ensure that one crop does not dominate and take vital nutrients from the other.

Later in the same report he returned to the subject of mulberries and made an exciting commercial proposal:

Whilst speaking of Mulberry trees I forgot to mention a circumstance communicated to me the other day by Mr Cambisi and since corroborated by other Greek gentlemen to whom I have spoken on the subject and if it is true, it is a most important communication for forwarding the establishment of a silk manufactory in the island, he says that the Mulberry ingrafts beautifully on Plane trees_ Now from the place along both sides of the river for 3 or 4 miles are thousands and thousands of plane trees, and therefore in two years from the time of ingrafting we might have a supply of leaf not to be laughed at even in Italy_ this is however private property, but near the convent at the upper part of the valley of Racli there are a great number of trees and as this belongs to Government the concern might be commenced there and extended by purchase afterwards to any extent thought proper_ I state this for the information of Sir F Adam who can carry the plan into execution if he approves of it_ I do not answer for the correctness of the information But I have ingrafted a few trees here and if I stay long enough, will hereafter give a faithful account of the result.

In this report, writing once more about the hidden value of the animals:

these bullocks which I am now fattening have put in all our corn this year, which when taken into calculation makes a wonderful difference in our favor, as when I was obliged to hire some greek ploughs last year I was charged half a dollar a team each day_ and as a penny saved is a penny gained our fattening bullocks may fairly be said to have turned well to account and that the 18 dollars a piece [sic] paid for them was money well laid out_ But I am not satisfied with the way in which they fatten, the fact is we have not yet sufficient food to give them as they do not digest the tares these may be considered as little better than hay, and this with the pasture they have in the day time is the only food they get which is not much of a diet for a fat bullock_ I will let the vetches stand longer this year, I will thrash them also and have them cracked at the mill, which must be a great improvement [to the cattle feed].

He continued to look for alternative cattle feed and resolved

early in the Autumn [to] sow lentils in all my young currants and this will also produce a good supply of food; we must also ingraft our wild Carubi trees which will then produce fruit, and with lots of Swede turnips also, I think in a little while, our bullocks will have no reason

*to complain, and that my dissatisfaction will be done away with also_
I have given a little cotton seed to those now fattening and it is
surprising to see how fast he [sic] is leaving behind all the others, in
a short time I will cut some of the green vetches which will help them
on a little.*

But the Maltese, despite the improvements Edward had made in their habitations
and working conditions, were still drifting away. Edward wrote

*I would have trenched the ground with the hoes of the Maltese but my
number of hands are now so limited that I was obliged to put in the
corn in any way I could_ that which was quickest I was obliged to
consider the best, or have half the ground uncropped.*

Nevertheless, Edward felt that the farming practices and innovations on the colony
were beginning to have an effect locally – the original reason for Napier's setting
the colony up:

*Cambisi at my recommendation also purchased two [cows] and is
quite delighted at the comfort and profit they afford him_, he
communicates this to every one, and people already begin to beg of
him to write and procure them some of the same sort, and I should
not be surprised, if, from the example set by the Maltese Colony, a
house without a cow will be considered a rarity in Cefalonia.*[203]

Although Cambici was hardly a new convert, his demonstration of support for
Edward's example would have had a considerable influence on other local farmers.
    In order to manure the ground, Edward had, he wrote, sheep and goats from the
convent, grazing

*a considerable quantity of land which had vetches last year, & which
I am soon going to sow with Indian corn and I hope to get a tolerable
crop from it.*

---

[203] This may be the source of the theory put forward by Angelos Debonos that prior to
Edward's arrival there were no cattle on the island. It is clear from Edward's journal
that the monasteries (or convents as he called them) certainly had cattle, but perhaps, it
had been customary for only these religious communities to have them. What is also
clear from this passage is that Cambici bought a particular breed, presumably on
Edward's recommendation, probably chosen for their milk production and maybe for
the quality of beef.

Fig. 22. 'Flint corn' or 'Indian corn', more colourful than sweetcorn

Indian corn was his most important crop for feeding to livestock. Both significant acreage and many hours were devoted to nurturing this essential crop. It is a form of maize,[204] whose cobs may have made good food for the workforce as well as the cattle, although the kernel skins are much tougher than modern maize cultivars. The rest of the plant would make good compost. Because the mature plants are large, this crop needs considerable stretches of land, so a great deal of effort went into preparing the territory, clearing, ploughing and manuring it prior to sowing the seed.

Named visitors to the colony were less frequent in Edward's second year, but he hinted at regular visitors in this passage in his report:

> *When I came here first I had heard only of the heavy rains of this country, but when I saw them, my whole attention was engrossed endeavouring to invent some means to protect the land against them, as I already foresaw that if something was not done the land in a short time would not be worth a straw_ Stones we had not on the land and we could not afford the labour necessary for the carriage of them from the mountain, and therefore I made the slanting water furrows which I have before described, and I give myself credit for having by means of these preserved the land very nearly indeed in the same*

---

[204] Alamy stock photo. There is information about flint corn here:
https://bit.ly/Ch8BIndianCorn

condition in which I found it, and this assertion every one will and does admit that visits the Colony.

Elizabeth Napier's health

William Napier reported:

> Mrs Napier became ill, and her husband was forced to take her to England so suddenly that he left his children behind. He touched at Corfu, and was received by the lord high commissioner with all demonstrations of friendship, his lodging being the palace. A passage in the government steamer was offered. Sir Frederick went with them to the sea-side, and took leave with these words, 'Good bye Napier. Stay as long as you please, but remember that the longer you stay the worse for us.'[205]

Elizabeth's state of health must have been dire for Napier to consider taking her back to England. The journey itself would not have helped her condition. The first leg of the journey, by sea, was from Argostoli to the port of Ancona in Italy, and they had broken their journey in Corfu, staying with Sir Frederick Adam.

In Ancona, Elizabeth wrote on 2 June 1830, in great distress, to her daughter Mary, who was travelling in Europe with Samuel Laing (Elizabeth's widower son-in-law) and his children:

Ancona 4 June 1830

My dear Mary I received your letter of 10th April just after I got on board the vessel at Corfu. We arrived here only the 2nd June We had a long and bad voyage and I am still much exhausted by sea sickness but by the time our quarantine is out which will be the 9th I expect to be restored and able to travel and to find benefit from change of air and scene I was not at all prepared for your refusal to meet us on our way, nor can I understand how our meeting is "out of all question" and now particularly when there is great chance (if you leave Tours near the time you say for the north of Germany) that we may cross on the road. However I will not urge you indeed my dear Mary it is hard for me to understand your letter or how it is possible for any one to find so much fault with all I say or do towards every one. I must however remind you that it was not as a visitor that we asked you to come to Cefalonia but to live and share our home and our means as a child who had been away from home and who we wished to return to it and you should have recollected too Mary that my leaving

---

[205] *Life and Opinions*, p. 428.

115

Cefalonia did not rest on any wayward fancy, that you had refused to come to us, that I had been as near death as one could be and not dead and that the cost of yours and Eliza's coming was never even thought of when put in competition with a wish so natural for a mother to feel. Thank God I believe and have good cause to do so that were it to give me comfort and afford a satisfaction so natural and so sacred to a mother my husband would not hesitate at any price within his possible means. do not then puzzle yourself more or calculate for us and for God's sake Mary consider that I am your mother your old and sick mother and that I have a right to your duty and respect and a consideration for my shattered nerves

I cannot tell whether this will reach you but you can direct to me as you do to Eliza_ God bless you my poor Mary and give you power to control your temper_ your affectionate mother

E Napier[206]

The final paragraph of Elizabeth's letter seems to indicate that her daughter Eliza might have been with the Napiers on their journey home, but there is no other indication that she had been staying in Kefalonia with them. The rift between Elizabeth and her other daughter, Mary, must have been a major contributory factor in Elizabeth's decline. Samuel Laing's unyielding opposition to his mother-in-law's marriage prevented Elizabeth from seeing not only her daughter Mary, but her grandchildren. It was a kind of torture for her to know that Mary and her grandchildren were near enough to meet up en route and yet to be actively prevented from doing so. Laing almost certainly wielded undue influence on Mary. In February 1834 he wrote 'My sister-in-law Mary Kelly a few years before, when at Cookham, was so bent upon going abroad with Elizabeth [this Elizabeth was Laing's daughter] that we almost separated on that very point.' It may be that Mary had thought of going to Europe to be within easier travelling distance of a meeting with her mother, but been prevented by Laing from doing so.

The Napiers had chosen to make the majority of the journey back to England overland. Possibly the sea journey would not have suited Elizabeth's delicate condition, but the overland journey was by no means an easy option. From Ancona to London is 840 miles, and even with all the comforts today's travellers enjoy, that would be a major undertaking for a woman, aged sixty-five, then seen as elderly, in poor health, necessitating several overnight stops. For comparison, Catharine Curling's journey by coach from Cookham to Sandwich in September 1819, a journey of about 120 miles, included an overnight stop in London, and as London

---

[206] BL Add MS 49111 f. 96.

to Sandwich then took eleven hours, a journey of 840 miles by coach might reasonably have been expected to take at least two months, and probably took longer with resting intervals for Elizabeth.

Fig. 23. Zollstation am Simplonpass (Customs stop at the Simplon Pass)[207]

Without the benefit of cars, buses or trains, they would have had to travel from Ancona through Switzerland over the Simplon Pass to France; then traversed the full length of France, to arrive at Calais, all the land travel done using a series of horse-drawn public coaches. At Calais they would have boarded the paddle steamer *Rob Roy*.[208] Once on English soil they would still have had a substantial journey to take them to the Napier home in London.

Back in Kefalonia, things were not looking good. William Napier asserted that Sir Frederick Adam seized the opportunity of Napier's absence to halt many of the works which Napier had instigated:

---

[207] Image © Eugene Pierre Francois Giraud, 1886, Art Renewal Centre, Port Reading, NJ. https://bit.ly/CustomsAttheSimplon

[208] The InspirationHub blog has this excellent page on the history of the English Channel ferry crossings between Calais and Dover: https://bit.ly/Ch9ChferryHist. I was surprised to find that *Rob Roy* was assigned as a mail or packet ship as early as 1821. Another surprise was to find that her owner was marine engineer David Napier; not, however, a direct relative of Charles James Napier, but from another branch of the Scottish clan.

first he stopped all the works of Cephalonia, and then removed the Maltese colony … thus stamping out the glowing spark of agricultural knowledge! Mr Curling offered to continue it at no more cost than one hundred pounds yearly, with the certainty that in four years it would make enormous returns, besides the moral advantages of increased comforts and improvement in the character and habits of the poorer classes.[209] [210]

William Napier was incapable of attributing even the slightest fault to his eldest brother Charles, who had been his hero since childhood. Charles was implacably convinced that Sir Frederick Adam had, from jealousy, contrived to besmirch his name and destroy all of the public works he had instigated. The perspective the two Napiers give on the affair is inevitably skewed. While there were certainly major irregularities in the way Adam had treated Charles Napier, William's account has the hallmarks of a full-blown conspiracy theory, complete with spies:

> Five months after Charles Napier's departure, a disturbance in Cephalonia brought Sir Frederick to that Island. It had arisen from a belief, propagated by Russian agents, that Adam's new and foolish code was designed against their religion; and one mode of showing their discontent was refusing to sign an address to the king on his accession. Sir Frederick publicly acknowledged in the island, that this religious fear was the cause, and he sought to remove it: but to the secretary of state[211] he said it arose from what he called Colonel Napier's oppressive and illegal conduct, and his means were [as] base as his end to give that charge plausibility.[212]

William continued the account of the dispute at some length, and Charles himself spent considerable time writing his own fierce outline and rebuttal of the accusations, which he published in 1833.[213]

The dispute between Napier and Samuel Laing also remained unresolved at the time of his departure from Kefalonia.

At the Maltese colony

By the summer of 1830 things were looking up again in the colony. In June, Edward was *selling much garden produce to the Maltese,* and in July, apparently still

---

[209] *Life and Opinions*, p. 428.
[210] Sir Frederick did discuss the possibility of moving the colony to Corfu with Edward, but nothing came of it; see later in this chapter.
[211] Viscount Goderich in England.
[212] *Life and Opinions*, p. 428.
[213] *The Colonies*, pp. 70–603 C J Napier.

optimistic that Napier would be returning, he commenced a second major building project.

> *Mason building reservoir for water at St Nicolo_ this is an important work ... by means of this reservoir I shall be able to irrigate the whole of the garden and all the land under it as far as the sea.*

In August 1830 he had *Men constantly employed terracing_ women collecting herbage for manure &c Mason building reservoir.* This was a highly skilled task, and one which the mason would doubtless have relished as a major source of income for some time. In fact, this project occupied the mason and assistants for ten months as recorded by Edward periodically until finally, in the third week of October 1830, he wrote *Mason and Assistant finished the reservoir in the garden.* You would naturally think that this project was now complete. However, curiously, in the first two weeks of May 1831 he *Employed the mules & donkeys to fetch lime and [porcelain] for the reservoir at St Nicolo and hired a Greek mason to finish this important work.*

But, disturbing the harmony of several months, in September 1830 Edward found that

> *Mr Stevens with the sanction of the Senate at Corfu, <u>sold the whole of the produce of the Colony,</u> and <u>effectually put a stop to all my schemes for collecting manure and improving the land</u>_ On this account I protested against it to Government, but to no purpose this has quite put me out of heart, and destroyed all my hopes of bringing the grounds into a good farming state_ as manure was our chief stuff, without stock we cannot have manure, and without the produce we cannot feed or fatten stock_ Besides this I was <u>selling the corn at nearly double the price that Mr Stevens got for it</u>, as he put it up to Auction and took little pains to sell it well, however the policy of those who are now intriguing against the Colony is to decrease the produce as much as they can in order to have some handle to do away with it entirely which is easily foreseen they aim at.*

Edward had received no prior notice of this. All his innate energy and ebullience was finally defeated by the machinations of local government. No wonder he was, albeit only momentarily, utterly dejected. However, he did not give up. He, along with most other people on the island, was still fully expecting Napier to return and set matters to rights on all fronts.

Chapter 11 – All as contented as possible

It is possible to make a rough judgement of how important a crop was to Edward by the number of times he mentions it in the journal, but some plantings, particularly of fruit trees, were bound to be long-term projects which would not be harvested for many years, so there was nothing to record beyond their planting. This table lists all the crops of which he wrote, with the number of mentions. Cabbages, however, he considered to be partly a fodder crop, and grew them extensively at St Nicolo and between the currant rows.

Crops	Mentions	Crops	Mentions
Wheat	79	chickpeas	9
Tares/Vetch	63	mulberry	8
Potatoes	59	Lucern	5
Currants	54	Indigo	5
Barley	50	Cucumbers	5
Indian corn	49	Lettuce	5
Swede turnips	46	Grapes	4
Cabbages	24	Apple *	4
Cotton – used for fodder	24	lemon *	4
Guinea grass	20	Nua Papa	4
Pear	19	Olives	3
carubi/cambi	18	cherry*	3
Beans	18	Radishes	3
Charcoal	15	celery	2
Straw	12	Lentils	1
Peas	11	Walnuts*	1
Clover/trefoil	11	almonds*	1
'natural grass of Cefalonia'	9	artichokes	1
* these were tree saplings which would not be cropped until years later.			

Fig. 24. Table of crops

The most important vegetable crop Edward grew was potatoes, underlining that although harvested crops were sent by gunboat to Argostoli for sale, potatoes may have been the main food source for the workforce, particularly in the early days of the colony. The larger crops were field crops, while those which he grew on a smaller scale were grown in the garden. For example, beans were a field crop which he started to sow two months after his arrival in the colony, but peas he grew in the garden, and his first sowing was in March 1829. Other garden crops included cucumbers, cauliflowers, lettuce and radishes.

Only three months after his arrival, at the end of December he *put some walnuts and almonds to day in the ground in a basket of manure_ Cambisi tells me they will be ready to plant out in March.*

Periodically he ran trials of seed, either because he was not sure whether the climate would suit the plant or because the plant was new to him, something recommended by one of his local advisors. Occasionally he received plants from further afield; for example, the governor of the Ionian Islands, Sir Frederick Adam, sent a few Guinea grass plants from Corfu for Edward to try. At the time, Edward had no suitable land apart from a rather wet area so, having manured the ground, he brought dry soil from elsewhere and the grass got off to a good start. Receiving a number of currant cuttings in January 1829, he had them buried until they could be planted out in warmer weather.

Although, as mentioned earlier, currants had been the primary established crop on Kefalonia long before Edward or Napier appeared on the scene, the traditional method of cultivation which can be seen in Joseph Cartwright's painting (Fig. 25) was inefficient in a number of ways. The plants were not trained or planted in rows, but merely grew in low mounds, the fruit liable to trail in the soil.

Fig. 25.   Town and harbour of Argostoli (Cephalonia)[214]

Edward addressed this from the outset. It is surprising that grapes, which were a separate crop from currants, were not seen as commercial, given that currants did

---

[214] Joseph Cartwright, 1821. Adapted from
https://theolabrinos.blogspot.com/2017/12/joseph-cartwright.html

so well for the islanders. Edward did however, grow sufficient grapes to have *gathered and made wine of our grapes*.[215]

Edward liked to make maximum use of available resources. He was also eager to take useful advice from local landowners including, of course, Cambici. In March 1829, Cambici recommended a grass crop to Edward:

> *Mr Cambisi showed me some natural grass of Cefalonia, which seems a species of Guinea grass_ he says he can cut it in the summer almost every fortnight, the leaf and taste are like the guinea grass_ Cambisi's mules &c eat it voraciously_ if it is not Guinea grass it is quite as good and I shall have some of it transplanted into the Colony immediately.* [216]

There was some confusion here, as Edward referred to 'natural grass' in other contexts, when he was clearly writing about the wild grass growing on uncultivated land around the colony: *the women and 6 boys are cutting the natural grass with which the Colony abounds, I am in hopes we shall make a good stack of it*. Cambici on the other hand appears to be cultivating the 'natural grass' which he showed Edward.

Asserting his authority must have been an uphill struggle for Edward at first, especially as the nascent colony had been neglected for so long. We already know about the eleven Maltese workers who absented themselves in March and who had returned to work the following day. At some point a group of Maltese asked to be repatriated. This was, of course, a matter to be referred to Napier, who was eventually forced to begin making arrangements. On 21 April 1829 [217] he wrote to Captain Mawdesley, his counterpart on the island of Zante,[218] asking for details of the Malta packet.[219] Napier had been instructed by Sir Frederick to allow the returning Maltese only to go straight home; they were not to spend time on any of the other Ionian Islands: they all had unpaid debts to the convents on Kefalonia,

---

[215] Kefalonia has its own grape variety, Robola, and a distinctive fine wine from it is still available on the island https://www.orealios.gr/en/robola/. Wikipedia says 'Robola is a white Greek wine grape variety that is grown primarily on the Ionian island of Kefalonia. Historically the vine was thought to be the same variety as the Friuli wine grape Ribolla and was thought to have been brought to northeast Italy by Venetian merchants trading with Kefalonia in the thirteenth century. However, DNA profiling in the twenty-first century has cast doubt on that theory and today Robola is classified by the Vitis International Variety Catalogue (VIVC) as a separate variety', see their online database, https://bit.ly/Ch11Robola

[216] 'Guinea grass (Megathyrsus maximus (Jacq.) B. K. Simon & S. W. L. Jacobs) is a major pantropical grass used throughout the tropics for pasture, cut-and-carry, silage and hay. It is a fast growing and leafy grass, which is palatable to livestock with a good nutritional value.' https://bit.ly/FeedGuineaGrass

[217] TNA CO 136.1274 – bundle of correspondence in date order; individual items do not have catalogue numbers.

[218] Zante is now known as Zakinthos.

[219] See **Appendix 7a – Packet ships** p. 200.

and Napier felt that they should be made to pay off those debts in instalments before being allowed to leave, *however one don't like to be over rigid towards poor devils, though they do try one's patience severely by their folly and knavishness_* [220] He seemed to have been oblivious to the fact that he had been responsible, however unintentionally, for the downturn in the fortunes of the Maltese prior to Edward's arrival. He outlined to Mawdesley the provision he had made for the Maltese:

> *I never met such a damned set_ they have a house, clothes, and pay found them and yet they are discontent and want to get back to starve at Malta! Every child has three pence a day; every woman 4d and the men 6d, 9d, and a shilling a day according to their conduct, besides being taken care of in the public hospital if sick.*

But his prolonged absence in England, winding up affairs after his mother's death, which happened just as the Maltese were arriving and when things were very chaotic for them, had meant the project had got off to a very poor start, and they had been left adrift for too long.

However, the following month, May, Edward wrote: *the Maltese seem all as contented as possible it gives me pleasure to see them all enjoying themselves, dancing and singing as they were to day.* It must indeed have been very satisfying for Edward to see his workforce content, although he may also have been making this record for any government officials who might want to read his journal, as a way of showing that not all of the workers were homesick. Again, at the beginning of July, there was merriment: *Celebrated today the feast of harvest home_ the Maltese all dined together at one table which I supplied with plenty of bread meat & wine_ they enjoyed themselves exceedingly.*

A major benefit of improved relations between Edward and his workforce was their loyalty, even to the extent of supporting Edward in a court case brought by their priest in July 1829:

> *Absent from the Colony being obliged to attend in town to face the falsity of some accusations which our worthy chaplain had thought proper to make against me to the bishop of Zante_ thanks to the Maltese who would not support their priest in falsehood I succeeded in convincing the Municipal Court that the whole of the accusations were infamous lies_ he accuses me of forcing the Maltese to work on feast days_* [and we know from his journal that Edward did at least put pressure on them to do so] *of irreverence in church_ of persuading the girls not to confess &c &c the cause of all which was that I would not let him rob the poor Maltese of their money for services for which he expressly receives a salary from Government.*

---

[220] This quotation and the next are from a letter in the Resident's Letter Book, TNA CO 136/1310. This is Napier's official correspondence as Resident of Cephalonia. CO 136 – War and Colonial Department and Colonial Office: Ionian Islands, Original Correspondence.

The drawings of the extraordinarily imposing building in Fig. 26 and Fig. 27 indicate Napier's grand plans for one of several buildings he had in mind for his little 'autocracy'. The given title of the first is 'Elevation of the East Front proposed for a Building to contain the Courts, and Public Offices in Argostoli. The annotation on the left says 'designs by Captain Kennedy' and on the right 'Transfer Litho. 11 Charlotte Stt., Fitzroy Sq'. Given that the title includes the word 'proposed', we should probably assume that this was not the building Edward attended for the court hearing.

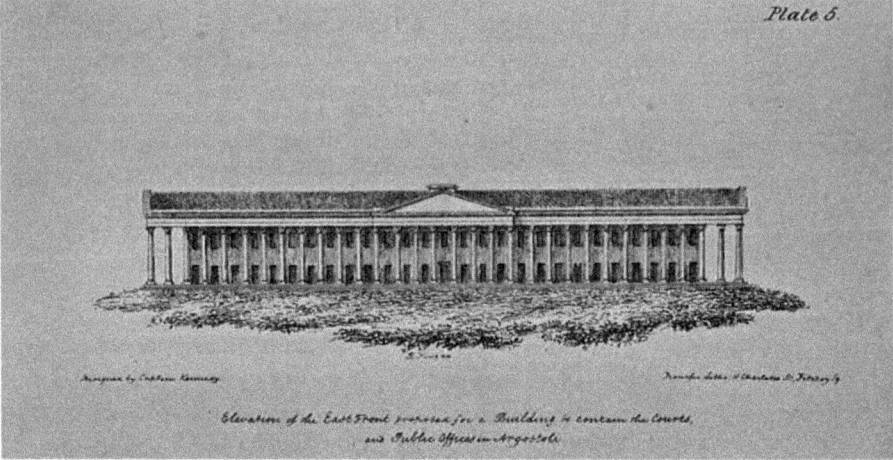

Fig. 26. Proposed court house in Argostoli[221]

Fig. 27. South elevation of proposed court house in Argostoli

---

[221] Captain John Pitt Kennedy's drawing of the court house which he designed under Napier's direction. *The Colonies*, C J Napier.

'Beautiful' was a favourite word of Edward's. He appreciated beautiful weather and the beautiful fountain at St Nicolo, and his projections for plantings were made with an appreciation of aesthetics as well as productivity. An aspect of agriculture dear to a Kentishman's heart was the growing of fruit trees. On 30 December 1828 he *Planted carubi and olive trees on each side of the road from one end of the Colony to the other_ these will be beautiful when they grow and the Cambi [Carubi?] trees will bear plenty of fruit for cattle_ the Maltese eat them.*[222]

The Carob Bean Tree (Ceratonia Siliqua).

Fig. 28. The carob bean tree, Sargent[223]

Edward would have had in his mind's eye the fruit orchards of his childhood as he planned and organised the tree planting at Rakli. In mid-February he received a batch of young trees from Argostoli, necessitating a flurry of activity. Over two days he *planted a row of lemon and cherry trees in front of the houses.* The

---

[222] The trees which Edward calls carubi or cambi trees were almost certainly carob trees. The fruit of the tree are pods. See **Appendix 11 – The carob tree** p. 219. These were fed to cattle. In the present day they are ground to a flour which is used in a variety of ways as a substitute for cocoa – this page has information on its nutrition benefits: https://bit.ly/App9Carob. Surprisingly, the tree belongs to the legume family, see next footnote.

[223] Illustration from *The Garden: an illustrated weekly journal of gardening in all its branches*. London, May 4 1878. https://bit.ly/CarobTreeGardenJournal

following day he *planted the remainder of the lemon and some pear and prune*[224] *trees at St Nicolo*, and five days later he planted a number of prune and cherry trees there. In March he *grafted a number of pear trees of different sorts on the wild crab apple with which the colony abounds*. Edward observed his saplings carefully, and only six days later wrote *some of the prune trees I transplanted the other day are in blossom, whilst those I have not removed have hardly any buds on them_ this is a circumstance I never noticed before.*

Edward was pleased, too, with progress the Maltese made in learning agricultural skills. In July 1829: *The Maltese learn thrashing*[225] *tolerably quick and would now beat the Greeks hollow_ on account of the superiority of our flails*, and in March 1830:

> the Maltese have beaten the Greeks hollow in ingrafting_ those trees done last year by the Greeks have shot out about 2½ feet, whilst those done by the Maltese have some of them taken a start of 8 feet_ the Greeks graft high, the Maltese low_ the Greek inserts the cutting between the bark and the wood_ the Maltese splits the tree and inserts the graft in the wood_

– an interesting illustration that not all the Maltese were ignorant of agriculture, and that some of them had in fact, as Napier had hoped, brought their experience of Maltese farming practice with them.

In clearing the land, many shrubs and small trees had to be dug up. At the beginning of December 1828 Edward had as we have seen, begun making charcoal. And been unimpressed by the workers' progress. He tried again the following spring. On 1 April 1829 he had *women & children piling roots together for burning charcoal*. Two months later, between 25 and 30 May, there was a flurry of charcoal burning, the job assigned to Greek workers. Somehow the product of their labours was taken to the port, possibly on pack horses as he had no cart, and on 13 June he *Sent into town by the gun boat 136 bushels of charcoal.*[226] The burning continued, and in August he *sent in another cargo of charcoal*. Edward obviously considered charcoal important enough as a product to have built a charcoal house, as he wrote in October 1830 *Sowed three bushels of wheat on the land near the charcoal house*

---

[224] As in the twenty-first century there is no fruit tree called a prune tree – prunes are dried plums – a guess would be that he was planting *prunus* trees, grown principally for their flowers; that he would do that is quite surprising in one so assiduously concerned with productivity and the potential for profit in a crop.

[225] Threshing. Edward uses both spellings.

[226] Using the transcript, in **Appendix 2 – Castlereagh's Cabinets of Weights** p. 192, of the technical information associated with Castlereagh's cabinet of weights, 1 bushel = 60lbs; 136 bushels = 8160lbs = 3.64 British tons, which seems like a very significant amount.

... In his 1829 end-of-year accounts he was able to report that charcoal had realised £15/16s/3d.[227]

For a period from April to July 1829 Edward kept an almost daily record of the number of people working. Although he recorded numbers for men, women and children separately and on two occasions mentioned three or four soldiers helping, he did not say whether he was counting only the Maltese or including Greeks. Putting this data into a table (Fig. 30), we see that although he only had about fifty workers in his records for April, the average for the period May and June was about seventy; the single entry in July gives seventy-three, but a month later there are only forty-five. The reasons for these variations are unknown but indicate that he must have been making regular use of labour from the Greek community, probably the calogers. The dates have included church feast days in either the Greek or Maltese communities, and there may have been widespread brief illnesses, although this is unlikely in August. One day he recorded seventy-four and a half workers – possibly someone working half a day.

[227] The National Archives (UK) old money to new currency converter, offers an equivalent present-day value of £782.56. https://bit.ly/Ch11CurrencyConverter

Date	Maltese Colony - numbers working the land [Edward's own words]	Daily Total
April 6th	*On my list to day there are 29 men 5 women 17 children*	51
7th	*2 more men.*	53
8th	*Same numbers as yesterday*	53
13th	*Six men working in garden_ 10 earthing up potatoes the remainder with the women and children terracing the newly cleared land ready for planting currants_*	
14–17	*All employed as yesterday_ on the 15th four men fell ill while at work_*	
May 12th	*On my working list 49 men 7 women and 14 boys_*	70
16th	*At work 31 men, 19 boys, 6 women, 11 children*	67
18th	*33 men 19 boys 6 women 11 children*	69
20th	*at work 33 men, 19 boys 17 women 10 children_*	79
22nd	*35 men 19 boys, 7 women 11 children*	72
26	*on list 34 men. 22 boys. 3 women 10 children_*	69
27	*33 men 22 boys, 9 women 10 children_*	74

Fig. 29. Table of workers, April–August 1830

June 1st	on list 32 men, 21 boys, 7 women 11 children_	71
2nd	33 men 19 boys 8 women 11 children_	71
3	31 men 22 boys 8 women 11 children	72
5	On list 33 men 19 boys 9 women & 4 children_	65
8	31 men 24 boys 5 women 11 children_	71
9th	33 men 23 boys 6 women 11 children	73
11	On list 31 men 23 boys 6 women 11 children_	71
12	On list 29½ men 27 boys 7 women 11 children_	74½
15	On list 31 men 23 boys 7 women 11 children	72
22	31 men 24 boys 7 women 11 children_	73
23	31 men 22 boys 7 women 11 children	71
24	Same number on list as yesterday_	71
July 17–18	36 men 19 boys 8 women 10 children	73
August 11th	4 soldiers thrashing_ ... 2 Maltese thrashing the remainder assisting the masons making cob wall_	
12th – 13th	... on list including 3 soldiers 19 men, 10 boys 5 women 8 children_	45

Fig. 30. Table of workers, April–August 1830 continued

129

Chapter 12 – A Most Solemn Engagement

Edward stayed on in Kefalonia, managing the Maltese Colony and writing to Colonel Napier to report on developments. Most of his letters began with business information and concluded with news of the colonel's friends, the colonel's horse, Turk, and his two young daughters who had been boarding, since they were toddlers, at the girls' school run by Mr and Mrs Dickson, which Napier had set up at Agios Andreas monastery.

Fig. 31. Agios Andreas Monastery, Kefalonia, LAC

At the beginning of October 1830 Edward wrote in his journal

> *Manured and worked a second time the ground below the houses and sowed beans in rows_ planted out a number of cabbage on a part of this ground and also at St Nicolo_ 2 men working with pick axes a piece of ground below the house that has not yet been cleared_ in garden sowed carrots, lettuce, turnips, peas, cress, radishes, celery_ transplanted celery and artichokes.*

As it refers separately to 'the houses', the workers' homes and 'the house', this entry would seem to confirm a hunch I had that he was no longer living in one of the workers' cabins but had moved to a house in Agios Nikolaos, although he never recorded such a move. In mid-October 1830 he

*Put in 8 bushels of wheat at St Nicolo in ground that was manured
with sheep for Indian corn_ ... Mason and Assistant building
reservoir_ put in more beans and some peas_ clearing more ground
under the fountain at St Nicolo_ ... started cultivating land under the
mountain overgrown with wild oats.*

To kill these weeds he ploughed the area, then covered it with leaves and finally
reploughed it. At the end of the same month he ploughed between the currant rows
to improve the land and to

*prevent the soil being washed away by the rains, sowed mustard &
onion seed in the garden and had some men employed trenching and
terracing to extend the garden.*

At this point, probably for the first time since November 1828, Edward wrote, a
long letter, to Napier:

Argostoli – Nov' 11th 1830

*Dear Colonel_*

*After waiting nearly a fortnight I have at length had a
conversation with the General[228]_ he has not yet he says quite decided
about the colony but appears decided to give it up entirely. The points
he argued are more the situation and the expenses; the situation he
said prevented anyone from seeing the improvements_ & experiments
going on. I told him Cambisi was following us as much as possible &
that he spread the thing over the whole of Levato etc and that a
journal published would certainly give everyone in the islands every
information that the expences [sic] were occasioned by the improvements and by the clayey state of the land which required more
cultivation than any other sort of soil_ but I saw clearly that his mind
was made up and that anything I could say could not alter it_ he then
asked me what my personal views were, I told him that these
depended entirely on you_ he told me he had a piece of ground about
70 acres within a mile from Corfu and he thought this a most eligible
spot for a model farm as every one would see it, it being the usual
walk for the public on all Feast days, Sundays etc. he asked me if I
would look over it for him saying that he could provide me with able
assistants and that it would be more comfortable for me_ I said that
if he was satisfied with what I had done at Pronos I had no objection.
He answered that he was perfectly satisfied of my knowledge of my*

---

228 Sir Frederick Adam.

131

subject, and decided that I was to go to Corfu to look at the spot & in the mean time he would decide about the Colony_ I am sorry to give up Pronos notwithstanding that Corfu will I think be more advantageous for me. One gets so interested in the improvements & experiments that it is really difficult to bring one's mind to leave them_ however, I think the General's plan is a good one_ 1st because he informs me that the land is nearly on a level, [so] we can use to advantage all our English instruments & 2^{ndly} because from the town of Corfu we can immediately procure as much manure as we want and perhaps the General's idea, that it being seen by every one, will give it the advantage of Pronos as a model farm, may be right, but then one of our principal objects, that of bringing the fine district of Pronos into cultivation must be abandoned which is a great pity_ but all I can say will be of no use against a General's opinion, and therefore I may as well as [Monferath] says "navigare un pass col vento" especially as it appears likely to bring me to grand anchorage_ Now as to the Colony_ the Guinea grass this year thrives admirably I have cut it three times this summer and it is now as high as my head, you will recollect that this is under the Spring at St Nicolo, yours behind the new prison has done very badly and a few roots only living. I have since you left, got my harvest in which was not much better than the preceding one, and afterwards have been [clear]ing as much land, in the most favourable positions, as possible_ at St N... I have built a resevoir [sic] for water, the stream not being large enough in itself to irrigate the land and have extended the garden very much_ I thrashed the tares I grew this year & gave them to two bullocks in the shape of [bread], and I found this experiment perfectly to answer as the bullocks fattened uncommonly fast on them_ I intended to have consumed the whole of the tares in this manner in order to get as much manure as possible, but Mr Stevens stopped me by selling not only these, but every bushel of our other produce, in consequence of an order he had received from the Senate to give them a precise account of the "netto ricuvato"_ as this exactly upset all my intentions I protested strongly to the Resident against it but he was of opinion that Stevens did not exceed his riders_ I have a great many [Carubi] trees from seed ready to plant out_ I have planted poplars all along the wall under the houses and also behind them, I have made three capital terrace walls also under the houses_ straight according to your directions. I have been able to manure a good piece of ground this Autumn and have a considerable quantity more collecting. Turk goes on famously and is quite fat. Of course Capt Kennedy has told you of my proposal for reducing our expenses but even this though seconded by Colonel [Pitt][229] is not sufficient to induce the General to adopt it_ I have already decreased our daily pay of workmen from $5 to $2 a day, but my proposal limited us to $½_ Cambisi goes on just the same he has made an addition to his garden since you left.

Capt Kennedy removed to the mountain immediately you were gone and the change of air did him a great deal of good_ Latterly however he has caught a severe cold which brought on fever and afterwards jaundice and his appearance altogether is altered very much for the worse, I am glad to say he is determined to go to England as soon as possible either on leave or by giving up his employment when you write induce him to leave this place as much as you can, as the disagreeable business of answering the memorials and other things are worrying him to death and you know him too well to think that his mind can possibly remain quiet while he has anything to do, therefore the best thing is to get him home as quick as possible_ Charles is quite well but he also has had one touch of fever, but it soon left him[230] – Both Colonel and Mrs Pitt have been remarkably kind to me & have given me a general invitation to the house, I always ..... in the evening when I am in town_ I am getting on tolerably with Greek but much better with Maltese which I can speak as well as Mr Rowcroft, he said he had seen you at Cadogan Place & that my Aunt was rather poorly but nothing of importance the matter with her, I hope she is now recovered even of this slight attack and that she is going on well_

I saw Susan and Emily about a fortnight since they were both quite well_ Susan as fat and strong as ever_ Capt Kennedy seems inclined to take them home with him & I am of his opinion, perhaps however he will receive a letter from you before he goes to determine him_ Write also what you think of the situation the General offers me_ Whatever it is I owe it to you and my Aunt and to you both to the end

---

[229] Colonel Pitt was appointed by Sir Frederick Adam to be Napier's *locum tenens* while Napier was taking his wife Elizabeth to England. See *The Chartist General: Charles James Napier, the Conquest of Sind and Imperial Liberalism*, p. 93, Edward Beasley, Routledge, 2017.

[230] It is not clear who this 'Charles' is. John Pitt Kennedy had a brother Charles who might have visited him in Kefalonia – but Edward also had a brother Charles who might have been there.

of my life I shall be most heartily grateful_ the thought of Delmar's
*office always makes me doubly so_*[231]

Pray give my kindest love to my Aunt & beg of her to write to me
if she is able. I want to know what she thinks of Mr Rowcroft & my
*sisters_*

> *Believe me*
> *Ever yours most faithfully*
> *And truly*

Ed^w Curling[232]

Napier's note: *Agonies of the Maltese Colony which seems to be refused even*
extreme unction![233]

There might have been some justification in Adam's argument that the colony was
not getting enough 'exposure' – but, having reached the verge of breaking through
to profit, that argument would hardly have justified closing it down and beginning
again. Edward sounds strongly tempted, and we can imagine that Napier's reaction
might have been fury at Adam's attempt to claim Edward's allegiance to create a
similar enterprise to the detriment of the Pronos project. Given Edward's awareness
of the friction between Napier and Adam and his declared gratitude and strong
allegiance to Napier, it is surprising that he gave Adam's suggestion serious
consideration, but he needed to make provision for the time, which was fast
approaching, when he would finally be asked to leave the colony.

The delay in the transport of letters between Kefalonia and London greatly
increased the difficulty for Napier in dealing with what was a major issue of
principle for him. He was absolutely convinced that Adam was scheming against
him, and he was already fighting the battle on another front by addressing his
concerns to the Secretary of State for War and the Colonies, Viscount Goderich.
As the matter rumbled on for many months without much hope of redress, Napier
recorded and eventually published an account of the dispute in 1833 as part of his
book *The Colonies*, whose subtitle includes the phrase '*Strictures on the*
Administration of Sir Frederick Adam'. His own assessment of the situation was
far from being objective. He wrote to Lord Goderich:

---

[231] Edward's uncle, Michael Becker, with whom he appears to have been staying before
going to Kefalonia, leased Upper Goldstone farm from Charles Delmar who was
Becker's brother-in-law, married to his sister Mary Becker.

[232] BL Add MS 54536 f. 106.

[233] Extreme Unction is a former name used in the Catholic Church for the sacrament of
Anointing the Sick. It is one of the seven sacraments of that denomination, which mark
important stages in life. Extreme Unction relates particularly, although not exclusively,
to people who are dying.

I have ruled Cephalonia for nine years, changed the face of the island, encreased the revenue and established justice. All I did was approved by Sir Thomas Maitland, and all has since been effectually overset by Sir F Adam ... [who is] ... a weak and vindictive character ... He is perfectly despotic, his will is law, there is no appeal, his character is feeble, his disposition jealous and insidious: he is a tool in the hands of Greek knaves who excite his passions.[234]

In November 1830 Edward sowed tares and still had men terracing land. He was not in denial about the imminent demise of the colony – he was simply keeping it going in the hope that Napier would return to rescue it, and in the meantime Edward was waiting for specific orders from Corfu.

The most significant friendship Napier had made on Kefalonia was undoubtedly with Captain John Pitt Kennedy, the engineer assigned to Napier's command to supervise road construction and other building works on the island. The two men respected each other's work, and shared a similar sense of the absolute necessity of fair dealings in everything, as well as a wry sense of humour. When Napier was away from the island, Kennedy wrote him letters detailing progress in every area of concern to Napier. In the new year, he wrote once more to Napier and after the opening assurances about the little girls, broke a thunderclap of news:

Cefalonia, 6 Jan'. 1831

My Dear Colonel,

I have just received your letter of 7 Dec'. which I most anxiously looked for, that I might know your wishes about the little girls who are both as well and strong as possible; The Dicksons Establishment goes on extremely well and there is no likelihood whatever of their moving, consequently I shall leave the Children quietly where they are when I start from this, Edward of course will look to them as long as he remains, and on his removal to Corfu Colthurst has promised me that if any thing extraordinary should occur he will act for you; And now having told you that we are all well in health, I must give you a piece of Intelligence which I fear will worry you very much namely that Edward Curling has connected himself with one of the Maltese Girls in a way that it will not be easy to remedy; This girl has always conducted herself extremely well, & after making a Most Solemn engagement in the presence of her Father & Mother and two other witnesses that as long as they live they are to continue to live

---

[234] Quoted in *A True Romantic: General Charles James Napier 1782–1853* unpublished work by Walter Little.

together as man and wife, he walked her quietly into his House and they have been living together for these ten days past; None of us had the least idea of this until it was all over, & both He and She Conceive themselves as perfectly married as it is possible to be; Edward appears fond of her and will not hear of separating from her; However I have no doubt that whatever you and Mrs Napier point out to him he would follow_ I find myself curiously circumstanced as I have no doubt his friends' advice and wishes would be to separate him from her and had her character been at all doubtful before his acquaintance with her this might be easily done, and I should use every means in my power to accomplish it. But I confess it goes monstrously against my Conscience to advise him abandoning her when I consider that she was a well conducted girl until he persuaded her to take the step she has taken & that, with her Father's & Mother's Consent and under the Most Solemn engagements_ In short it appeared to me that unless she voluntarily released him he could not throw her off, and it is not likely she would do so_ You will Judge better what can be done under the circumstances and write to him, & whilst I am here should I find it practicable to separate them by his giving a sum of Money on condition that she releases him from his engagement as formally as he made it, I will not lose the opportunity; and this is more than I would do for Charles, for had he got into a Similar Scrape I think I should have done my utmost to have given the Lady the legal claim of a wife upon him an hour after I had heard of it.

... believe me ever Yours

J. P. Kennedy[235]

We do not know what Rosa looked like, but **see Appendix 12 – Life in nineteenth-century Malta** p. 222 for a selection of images of Maltese girls of the period engaged in spinning processes. The arrival of the group of Maltese people was officially documented at the time, and the records are still in the municipal archives in Argostoli. There is a page for each family, listing the adults in one column and the children with their ages in two further columns. Rosa had arrived aged 16 in 1826 with her father Nicola, mother Rosaria and siblings Giuseppe (19), Francesco (15), Vincenzo (12), Paolo (10), Raffaele (5) and Angela (3). A man named Angelo Dimech was also listed with them.[236]

---

[235] BL Add MS 54535 ff. 47, 48.

[236] Information passed on to me by Kefalonia historian Angelos Debonos from manuscript documents which he had found in the municipal archives of Kefalonia.

It is clear from how Kennedy outlined his own reaction to the situation that he felt that Edward should ideally see the error of his ways and extract himself from the relationship. This would probably have been the majority view of British society both on Kefalonia and further afield at the time. Napier kept on file a copy of his letter to Edward on hearing Kennedy's news. It was his own draft copy, and is the only surviving Napier letter to Edward. It gives tantalizing glimpses of Edward's prior communication, and is a dramatic and strongly worded rebuke for what the colonel clearly saw as Edward's ungentlemanly and foolhardy behaviour.

London Feb[y] 15 1831

My Dear Edward

I fear your folly will punish you sufficiently and I am more disposed to help you than to add to the burthens you have so madly assumed ... The first thing to be done, is to get a distinct view of your situation_ your family are in distress, your duty was to endeavour to relieve them, instead of this you have abandoned them! You have therefore done wrong. Stop there and act wrongly no further. The girl you have married has no reproach to make to herself nor have you any to make against her; for her conduct has been correct; she is your wife as much as if you had been married by a Bishop, you ought now to have the ceremony performed at once and as she is a young woman, you should endeavour to educate her: being virtuous she has only to acquire knowledge to make you proud of her_ Thus you at least act with the best chance of correcting your fault in some degree and have the consciousness of behaving like a gentleman, and bear in mind that in that character you have but one path, namely not [to] sink your wife to the level of a prostitute but raise her character by respecting it and instruction, so as to make her a gentlewoman: for virtue and education are the only things which make one human creature actually better than another and the first of these desirable qualifications it seems she already possesses and therefore this poor girl has a claim upon you which you cannot get rid of, or wish to get rid of without meriting a name that I will not one moment believe you deserve. I ~~conclude by warning~~[237] will tell you fairly that this act of folly has shaken the good opinion entertained by your best friends of you and has injured your prospects in life; a second such false step will probably ruin you past redemption and reduce you to a state from which you would look back on your employment as an attorny's clark,

---

[237] Napier's correction.

*as one of comparative ease & happiness_ you were pitied my d'
Edward, because adversity was your misfortune not your fault_ If you
reverse the picture the world will laugh at you in just derision. I did
my best to pull you out of the water, when you were thrown in by your
bad fortune but I will do nothing for you if you choose to jump in out
of pure folly and weakness of character. I expect to hear from you
what you have to say on this business and I am my dear Edward, as
yet*

    yours sincerely

CJ Napier[238]

*Write to me directly, or I shall have left London to return to the
Islands before your letter comes.*

Remarkably radical for the time, Napier's advice completely ignored Kennedy's
suggested response of paying Rosa and her family to release Edward from the
relationship. Instead he strongly recommended legitimizing the marriage as soon
as possible. Napier himself annotated this copy at a later date, giving the end of the
episode on the address page of this draft:

*Copy of a letter to Edward Curling on hearing he had seduced a
young Maltese girl by a solemn promise before her Father & Mother
& two witnesses never to part from her*

*Edward Curling married Rosa and behaved in every way like an
honest good man. He cannot stand higher than he does in my opinion.*

C Napier [signature]

This extraordinary letter, and particularly its additional note, could not but warm a
descendant's heart. To me it felt as though Napier's footnote was addressed directly
to posterity; why else would he have bothered to add his signature to what was
ostensibly a draft? His opinions on the treatment of women were radical for the
period, and he backed them up in his actions.[239] However, the contrast between his

---

[238] BL Add MS 54536 f. 108.

[239] The best-known instance of this dates from a much later period in Napier's life when
as governor of Sindh in India he prevented the customary act of *sati*, the burning alive
of a widow on her husband's pyre. There is an interesting online article which looks at
the complexities around the practice seen from the British perspective, by Maninder
Jarlesberg, *Widow Burning: The Burning Issue of Colonial Britain and India*:
https://bit.ly/Ch12Sati
In a more personal illustration of his views on the equality of women, he insisted on
his daughters being properly educated; his letters to them in their teens included
complex maths problems for them to solve.

138

advice to Edward and his own behaviour with Anastasia indicates at the very least a major blind spot in his conscience.

On reading Kennedy's account, Napier wrote to Edward a letter fearsome in its emphasis on Edward's responsibilities to the woman he had chosen to be his lifetime companion, and the consequences which as Napier saw it would ensue should he not live up to them. If Napier told Elizabeth the contents of Kennedy's letter – and we do not know whether he did so – she would no doubt have concurred. Whatever was of interest or concern to Elizabeth was important to Napier. Because Elizabeth was steadfast in her commitment to her dead sister Catherine's grandchildren, they came to be, through Elizabeth, almost a surrogate family of offspring to Napier, and he looked after the Curling boys like a father, ensuring that each of them found a suitable career. In his professional life, Napier kept copies of all his outgoing letters. He did not, however, do this with all his personal correspondence, and this indicates that the letter to Edward was so significant that he felt it necessary to keep the draft and to annotate it at a later date. It is the only extant handwritten letter from Napier to Edward.[240] From it we also learn the crucial information that as late as mid-February 1831 Napier was still expecting to return to Kefalonia.

That same month Edward was still apparently hoping that the enormous effort put in by himself and his workers over the preceding two and a half years was not going to be wasted. In March 1831, he

> manured the land under the mountain in preparation for sowing corn, sowed lettuce peas onions &c in garden and Ploughed again the land destined for Indian corn and sowed it ... This land has been well cultivated, that is, it has been worked deeply and often, and has been properly manured, and let the result be what it may this may be considered a fair trial of the capability of the colony, to produce good crops_

This feverish activity continued:

> Manured well some ground in the garden and planted 150 lb of potatoes as a trial_ planted out lots of young onions in the garden prepared ground for melons, put in pumpkins, sowed more peas

---

[240] Every one of Napier's letters to Edward would have been treasured by him and filed in the appropriate 'letter book'. They would no doubt have been handed down to posterity had it not been for the intervention of the Irish Civil War. In 1922 the Curling family home, Castle House in Newcastle West, was destroyed by fire. The incumbent at the time, Edward's grandson, bachelor Richbell Curling, had retreated to Ahern's Hotel in the town. Most of the Curling belongings were destroyed, although a few were saved.

beans & French beans cucumbers salad & leeks_ planted out more strawberries.

Chapter 13 – A bottle of smoke

It is apparent in Edward's next letter to Napier, written on 1 March 1831, that he has not as yet received any reassurance from Napier following what would have been Edward's attempt to explain his liaison with Rosa. The main focus of this letter is Napier's and Kennedy's business matters, mentioning Edward's personal life only in passing. Edward had pressed Napier to encourage Kennedy to leave Kefalonia, and Kennedy had done so, entrusting the management of his financial affairs to Edward, who was now agent for both men. The study of Greek and Maltese continues, Edward comparing his progress in the latter language to his step-father Charles Rowcroft's proficiency. This is strange, as we have no other indication that Rowcroft spoke Maltese

It is a lengthy epistle. Edward has a mixture of news, some of it gossip, some official. He is managing both Napier's and Kennedy's finances on the island, and we discover exactly what monthly salaries the two men were receiving. The Ionian government has decreed a reduction in the rent of houses hired to accommodate its officials. This seems to have included Napier's own house, although we know that he owned it, so he must have been letting it to the army rather than continuing any rental payments of his own. The Greek population seems to be volatile, apparently disliking Captain Kennedy while, to Edward's face at least, being civil to him about Napier. Edward, however, doubts their sincerity. He reports for the first time on the welfare of Susan and Emily, the measure of their good health – perhaps alarming to a twenty-first-century reader – being their fatness.

Argostoli March 1st 1831

*Dear Colonel_*

*I have this moment received your pay for January £32.11s_ and also for February £29. 8s_ which for the sake of security I have deposited in my name in the treasury_*

*I have also received Capt Kennedy's pay for Feb^ry £16.4s.4d which after deducting five dollars & 94 soldi which I was obliged to leave on his account at the Treasury I have paid the remainder to Costantine Valsamachi as the Capt directed_*

An order came from Corfu yesterday to reduce the rent of houses hired by government, and also the allowance to people in Gov^t service to about one half_ I have been served as your Agent with a notice to this effect_ A Commission will sit to determine the rent, and I think it will be better, unless the reduction is very great indeed to leave your house in the hands of the Military_ Rents must fall_ Toole has hired *the Mess House for 12$ a month & the Landlord lays out 150$ in improvements_*

*I saw Susan and Emily the day before yesterday, they have been much troubled by chilblains but are otherwise uncommonly well I never saw Emily so well, it is difficult to decide which is fattest her or Susan_ they appeared to be very comfortable and happy_ Emily sends her love and a kiss to you, but Susan would not say a word to me being for some cause or other in a bad humour_ they got the worsted stockings ordered by Capt Kennedy last week_*

*I hear no news in town of any description. Angelica tells me that not a Greek in town speaks well of Capt Kennedy_ Every Greek is much more civil to me now, as they expect you back in a short time_ damn them I would cut them if they were worth noticing_ I am staying with Rankin who I believe to be the best fellow in Argostoli as Capt Kennedy can tell you. The Marsh at Cranea is going on famously_ the corn sewn , contrary to my opinion thrives well for the present but I cannot yet believe that it will continue long to do so_ The new Theatre [241] advances slowly the ground flooring however is on_ Thompson is gone to Corfu and report says will get through his difficulties [Currants] are $25 still_ so much for town news_*

I will not enter on the subject of my own affairs, as both by letter and personally you will have had before this a full account from Captain Kennedy_ I am daily in hopes of receiving a letter from you and yet dread it, from the fear of having incurred your displeasure, not however for the moment conceding the point that I had not a full right to act as I thought fittest in the step I have taken, and the only thing I assure you that can make me regret the step will be its depriving me of your esteem and confidence.

The Colony goes on but poorly_ I have not sufficient hands to crop the lands even, and Gov^t will not allow me to let the land to Greeks as I proposed as no answer has yet been received from the General concerning it, although <u>six months ago he promised to decide on it in a week</u>, however I really believe we shall have an answer soon, as yesterday he by letter asserted to the Resident that the next steamer shall positively bring his decision_ Every day I am more convinced that the Colony would prosper <u>if it was allowed to do so</u>_ I shall

---

[241] One of many public buildings planned and constructed by Napier and Kennedy.

manure this year 12 acres or more and have chain walled[242] *a considerable portion, but of course improvement you can hardly expect when I tell you our pay for labour is only 1½$ per day_ If the General had allowed me to do as I proposed, I would much more than have paid the expenses this year, my few Maltese would have been for at least [9] months constantly employed in improvements, and consequently a considerable portion of land would have been brought into a high state of cultivation_ Now I greatly fear that we shall not pay our expenses, very little land in cultivation has been terraced, and the men have been constantly employed cropping the land, most of which not being manured, nor terraced, and only having the seed simply ploughed in, will not pay the expence [sic] of cultivation. What I am to do for the young [Nua Papa] I know not, if not properly taken care of this year, our expense for the two last years will be entirely thrown away_ I have represented all these things to Colonel Conyers,*[243] *but he will not authorize any expenses particularly as the general is fully aware of the situation of the grounds at Pronos I am therefore relieved of any responsibility_ I of course preserve his letter_*

Cambisi is going on famously, and following as nearly as possible my example, he does not however yet understand the advantage of a succession of crops, which would of course prevent his leaving his land fallow however he is doing a great deal, as you will see when you come back_ He has another daughter which increases his number to 6 He told me the other day that he knew for certain that Stevens & Co had actually sent deputies to the different villages to excite the peasants to present Memorials against you, which he says he will prove to you when you come_ I believe Cambisi himself to be really attached to you as he has never since your departure altered either his professions towards you or his conduct to me_ Bess and the cow that Capt Colthurst has have both calved, and I have requested Capt Conyers to arrange so as to preserve Bess' calf which will be valuable either to the Colony or Cambisi_ Turk goes on capitally, I have lately put him in stable every night_ Tell my aunt I fattened a pig this year to nearly 12 score_ and would have fattened many more and, bullocks

---

[242] A 'chain wall' is normally used in buildings which might be liable to flood, to lift them above the likely flood level. As Edward is writing here about agricultural land we can only guess that he was building walls with extra strength in the foundations. These might have been the walls supporting terraces or field boundaries.

[243] Conyers had been appointed temporary Resident in Napier's absence.

*too had not Stevens sold all the produce_ Haynes and Hay too are both well though Angelica tells me the former is much cut up on account of Capt Kennedy's departure_ Angelica has not been well, but begs me for my souls [sic] sake to send her … both to the Capt and yourself_ I had a letter from Chas Kennedy from Malta where [Repel] put in from [stress] of weather_ you will find Charles wonderfully improved and a better fellow than ever_ The General[244] stayed one day here in passing from [Gourte] where he had turned out the head of Police & hung a Signore for murder_ I only saw him for a moment & he did not enter on the subject of the Colony. I think he must have got some idea of your coming back, and I think the long delay will turn out favourably for the Colony, at all events I hope so_ I will not forget to plant Guinea grass. I do not like to commend myself but I think you will say when you see the colony that considering our number of labourers we have not been idle_ and for my good Directorship the quantity of manure will speak_*

On the endpapers of the address page:

With regard to my affair you can do as you like about mentioning it to my mother and Mr Rowcroft_ I have not yet written to them myself_ indeed I think it will be much better for you to communicate it if you will take the trouble_ as I know their opinions I am almost sure they will be extremely angry from you I do not expect this on account of my mode of conduct but I do think you will condemn me for having (considering my circumstances) acted too precipitately, but this in my opinion will entirely depend on circumstance, as at present I am living cheaper than before my connexion.

*Mary… … , Camso, Marcoran, Colthurst etc are all well_ I have never had a moment's illness since you went away_*

> *With kindest love to my Aunt Capt & Chas Kennedy*
> *I remain dear Colonel*
> *Yours ever gratefully & faithfully*
>
> *Edw Curling*[245]

[Postscript:] *Rankin sends his respects to you*

---

[244] Sir Frederick Adam.
[245] BL Add MS 54536 f. 110.

Granted that as Napier's agent Edward had pressing business matters to convey, it is still somewhat surprising that he left the mention of his liaison with Rosa to the very end of his letter and then only calls it his 'affair'. He admits to being too scared of his mother's reaction to tell her and his step-father Charles Rowcroft, about it, and asks Napier in a rather offhand way to speak to them on his behalf. His tone is almost belligerent – the only instance of such feeling in all his correspondence with Napier. This could be seen as a defensive response. Captain Kennedy had left Kefalonia at some point before Edward wrote this letter, and in it Edward assumes that Kennedy had already visited Napier in London.

Napier's reaction arrived almost a month after Edward wrote the above letter, and he responded, with huge relief, this time placing his personal life at the beginning.

Pronos March 30 1831

Dear Colonel

I wrote you a letter at the beginning of the month which I hope you have received as it would tell you of the health of your little ones. I have since had yours of 10th Jan^ry and no one can [tell] the pleasure it gave me_ to have gained your good opinion delights me, because I feel that the only way in which I can repay the debt of gratitude I owe you is by deserving your esteem_ you will believe me, that had I not received your caution I should not have been in danger of being seduced into dissipation_ I have a decided dislike to drinking, gaming I abhor and as to economy, my experience of what a man is in this world without money has too deeply rooted in my mind the necessity of it, ever to allow me to abandon it. I have always practised it and even when a Lawyer's clerk it prevented my running into debt_ to run in debt without having the means to pay is, in my opinion downright sobbery[246] a man should conquer himself, that is when he finds his income cannot support his expenses, he should immediately decrease them to the proper bounds_ As to your question whether I can look a life of labour in the face, I am sure you must have been persuaded of the affirmation when you wrote the question_ As to fame_ I am ambitious of joining it in a certain degree, for instance, I should think my life well spent in establishing a perfect system of farming in the Ionian Islands, and thereby increasing the welfare of the inhabitants, not that I think they deserve it (that is, at present) but it would render

---

[246] This word was difficult to read in the original. 'Sobbery' may mean 'unwarranted self-indulgence'.

*my name famous and that would satisfy me_ but I have no wish either to be <u>very rich</u> or <u>very great</u>_ A man's object should be content, and whether my past life, or observing others has taught me, I do not know, but I <u>have</u> learnt the art of being content on very little_ Now I think I rather differ from your idea of fame_ be it so_ you desired me to state my feelings and I have done so_*

*Since you left I have studied hard at Greek, though without I believe making much progress, to learn a language requires practice, I can neither speak nor understand Greek one quarter so well as I can Maltese, though I never studied the latter more than half a dozen times in my life_ so much is practice_ I have read the Agricultural Dictionary which is a very clever work, and has given me a greater insight into the principles of farming than I ever had before_ I did not continue my journals for many seasons, I am sorry I did not_ My accounts go on in the same way_ I always save a little_ I have now in hand about $400_*

Edward continued with upsetting news of his own family:

I was extremely distressed the other day to find from a letter from my mother, that Mr Rowecroft had failed in his school_ his kind endeavour and sacrifices to assist us, his affection for my mother and indeed to all of us, added to his not forsaking us either in prosperity, or adversity, has made me regard him with sincere affection and esteem,

This was a strong endorsement of Rowcroft. However, Edward also criticised his step-father:

*he is without doubt a very clever man, but fails in two points, he has too much pride, and too little economy, and these I have no doubt, are partly the cause of his failure, but with management of his own concerns I have no right to interfere, he has acted rightly by us and protected and fed my brothers and sisters when their nearest relations refused it_ he and my mother are of course in distress_*

Charles Rowcroft and Jane's school had first been in difficulty in December 1827 so they had clearly struggled on for over three years. In February 1831 Rowcroft advertised in the Morning Post:

RUSSELL HOUSE, Streatham, CLASSICAL and COMMERCIAL SCHOOL, conducted by Mr. ROWCROFT.—Terms, under ten years of age, 25 guineas per annum; above that age, 30 guineas. Russell House is situated five miles from town, on the Brighton road. The air of Streatham is proverbially salubrious, and there is, within a few minutes' walk, a Chalybeate Spring, long famed for its medicinal virtues.

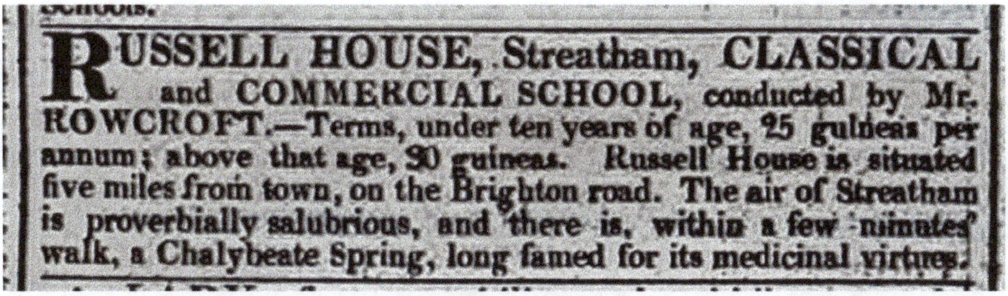

Fig. 32. Morning Post 18 February 1831

Edward's letter, written only a month after Rowcroft's advertisement, would seem to indicate that even when all the indicators were against him Rowcroft refused to accept that the enterprise had failed. Russell House, Streatham, was a large property, originally the home of Lord William Russell who had occupied it only briefly.

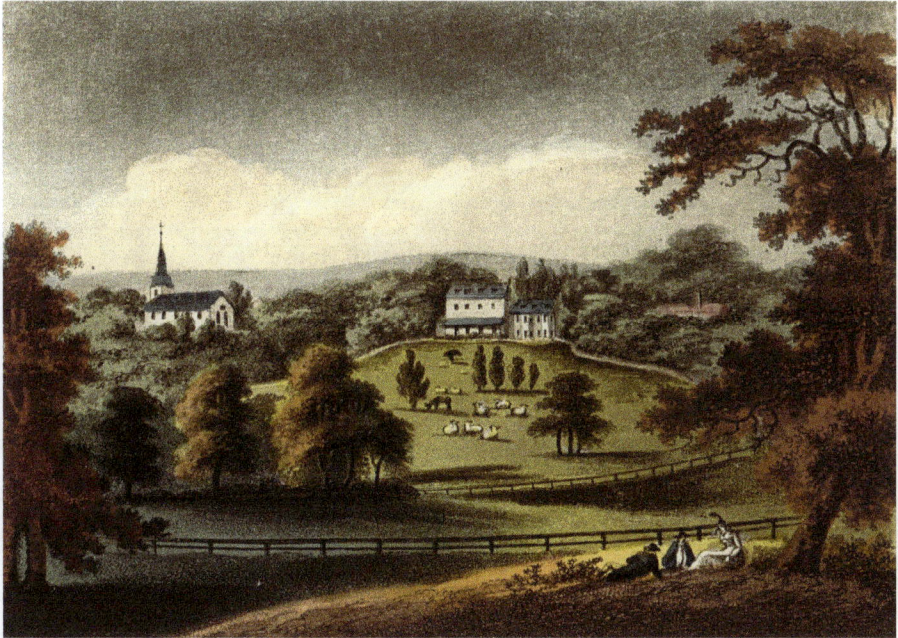

Fig. 33. The Seat of the R^t^. Honble. Lord William Russell, 1804 [247]

Hassell's engraving of Russell House, executed twenty-three years before the Rowcrofts took over the property, shows an idyllic setting for a school. However, the upkeep must have been considerable, and managing the school as a going concern was clearly too much for them. The property had a chequered history, and was eventually demolished in 1892 to make way for the Roman Catholic church of

[247] Drawn and Engraved by J. Hassell. London Borough of Lambeth, Archive department.

the English Martyrs, Streatham, but this evocative image of the interior of the house (Fig. 34) might well suggest the ordered tread of well-disciplined boys moving from dormitory to dining room and thence to classrooms. There would certainly have been 'no running on the stairs' in the Georgian era.

Fig. 34. Staircase at Russell House[248]

In looking for solutions to his family's financial difficulty Edward referred, for the first time in any of his correspondence, to his elder brother Thomas III, continuing from above:

> *my eldest brother, who is actually in the receipt of from £700 to £1000*
> *a year has refused to take charge even of one of my brothers_ I*
> *perfectly agree with you that a man has a right to cast [off] unworthy*
> *relations_*

As mentioned earlier, Thomas III had qualified as an apothecary in May 1827. Looking at his family's situation from his perspective, he may have felt that there had been many foolish decisions made by his parents, starting with the idea of going to Van Diemen's Land and including his mother's boarding school venture with his new step-father. He may also have felt abandoned by his family when they left him behind: his father had sold up all the family's assets, forcing them to leave the house which had been their home for three generations, taking all but himself to the other side of the world. When his mother arrived home with a new husband less than a

---

[248] From *A History of Streatham*, p. 165, Frederick Arnold, 1866. Alamy stock photo.

148

year after his father's death and both parties with recent bequests from deceased parents, there would have been some justification in his feeling that they should be able to fend for themselves. He was newly qualified, and while he was an apprentice was probably not in a position to accumulate any savings on which to draw to help his family. He may also still have had financial commitments to Messrs Jarvis and Waddington of Margate, to whom he had been apprenticed. There must too have been a strong sense of frustration that his father had left for Van Diemen's Land without finalizing the administration of the will which his grandfather Thomas Curling I had left on his death in 1819, compounded by the death of his grandmother Catharine Curling the same year. We know that Thomas III was very attached to Catharine in his youth.[249]

Returning to Edward's letter, we find that he himself had offered his mother practical long-term help, but had sought Napier's assistance in implementing it:

> *I wrote to my mother to send out my brother John to me, I can feed &*
> *clothe him, and he will have an opportunity of learning languages,*
> *and not knowing how to forward the money for his passage I directed*
> *my mother to apply to you, not doubting that you would advance the*
> *money necessary, and allow me to pass it to your account here, I did*
> *not write to you to save postage, but directed my mother to show you*
> *the letter_ Excuse the liberty as under the circumstances it was*
> *unavoidable_ will you be good enough to use your discretion as to*
> *the sum, you know I have no money to fling away_*

At the end of March 1831, Edward and his siblings were aged as follows:

Thomas	25
Edward	24
Henry	22
Charles	20
Robert	16
John	14
Jane	11
Catherine	10
Arthur	9

The five eldest boys might reasonably have been assumed to have been working. John would have been about to leave school with the hope of some kind of employment. We know that at least one of the older boys, probably Charles, had been working as an 'usher' at the Rowcrofts' school until its 'failure'. Henry had

---

[249] See their correspondence in *Curling Wisps & Whispers of History*, vol. 1, **Appendix 6a – The Letters of Catharine and Thomas Curling.**

been appointed, on 3 November 1827, to serve as a 'volunteer' aboard the East India Company's ship *The Mermaid* out of Calcutta.[250] Robert was also at sea, apprenticed aboard the *Lady Kennaway*.[251] So, apart from John, Jane Rowcroft and her second husband would have had three children, Jane (aged 11), Catherine (10) and Arthur (9) in their immediate care.

We do not know what happened to Charles in the wake of the closure of the school. At a later date John and Arthur joined the 4th Regiment of Dragoons. Charles's next appearance is not until 1839, when he surfaces in Egypt.

Edward continued his letter to Napier with news of the little girls:

> *April 2__ I passed yesterday by the [convent of Sᵗ Andrea], Emily and Susan both quite well__ Susan improves much in reading both desire their loves and a kiss to you and my Aunt__*
>
> *I have received your and Capt Kennedy's pay for March__ Baynes and the Vice President are here, examining memorials[252] and the Regent[253] is to make a report on the Colony, of course you can easily judge what sort of a one it will be__ I have written as strong a letter to the resident[254] as I could frame, in defence of the Colony and begged him to forward it to Sir Frederick__ Colthurst says he thinks it will throw them all on their backs I hope it may but I doubt the other side is too strong__[255]*
>
> *Mr Read tells me that the Memorials against Capt Kennedy are all decided in his favour__ some against yourself have been submitted to the Advocate Fiscal, and he has made favourable reports, in fact I believe the whole (with very few exceptions) will turn out to be, a bottle of smoke__ Baynes has said that you certainly will not*

---

[250] *Calcutta Annual Register and Directory*, 1831, under Pilot Establishment, p. 286.

[251] Although we do not know the exact date on which Robert's apprenticeship began, it is likely that at age fourteen he would have left school to sign up to an apprenticeship which would last seven years. Later in life, when Robert was applying for a Master's certificate, he was required to list all the ships on which he had served. Both his application and the certificate itself are preserved in the Caird Library archives at the National Maritime Museum, Greenwich, catalogue number MC5 166. The certificate was awarded on 12 June 1851.

[252] A 'memorial' was what we would now call a 'memorandum'.

[253] The 'Regent' was a local person, appointed, rather like the mayor of a local council. For further details of their local government at the time see **Appendix 13 – Government in the Ionian Islands** p. 230.

[254] Napier's replacement since his removal in absentia by Frederick Adam from the post.

[255] This phrase seems contradictory, but in Edward's time the meaning of 'I doubt' was diametrically different from what it is now: to express his meaning we might write 'I hope it may not be so, but I expect that it will because the other side is too strong'.

return, where he gets his information I know not, however I trust to your letter to me___ there is a talk of great reductions but as yet I have heard of none___ We shall, I believe have free pratique with the Morea almost immediately___ [256]

Reid is getting on famously with the marsh, the corn sown is not dead but begins to look sickly. The [theatre] appears to have come to a standstill___ the Commission has reduced the rent of your house to $5 a month___ Rankin has offered me $6 but I prefer leaving it with the Gov^t till you come back as thus it is certain to be permanently let___ The Colony and Park go on as usual___ the [rams] have much injured the road near [Coronus]___ The General[257] has sold, I hear, all his furniture etc and is expected soon to go to England___ Cambisi is doing wonders in cultivation this year___ he, [Monferratta] & [Marcocau] are well, also Mrs C but it is said she has had paynes in her bowels___ Fellaporte has married Miss Ciselli, but made a small mistake in consummating the marriage first by which he has obtained a dowry of $4000___

I trust my Aunt is well___ pray tell her that I always remember her kindness___ When you see Capt and Cha^{ls} Kennedy remind them of their promise to write to me___ I trust also that I shall hear from you, I almost count the minutes till May arrives___ I have nothing else to say but that

> *With kindest love to my Aunt*
> *I am*
> *Yours most gratefully & faithfully*
> *Edw Curling[258]*

Edward's mother, Mrs Jane Rowcroft, writes to Napier the same month, to follow up Edward's suggestion of having his brother John, then aged fourteen, to live with him in Kefalonia. In the first of only two letters she wrote to Napier she says:

---

[256] This would have meant that the British government was satisfied that the danger of importing the plague had receded so much that passengers arriving from the Morea would no longer need to go into quarantine on arrival in the islands.

[257] Sir Frederick Adam relinquished the governorship of the Ionian Islands in 1832. In October of that year he became Governor of Madras. (Wikipedia)

[258] BL Add MS 54536 f. 112.

8 Stamford Street
Blackfriars Road
April 1831

Dear Sir

The enclosed letter which I received from my son Edward a few days ago under very excited feelings evinces so much goodness of heart that I should be desirous of placing it before you for that reason alone.

We are very much disinclined to burthen Edward with an encumbrance, which might either press too much on him in his present position, or be a hindrance to the free motion which other employment might need.

But at the same time, we do not consider ourselves justified in neglecting this opportunity of securing for John, under our circumstances, the means of present subsistence, and the great advantage which he would derive from the acquisition of some modern languages.

The advice, therefore, which I take the liberty to ask, is, whether you think, from your exact knowledge of Edward's position – a position in which your kindness and liberality have placed him, that our acceptance of his offer would [tax] him more than his generosity had calculated – The duty of one brother to another is too sacred for mere worldly computation: but it would be shortsighted policy to allow Edward's offer to be the means of sinking him to the same extremity of distress as his brothers and sisters must very soon suffer
With kind regards to Mrs Napier
I remain
Dear Sir
Very sincerely
Your obliged

Jane Rowcroft[259]

Jane Rowcroft was touched and excited by Edward's offer to take his brother John under his wing, but she was unsure whether it was practical for Edward to take on this extra responsibility. Sadly, although it would have been a wonderful opportunity for young John Curling, in the circumstances it was not an idea which

---

[259] BL Add MS 54542 f. 38.

Edward was going to be able to follow through: there is no further correspondence in which the idea of John joining Edward in Kefalonia is mentioned.

Napier used the reverse quarter of Jane Rowcroft's letter to draft part of a rebuttal in his ongoing battle of words with Sir Frederick Adam:

> ... *My object in calling on Lord Goderick with the above observation is to say that I expect Sir F A "will order" me to [Zante] instead of Cefalonia which after his speech to the Cefalonians would be a stigma upon my Gov^{nce} of the latter Island and I therefore trust to his Lordship's fairness for my return to Cefalonia or an impartial enquiry into these asserted grievances that I am said to have inflicted upon the Island. However, I do not want to alarm Sir Frederick Adam my object is to defend myself and I do beg of [Lord Goderick] to do one of two things either/call on Sir F Adam to substantiate any charge he has to make against me before a commission of impartial men or/ insist upon my going back to Cefalonia and not being sent to any other Island, which can only be considered as an unmerited stigma after this speech made by Sir F Adam. If Lord Goderick will speak to Lord [Idray] Osborn he will fairly tell his Lordship whether I have either inflicted or countenanced grievances as far as his knowledge goes; which is very accurate because* [ends]

Napier's preoccupation with the matter of his Residency of Cephalonia had continued. He felt very aggrieved that Sir Frederick Adam had seen fit to remove him from the role without prior warning or consultation and in his absence, and although the offer of the Residency of Zante was 'on the table', he believed that if he accepted it that would be a tacit admission that he was at fault in his administration of Kefalonia.

Chapter 14 – My precious Elizabeth

On 16 April 1831, the fourth anniversary of their wedding, Napier wrote to Elizabeth:

April 16th 1831

Four years this day since we were married my beloved Elizabeth of all that has worried or vexed us I will say nothing like others we have had our plagues but not all like us have had the full affection of each other, and though the Almighty has given us some severe trials in common with other mortals I do hope he has in his mercy thought fit to let them finish in part, and that by your going abroad (in peace with your daughters) we shall have a more happy time than heretofore and you more health. let us hope so my love, let us trust to him and exert ourselves for those who do not do the one do not really do the other The first step is to look at what he has done for us_ we are given to each other our love has been tried and all is sound you are divided from your daughters in distance not in anger; Are not the most happy and fortunate mothers the same You go with your husband possessing all his love, what can a woman wish more? And to where? Exile? No, to a place where both are known and respected and the Scene of what he has done of good to man exceeding what falls to the lot of men in general. All these gifts are to me as well as to you_ We have also riches sufficient if our wants are kept in due bounds You have not good health and I have a ..._ these are evils but who is without evils? How many have greater! You I believe would not change me nor would I change you! Again in my power again I would marry you I blest this day in 1827 I continue to bless it in 1831 I pray for its constant return with each other, and as you are the oldest I pray to go first, because you would not suffer so long as I should but this is the office of a Higher Power not ours. We are together now and the time present is our own_ let us enjoy it. Let us foresee our amputation and thus show our gratitude long ere nighttime of the time entrusted to our keeping for assuredly it is not our own and to do this we must have a pursuit we must try to dwell upon what is given rather than upon what is refused; this last I am apt to do and this is not being resigned. Complaint is not resignation. My liver constrains me to lie low, but I think that I possess you my love and the tears of joy burst thro the Clouds of disease, and I think

the hours pass heavy and slow till I again clasp my beloved wife to
my bosom God bless you my precious Elizabeth Yr own Charles[1]

As well as Napier's touching and remarkably constant feelings of love for Elizabeth, we are reminded in this letter that it was not only Elizabeth who was beset by ill health but Napier too. He had suffered many periods of illness from childhood onwards:

> Charles Napier, sickly as a child from the misconduct of a barbarous nurse, was probably stinted of natural growth being of low stature and slight, though both his parents were tall and strong, his father gigantic: but rigorous temperance, through life inviolate, gave him an iron constitution, evinced by immense mental labours and the endurance of strange sufferings in every variety of climate.[260]

This was not helped by continuing trouble from old wounds he had received in various battles as a young man.

The rift between Elizabeth and her daughters must have been a major contributory factor in Elizabeth's decline: Samuel Laing's unyielding opposition to his mother-in-law's marriage continued to prevent Elizabeth from seeing not only her daughter Mary but also her grandchildren. When Napier had written 'by your going abroad (in peace with your daughters) we shall have a more happy time … and you more health' he (and no doubt Elizabeth) had clearly thought that some kind of truce had been established, at least between the Kelly daughters and Elizabeth, if not with him. It sounds too as though he himself, like Edward, was still expecting their imminent return to Kefalonia, and Napier's sister Emily had understood from him that their departure for the island was imminent:

[26 April 1831]

> since I must part with you I rejoice that your dear Bess feels equal to setting off so soon & glad I shall be to receive your first letter from Cefalonia to tell me you are all arrived safe there & have found your chicks well too. I can well understand your feel[ing]s at their being at such a distance from you

In 1830, at the age of forty-seven, Emily Napier married Sir Henry Bunbury. He was fifty-two when they married, and she was his second wife. She continued to take a keen interest in her brother George's family, having been their surrogate mother since the death of George's wife Margaret née Craig. George remarried in 1839, and from time to time took his family to visit the Bunbury home at Great Barton in Suffolk. Emily's marriage appears to have allowed her to relax a little, and judging by the letter extract above she had developed a greater affection for

---

[260] *Life and Opinions*, p. 2.

Elizabeth. Elizabeth's health fluctuated considerably throughout 1831, as letters from Emily and her husband Sir Henry Bunbury document: in October of that year Bunbury wrote in a note to Napier:

My dear Charles

Am very sorry to learn from your note of yesterday that Mrs Napier is so much of an invalid.

Napier's daughters

The little girls were still in Kefalonia; after Napier's departure the Dicksons provided intermittent reports for Colonel and Mrs Napier, and three letters survive. In the first we learn that the school had seventeen pupils:

April 1831

Sir

*I have just now received your letter and am glad of an opportunity to comply with your request It gives me much pleasure to gratify your affectionate solicitude with regard to the dear children_ Their continuance in health whilst it has been a source of satisfaction to us and of comfort to them has removed no small share of the anxiety necessarily connected with such a change. Miss Emily is much improved in her appearance. her fresh looking countenance speaks well of St Andrea's clear air and the happiness of her mind is marked by frequent and lively sallies of pleasantry_*

Miss Susan enjoys her usual uninterrupted state of health, goes steadily forward and uniformly cheerful_ She reads easy lessons correctly and now beginning to distinguish the sense of what she reads from mere signs and sounds, increases in attachment to her book. On the return of mild weather she commenced writing and bids fair to do well She has nearly finished her sampler which I am told is very well done for a child of her years

They have given less trouble than might have been expected. Mrs D's greatest inquietude has arisen from children of a larger growth. They are much pleased with the prospect of soon seeing you here and they do not appear to be insensible that there are those at a distance who on their return will be glad to find them well and improved. These notions often seem as a stimulus to diligence and obedience.

Our school goes on well. The number at present is seventeen. No applications from this Island. You have on all occasions given such unequivocal proofs of your interest in the welfare of this Establishment as prevents me from imagining this information [will be] uninteresting to you. Your presence will prolong its existence and prosperity._

The flannel and books for the children together with a letter from Mrs Napier reached this [sic] only a few days ago

Captⁿ. Kennedy is doubtless ere now in England. We miss his unremitted visits to see the children. Mr Curling called last Sunday. He is looking well amidst all his hard work. It is not easy to contend against a host of foes. M^{rs} D requests her respectful remembrances to Mrs Napier.

In the hope of seeing you soon in the Island I remain your most obliged & humb^l serv^t

G Dickson

At some later date, Napier annotated this letter: *Mr Dickson about My children, Cefalonia_ 8 April 1831.*

In April 1831, Napier's elder daughter, Susan Sarah, was aged about five or six, and her sister, Emily Cefalonia, was four: they were boarding at the school at what to us would seem shockingly young ages. The change Dickson refers to was the departure of the girls' parents from the island, Napier fully expected this separation to be purely temporary as he had a job which required his presence on the island, so leaving Susan and Emily at the school in his absence must have seemed like the obvious solution

It would appear from the Dicksons' letters that the school offered its services to girls of all the Ionian Islands, both British and local. It is not known how the school was funded after Napier left, but the likelihood is that parents paid fees, making it available only to educated and well-off families.

Daily life in the Maltese colony

Edward continued to expect his benefactor's return, and with him the hope that the colony might continue. His journal entry for April reads:

Finished hoeing the currants and sowing Indian corn_ carrying out manure and working in garden_ planted out many young orange plants_ still carrying out manure for cotton_ Boys with the stock as

157

usual_ Colonel Conyers visited the colony and called on me to make
him a report of the colony for his information.

None of this sounds as if it were written by a man who knew that the days of his treasured, carefully nurtured agricultural project were numbered. He firmly recorded on 15 May 1831 that he had *Employed the mules & donkeys to fetch lime and porcelain for the reservoir at St Nicolo and hired a Greek mason to finish this important work.*

But the following day he *Received a letter from the Regent to suspend immediately all labour in the Colony* and on the 17 May 1831 Edward *Made lots of all the tools stock &c and consigned them and the charge of the Colony to Mr Stevens.* Thus it was that Edward's employment by the Ionian government officially ended.

In his journal he followed this final entry with a copy of his report to Colonel Conyers with which he also sent his *Observations* on the project: an overview of its achievements; matters still in hand; what had worked well; and what had failed.[261] So much of what he had done demonstrated that he would have brought the colony to a successful outcome, providing evidence that well-managed land in a Mediterranean climate could produce strong crops, that the island might even be self-sufficient in grain. An objective observer would surely have thought that the project simply needed more time. Edward's letter to Napier of 11 November 1830, about being invited by Sir Frederick Adam to set up a similar enterprise on Corfu, demonstrated that Adam recognised (a) Edward's abilities as an agriculturist and administrator, and (b) the virtue of the project, showing that more efficient farming methods would be to the benefit of the islands' economies.

The following month, still writing from Kefalonia, Edward mentioned the Mary whom the Dicksons had written about at Napier's school. Even after the official closure of the colony which had taken place in May, Edward expressed a confident hope that Napier was on his way from England:

Argostoli June 24 1831

Dear Colonel

I only received your letter of 28ᵗʰ April last Monday, and hasten to comply with your request of addressing a letter to London though I suppose it will never reach you as I hear positively that you are at Ancona_ I saw Emily and Susan the day before yesterday they were quite well and appeared quite comfortable_ Emily some time ago sprained her foot which troubled her for a short time, but now she has

---

[261] For a transcript of Edward's final report, please see **Appendix 14 – Final report on the Maltese Colony** p. 231

quite recovered_ Susan gets on famously in reading and sewing_ they
*both appear fond of Mary which I was glad to see_*

He followed this cheerful description with a poignant note showing how long
Napier and his wife had been absent from Kefalonia

I told them that you would come to see them in a few days, but Emily
did not appear to recollect you Susan however was well pleased_ M^r
*& M^{rs} [Dickson] send their best regards_*

The rest of the letter concerns the winding up of the colony, Edward's own rather
bleak prospects, and the ongoing politics surrounding Napier's absence:

The Colony is at length done up a few men only being employed to
harvest this years produce, the intention of Gov^t in future respecting
it is not known_ I have been to Corfu to know precisely the Generals
intention towards myself, and have been much disappointed at
receiving from him almost in direct terms an intimation that I need
not expect any other situation under Gov^t_ If, a lawc^{rt} now depending,
about 70 acres of land, is decided in favour of Gov^t which cannot be
til October then he will recommend to Gov^t to establish a model farm
and to place me at the head of it with an adequate salary_ but could
make me no promises and would not give me the slightest hope of any
other employment_ this is anything but adequate to me, but it cannot
be helped I must either now take part of the Colony in assets or a
small farm in the Morea my 400$ must manage to establish me and
*with management & economy I still have hopes of living independent_*

I am in [favour of the] latter plan and am anxiously waiting your
[arrival] to consign you your affairs and start_ I have received your
& Capt Kennedy's pay regularly and have collected nearly all the
interest due on your notes of hand_ hearing that the Countess
[Aminos] affairs were rather embarrassed I took the liberty of
registering her bond & 24000$ have since followed my example_ Of
course you may easily imagine that there is no fear of my being called
on to vindicate you even if I thought it was proper to do so

No Greek ever speaks ill of you in my presence I hear nothing but
"quando Vena [sic] il Collonello" "che disgrazia per il paese chi ha
mai lasciato Cefalonia" "quell uomo e nato per guvernare"^{262}_ etc
etc_ I hear positively from Colonel Conyers that you are not to be

---

262 These Italian phrases mean: 'when will the Colonel come?'; 'what a disgrace for the
country that he ever left Cefalonia'; 'that man is born to govern'.

Resident here, people say Zante will be offered you_ The Regent &
many others are in a devil of a fright now that they hear you are
coming back_ the old fool made me a long palaver the other day of
his attachment to you and the attempts that had been made to force
him to make a public accusation against you_ I nearly told him that
when you returned you would soon know both your friends &
*enemies_*

On the address side:

the cause of his alarm is that you never desire to be remembered to
him in your letters_ As I do not expect this ever to reach you I do not
write a long letter_ I forgot to mention that my marriage [will most]
likely take place in a few days as the Licence from [paper damaged]
came and a clergyman expected daily

I hope that your delayed arrival is not occasioned by any illness
of my Aunt_ pray give my most affectionate love to her & believe me

ever yours most gratefully & faithfully

Edw Curling

Edward's and Rosa's marriage, according to the Corfu parish register, was delayed
for a further three months after this letter was written. He wrote again, at length, to
Napier less than two weeks later. The letter provided Napier with a summary of all
the work done in the colony since Edward's appointment, together with a copy of
Edward's report to Colonel Conyers.

Pronos July 3rd 1831

My dear Colonel –

yesterday I got yours of 19th May_ I confess I have done wrong in
not continuing my journal and though there may be some excuse for
me I shall leave you to imagine it yourself, and proceed to the remedy
of my error_ I can easily from memory make out a statement of the
whole of the operations of the Colony from the time of my assuming
the Directorship till the present time and as you wish, will
immediately do so_ the history since you left is told in few words_ the
first blow struck against us was Stevens selling the produce by
Auction_ this completely upset my intention of fattening the stock and
thus preserving manure, and not mentioning this latter advantage
which was thus lost to us, I should certainly in addition have made
much more money of the produce than he did and would not have had

the trouble and expense of bringing the next years seed from the Convents My labourers were then reduced to a number wholly inadequate to the cultivation of the whole of the Colony_ but sufficient to have acted according to my proposal to Gov^t of letting part of the Colony to Greeks_ but to this proposal no answer from Corfu could be obtained. I spoke several times to Colonel Pitt but he would do nothing which might interrupt the General's ... which he expected daily to be made acquainted with_ I asked Colonel Conyers to speak to the General and also reported by letter to him, that unless my labourers were increased or the land let to Greeks, a great part of the Colony must remain uncultivated_ to this I received in reply "that Colonel Conyers would not authorise any further expense particularly as the General was fully aware of the situation of the ... at Pronos"_ What could I do more_ I cultivated as much land as I could but the greater part remained uncropped and now there is a cry against the Colony that after all that has been done this years produce should be so small_ indeed it appears to have been the policy to lessen the produce to have some excuse for doing away with the Colony_ why the General delayed so long I cannot imagine unless he was wavering between the influence of Baynes, and his fear of you, but the former hearing of your probable speedy arrival did I hear come down to Cefalonia on purpose to get patched up by the Regent on unfavourable reports and the consequence has been a suspension of all our works_ Colonel Conyers visited the Colony, that is, rode through it without asking a single question or making a single observation on the cultivation and called upon me for a report for his information in which I gave him a full account of the Colony etc and begged him to forward it to the General hoping it would act as a counter statement to Baynes'_ Colthurst who stuck up manfully got this done for me & therefore there is no excuse that the Genl did not know the actual state of the Colony_ I think this report so necessary to you that I even put you to the expense of postage to give you a copy of it_ the remainder is soon told_ the harvest was got in by Cambisi (my pay and direction being entirely suspended) in a slovenly manner_ the stock was sold by Auction by the Municipal body, two of whom bought 41 pigs valued at least 80 dollars for 30$ though Cambisi by letter offered 41 himself_ new surveys, fresh visits and other expenses took place for the information of Gov^t as if they had not been made 20 times before to prove the goodness of the soil and what cultivation and manure can do I shall only state this *fact_ that in one piece of my improved land there is Indian Corn at present 8 feet high whilst that of* [Racli] *with the advantage of water is only 2 feet_ Cambisi says there is certainly not such a crop in Cefalonia_from 1 bushel Gov^t will probably get 40 or 50_ potatoes I have grown capitally_ all my trees were coming on well_ our expenses were trifling and I was flattering myself that in one year more, if Gov^t would not again tie up my hands, we should conquer_ when all our improvements and operations were upset in one overwhelming crash by a few malicious people to gratify their own private enmity_ As for myself I thought that a sacrifice of 2½ years of hard work, without a single fault or neglect being found in me, might have merited at least a continuance in employment, but I alas am excavated as it were just as I thought I was taking root_ As for my fitness for being the Director, my works at Pronos are, I hope, sufficient proof of that_ and to establish that you were right in recommending me you can mention the General's own words after 2½ years trial_ "I am extremely desirous to take advantage of your talents and knowledge of Agriculture for the benefit of the islands" etc_ I do not dislike Stevens his conduct has I believe never been underhanded, he showed me his report, and always expressed his opinion openly_ not like the greek rascals like* [Gerasimo Lusi] *who to Stevens talks of your "cosé lunatice" and is I hear one of the most active partisans against you, and to me he is all blarney "quando verra il nostro Colonello" "qual uomo é nato per governance" etc Make Capt Kennedy tell you all he knows of* [Mairs][263] *conduct which through delicacy he will not do_ your desiring to be remembered to him in your last letter has certainly saved him from a fit of the cholic_ you will be glad to hear that* [Caruso] *has obtained the situation of Master of Ancient Greek in the public School*

I saw [Dellaporto] *the other day, he was quite well, but beginning to be tired of the cares of Matrimony which serves him just right for marrying a Signora for money_ As for myself I scarcely know how to act I was wishing for your arrival that I might consign your affairs to you and start for the* [Morea]_ *now as you are not coming for three months, by waiting, I shall lose this sowing season_ I will not pretend to disguise that your kind expressions have great weight in tempting me to remain, without the additional one, that of attending to your*

---

[263] Edward didn't use possessive apostrophes. This name is in brackets (as are others below) because I'm unsure of the spelling from his handwriting.

*affairs and giving you from time to time an account of Susan &
Emily_ I have decided at present therefore to stay at all events till I
can again hear from you_ I cannot too much thank you for your kind
intentions, all I wish is that you will not allow them in the slightest
manner to interfere with your other [business] if a favourable
opportunity should occur I am sensible that you will take advantage
of it in my favour, if not thank God, my economy has made me in a
manner independent at all events whilst I have health and strength
and can find work I am always so_ I am living still at Pronos at an
expence of less than $5 a month, supporting myself chiefly by shooting
and fishing therefore my waiting three or four months will not ruin
me_ Write me your opinion of my taking part of the Colony_ if I can
get it for paying Gov^t a third of the produce perhaps I may take it_ at
present the intention of Govt is not known_ I hear the General has
given up his intention of going to England_ I heard this in Corfu_ he
has said in Public that you will not be Resident at Cefalonia but he
did not know as to Zante_ now I am sure that you will say to him in
the words of the Gospel "If I have done wrong accuse me of the wrong,
but if right why do you strike me" If you have done right why does he
remove you_ Colonel Conyers told me positively that you would not
come here_ he is much disliked except by the Signori who from his
inaction now do as they like_ the Regent's yellow breeches shine
more than ever now_ he told me [he] had never deserted you except
by telling the General that he had seen you strike persons in your
office, and that he was not "persuaded" of many of your measures
although he gave his signature_ that he passed "giorni amari assai"
when Baynes and Condari were here, who threatened him with
expulsion from office if he did not make a public [account] against
you_*

    Cambisi [Marcocan, Fosetti and Monferratta] *are all well and
anxiously expecting you_ Tell Capt Kennedy that his friend Paulo
Valsamachi abuses him right and left publicly and privately_*
[Cosmetto] *Valsamachi and the others indicted for high treason for
writing a caricature & endeavouring to incite the populace are
acquitted except a certain* [Monfarretto] *who has 2 years imprison-
ment_ the public building goes on slowly_ poor Michele who finished
the stone columns according to contract with Capt Kennedy is likely
to lose $400 by Gov^t altering the plan and refusing his [alimony] you
see how justice is thriving in Cefalonia_ I hope you will receive my
letter sent by packet 10 days ago according to your wishes it would*

tell you that Susan and Emily are quite well and anxiously expecting you_ I cannot yet find a good opportunity for investing your money, [Gussibb Monferrath] & I will do so in grand security Pray give my kindest love to my Aunt_ in this long letter I have not had time to mention her, but as long as I live I should never forget her kindness_ remember me also to Capt K & Charles_ believe me yours ever faithfully_ Edw Curling

Edward follows on immediately with a copy of his letter to Colonel Conyers for Napier's approval; see **Appendix 14 – Final report on the Maltese Colony** p. 231.

Chapter 15 – The Residency of Cefalonia into what hands art thou fallen.

Another letter from Mr Dickson written in July indicates that rumours of Napier's return continued to run through the community and in Edward's letters too it is apparent that hopes are high that Napier will soon be back. Mr Dickson hints at the growing controversy about Napier's authority in the island and active attempts, as Dickson along with Napier's other loyal supporters see it, to blacken his name.

14th July 1831

Sir

The arrival of your letter of the 17th of May has put an end to the expectations we were rashly cherishing of your being near us. Report after report was brought of your having actually reached Ancona & every hour we expected to hear announced your arrival in Corfu or Cephalonia. A few weeks more will however I trust enable you to realise your intentions, fulfil the hopes of your friends in this part of the world as well as frustrate the charges of those who talk at random because they know you are at a distance. It is not unusually the lot of the greatest benefactors of a country to be repaid with the blackest ingratitude & the facilest calumny of those whom they have benefited. The modern Ionians have not in this respect wiped off the stain of their ancestors.

Many thanks for the hints thrown out in your letter. A recent circumstance confirms their justice. Whatever may be the sentiments of the present Gov^t. toward us and our employment one of our countrymen the immediate organ of the former has expressed <u>his</u> in terms too plain to be misunderstood. He declared lately at a party that education would never do the Greeks any good & gave a friend of mine to understand they wished us out of the Convent. I had always considered this gentle man friendly nor am I conscious in any instance of having offended him, but if according to his judgement, alas! for his [sapience] to teach be a crime _ then explanation is easy. Despite of these circumstances our number keeps up & is likely to do so for some time to come yet should such sentiments from such a quarter ... you know the character of the people too well to be told the result.

Misses Susan & Emily continue to enjoy good health. Susan is growing tall and we think her improved in her appearance. She is

doing very well in her lessons. She has read all the books sent her &
feels happy at the prospect of receiving others & says she will try to
read them too. Emily a short time ago hurt her foot a little whilst she
was playing in the room. Shortly after administering an application
prescribed by Mr Muir it got quite better. We have had an unusually
cool summer. The heat however has rapidly increased within a few
days. An increase of 18 deg. has been observed. There is a great deal
of sickness in Argostoli & throughout the Island St Andrea maintains
its usual character of [...]__ Monferrat is much obliged by your
attention ... one of them who look forward with [pleasure] to your
return.

My wife unites with me [in wishing you a] successful voy[age] ...
to Mrs Napier we hope [she] continues well & will be able to
[accompany] you. Mary is behaving well and is attentive to the
children. We are glad to hear Capt. Kennedy's health improves. We
felt we had lost a friend when he left the Island. Any intimation of
your commands regarding the children or of your future movements
I shall ever esteem a favor meanwhile I remain Sir

Your most obliged & humble servant

G Dickson[264]

The final report on the girls, this time from Mrs Dickson to Elizabeth Napier was
written in August 1831:

St Andreas August 23rd 1831

My dear Madam

A few weeks ago Mr Dickson wrote to Colonel Napier in answer
to his kind favor dated May 19th and acquainted Col N with the good
state of health of the Misses Susan and Emily as well as their progress
in their education It gives me much pleasure to continue the same
good accounts. Notwithstanding the sickness which has prevailed in
the Island this Summer our large family has enjoyed uninterrupted
health which is no small comfort to us who are entrusted with children
whose parents are at a distance. We had some fears at the
commencement of the warm season with regard to Miss Emily as she
was rather delicate last summer but she has continued up to the
present perfectly well and is growing stout. They often enquire when

---

[264] BL Add MS 54542 f. 44.

their papa is coming again and what their Mamma will bring them from England_ if they shall receive any more pretty books – a Doll or sweetmeats They talk to one another of going to Argostoli in a carriage to see their papa and mamma and sometimes they are to go in the steam boat to Corfu for that purpose. A few mornings since after they had been out to walk Miss Susan came to me saying that Emily had told her that their papa and mamma were coming on the morrow and asked if it was true I told her that perhaps you could not come on the morrow but that I hoped you would come soon She was quite satisfied. She is going on with her second sampler and is doing it very nice [sic] Miss E has lately begun to get regular lessons in reading Mary is doing very well_ much better than at one time we expected She hears regularly from the friends in Corfu who seem anxious about your return She caught a cold in the spring which left a soreness in the inside of her nose it continued for some time which made us uneasy. We took her down to Dr Muir who thought by washing it regularly with a little milk and water it would soon get better. It is now almost completely well. She is complaining today of a pain in her knee and there is appearance of a tumour which perhaps indicates a bad state of the blood and may make medicine necessary which we shall ask from Dr M without delay. You will excuse me for being so particular I know your kind interest in the girl and would wish every necessary thing done for her health and comfort. Our school continues to prosper We have still with us the Misses Monferato & Stevens [We] were much gratified by your kind rememberance [sic] of them

I am my dear Madam
Your obliged and [humble] serv^{ant}
H E Dickson[265]

The girl, Mary, whom Mrs Dickson mentions, is a mystery. She may have been a pupil at the school or possibly an assistant. It was not Elizabeth's daughter Mary Kelly who was still, in 1831, living with her brother-in-law Samuel Laing.

Edward was turned out of his house when the government closed the colony and from then on was reliant on friends for hospitality until he heard the final decision on Napier's returning to the island. He stayed for some time with Rankin and in August was living at Kennedy's house on the Black Mountain (Mount Ainos). In August 1831 he outlined in detail the various duties he had taken on for Napier,

---

[265] BL Add MS 54542 f. 56.

and it is clear that he was managing all the colonel's business and personal affairs on the island.

Kennedy house, Black mountain
August 10th 1831

My dear Colonel__ I wrote to you about 3 weeks back giving you an account of the colony &c and shall be glad to hear that you have received my letter__ I saw Susan and Emily last week, they were as hearty and happy as possible and quite growing out of their clothes, so much so that if you do not come in about a month I must provide them with entire new suits__ they also want socks__ Mr Dixon I believe has given up his intention of visiting the Morea chiefly in consequence of your letter to him, which I am very glad of, as it will make you more easy in your mind in regard to the children__ I should have written some days back but I wished to be more certain of the day of Sir Frederick Adam's departure for England which appears fixed for the 15th inst certain_ i.e. every body says so__ the steamer is expected to day therefore before I close this I shall be able to give you the latest reports from Corfu__ People here have an idea that you are waiting to see the General and are calculating that winter will be setting in before you can leave, [they] are fondly in hopes that you will not come, at all events till next year__ 'tis' also said that Sir F intends to recommend the reduction of Inspector and Sub Inspector on account of Economy, but these are only Greek lies I believe and not worth your crediting__ Combotecra's fishery has followed the fate of the Colony, Government having chosen to break the contract without even giving him an indemnification of his expenses this is chiefly owing to the Regent who has in every way possible oppressed poor Combotecra since your departure__ the latter has in a very spirited manner presented a memorial addressed to the Government of the Island to be forwarded as therein stated "ai priedi dei re"__ the Regent tried in an underhand manner to stop this but did not succeed__ the Port of Pronos was shut when the Colony was done away with and Cambisi proposed a memorial already signed by some thousands petitioning for its being reopened which of course will not be done under the present administration because it was your recommendation that it was opened before__ Combotecra tells me that he has also received notice to quit Trapano __

*Mr Smithson has forwarded the strongest memorial possible to "His Majesty"[266] as he could get no redress from the General__ I have heard that his petition is well written__ in one part he says "Sir F Adam will say that I am mad, but I hold in my hand a letter of Sir F written three months back <u>inviting me to a consultation on the affairs of the island</u> which shows that <u>he did not think me mad then</u>"__ Mr Gerasimo Lusi is getting up a memorial to do away with the market and to allow people to sell things where they please__ when you come back you will find things in strange confusion. The policy appears now to work as hard to upset your works as you did to create them in fact I should not be surprised to see parties employed to destroy the roads because you made them__ there is no road work at present going on across the whole island__ I am now staying in the Black mountain__ the present forest guardian does not do his duty in the least__ I see trees cut down in every direction and sheep and goats range through the forest at pleasure. What a pity this is! But no one now takes the least interest in the matter__ there are some fine young trees about 5 years old growing beautifully and as straight as a dart and they show what a fine forest ~~might~~[267] this would become if care was taken of it__ I unfortunately injured the stock of my gun, and as from this I used to provide myself with at least three dinners a week, particularly here amongst the hares, I took the liberty of borrowing your double barrelled one which I will take the greatest care of_ feeling assured that you would not object lending it to me__ A Tin Cannister supposed to contain "tops & bottoms" has arrived for you. I have paid the freight and am taking care of it for you__ The people on whose notes of hand the interest is due hold off, until after the current crop is harvested__ I have however received your pay and that of the Capt up to the end of July__ Monferratta advises me not to put your money out at present, and as he knows I suppose all about these affairs, I of course follow his advise [sic]__ the whole of your money and that of Capt Kennedy remains therefore in the strong box in the treasury__ you can give me any further instruction about it in your next letter_*

I am delighted to hear of Charles Kennedy[268] having attained his Com^n in the 96th Reg^t remember me to him most kindly and tell him I

---

[266] It is not known to whom the epithet 'his majesty' refers, although it is clear that Edward cannot have meant Sir F Adam.

[267] EC's strikethrough.

[268] Charles Kennedy (1810–1862) was John Pitt Kennedy's youngest sibling.

wish him every success__ I shall not write as he may have changed his residence__ Nothing has yet been done with regard to the Colony and there is every appearance that from the dilatory manner of conducting affairs at Corfu the land will alas be left uncropped this year__ I have given up the idea of taking any part of it as I think going to the Morea will be a much better speculation, as there a pair of bullocks 40 or 50 sheep and a little hard work will render me independent at once__ I am not yet married according to law as no clergyman has visited the island and I cannot afford the expense of going to Corfu__ I am very anxious to hear from you again and particularly to know whether you have received my last letter, which I hoped would suit your purpose as well as if I had kept my journal__ I have finished the latter [...] up to the time of my being superseded and there [...] only remains to make my remarks which can be done at any time, indeed the knowledge which I am every day gaining from books will make me more competent to write them a short time hence__ I am sending Greek exercises to Caruso regularly by the ice Mules[269] and studying also law as hard as I can__ It will not be long I hope, if a Maltese or Greek interpreter is wanted before I shall be competent for the situation__ Hayton says "they are trying all they can to get me out of my place before the Colonel comes back, but I'm too wide awake nobody can hurt me" Haynes gets drunk as usual__ Turk is getting on capitally__

August 11th The steam packet did not come yesterday therefore I can say no more as to the General's departure__ Monferratta begged of me to advise you to bring out your appointment as Resident from England as the General was so bound both by letter and verbally not to allow you to return to Cefalonia as Resident, that it was useless to expect that he would appoint you__ The new criminal and civil codes have been passed in the Ionian Parliament & they are now working at the commercial code__ Capt Colthard has received your letter and

---

[269] The term 'ice mule' appears in a few 19th-century contexts; see for example the article 'Ice: its history preservation and use' by 'a Traveller' in *The Watercure Journal*, vol. XV no. 1. It refers to mules used as pack animals to carry ice from mountain tops to centres of population, where it would have been stored somewhere cold, probably below ground. Several large estates in England had 'ice houses' for this purpose. Presumably ice mules on Kefalonia brought the product down from the top of Mount Ainos and no doubt carried it not just to the town of Argostoli but to the rural estates of affluent.citizens like Dimitri Cambici.

is writing to you in answer__ Give my kindest love and affection to
my Aunt & believe me yours most faithfully
and gratefully
Ed^w Curling[270]

Even at this late date (10 August 1831) Edward was expecting Napier to return to Kefalonia. However, at the very end of the month everything changed. Two letters – one from Edward to Napier and the other from Napier to Captain Colthurst – must have crossed in the post. Napier was worried that Edward might already have left Kefalonia, but told Colthurst that he wanted Edward (1) to bring his little daughters to England and (2) to be warned against going to the Morea[271], probably because of the continuing instability on mainland Greece, resulting from the 'Greek War of Independence' [1821–1832] where the Greeks were fighting the Ottoman Empire to repossess their lands.

Napier's letter to Colthurst:

Maidenhead

26 August 1831

My dear Colthurst _ I am not sure that Edward Curling will be at Cefalonia when this reaches you so I direct to you and ask Montferat [to] pay you the postage _ giving my best regards to him_ will you tell Edward to come home with my children if he can get off by the October packet not otherways – tell him not to go to the Morea on any account I am not going to take him by the hand and thus let him be stuck up to his arse in this clay by my enemies to spite me I know the fools too well to trust to them or rather the fool adam whose father was wrong in calling his place Blair Adam, he ought to have called it Bray Adam as he meant to breed jackasses – well men can't help being fools and falling into the hands of rogues as he has done. if Edward is prevented from coming home in October tell him to write me word if he thinks he can get a good farm cheap at Cefalonia and as I shall be back some fine day, I would buy it. tell him to write to me what he thinks could be done for 700£ there & to use my money to live on, not his own till we settle something for him_ give my love to all friends tell Rankin I hope he likes my prison! he is a good fellow and I hope this time his lying in did not interfere with his currants as the time before did. well after all my jail is a better place than a watch house – I am waiting to see if there is a ... on the 8th I dare swear

---

[270] BL Add MS 54536 ff. 118, 119.
[271] The large area of land now known as the Peloponnese.

there are those at Cefalonia who will not regard my promotion if it
keeps me away! my action all depends on my wife's health. she
desires her love to you and her God daughter

We both desire to be kindly
Remembered to your wife
Yours ever truly
C Napier

Kind regards to all my friends for I believe I have some *at*
Cefalonia I know them and my Enemies too. Write to me and tell me
all the news but remember that fool Adam is your Enemy and that that
half Maltese half French half Greek Bugger Baynes ... will open and
read your letter as they will this for which reason I am so
complimentary to them that the drivelling Lord High and his [sacks?]
[pudding?] interpreter may know the value I set upon them! you have
not gentlemen to deal with._

Addressed to

Captain Colturst
Cefalonia
Ionian Islands
By Falmouth[272]

Napier need not have worried. Edward had received his instructions regarding the
little girls, and had already taken steps to put Napier's wishes into action:

Argostoli August 30th 1831

My dear Colonel

I received your letter of August 2nd the day before yesterday and
of course immediately decided in complying with your instructions
with respect to bringing the children home__ the packet that brought
your letter has sailed therefore I must wait for the next__ I purpose
[sic] therefore in about 20 days to go up to Corfu by the steamer and
there wait the arrival of the Packet which from what I can learn here
is expected the latter end of the month__ however I write to Mr
Woodhouse[273] *today and my movements will be governed by the*
information and advice which he may give me__ I saw Susan & Emily
yesterday__ they were quite well, but I thought Emily looked rather

---

[272] BL Add MS 41063 f. 47.
[273] This was probably the same Mr Woodhouse who was the official auditor for the Ionian
Islands at the time; see **Appendix 2 – Castlereagh's Cabinets of Weights** p. 192.

more delicate than usual, however Mrs Dixon assures me they have both been extremely well__ There will be no danger of their Mother's knowing of their departure as it appears from Mr Woodhouse's last letter to me that she is in Missolonghi reports here says she is dead, but I will take all the precautions you wish__ I will pay the passage money from the funds of yours in my hands, and bring the remainder & Capt Kennedy's pay home in Bills unless Monferratta should previously advise me of a good opportunity for investing it here__ I have already sold your white horse to Hayter for the same money that you gave for him, the cows I shall most likely sell today, as for Turk I must leave him with Cambisi and if Government should remove the man from [Cfi Merli] that at present takes care of him, Cambisi must pay a boy for that purpose__ I do not see what else I can do with Turk who is in excellent condition, and does not allow any horse mule or donkey male or female to enter the yard without wishing to form improper connections__ I leave Rosa at St Andrea under the protection of the Dixons__ I was rather in doubt as to whether it would be better to bring her home with me, as I have no further employment here, __ the arguments pro and con appeared nearly equal, however the small chance of finding any thing to do in England and the smallness of my stock of money, prevailed and I determined to leave her__ I hope still to receive a letter from you before I go about this, as you must long before this, know of my dismissal from the Colony__ The General I suppose will be with you before you receive this, he started for Ancona a week since__ it will not be difficult to bring you an account of the public works, I do not think any at all are going on in Cefalonia__ Colonel Conyers does not interest himself at all, in fact the residency of the island is a nullity, everything passes through the Regents office where the Municipal court is now held__ Colonel C said to Capt [Worsley] the other day "Mr Reid appears too independent of me have I anything to do with the Enginier [sic] department" "No Sir I am the head of <u>that</u> Department" was the reply__ in an altercation the other day between Mr Reid & the Colonel "<u>Mr Reid you speak so loud that I must leave my office</u>" "<u>No sir, I will go out if you wish it</u>" "<u>No I insist on going</u>" "<u>Well then Sir if you please we will both go out together__</u>" The Residency of Cefalonia into what hands art thou fallen, and where is thy ancient dignity!!! I have been living in the mountain this summer, twice I came into town for a day, twice I caught the fever, and twice the mountain air cured me immediately on my return__ there has

been very great sickness in town this year___ the Noa Papa crop is
got in safe and is calculated at 11 millions, and is of the best quality___
the Morea crop is much injured by rain & Zante partially___ With
kindest love to my Aunt & the Kennedys I am

ever yours most faithfully
Ed^w Curling[274]

Edward indicates how precarious his circumstances have become, with no permanent abode and no prospect of employment either in Kefalonia or in England. Napier and his wife Elizabeth were doubtless alarmed when they read that Edward was thinking of leaving Rosa in Kefalonia, even under the care of the school teachers, Mr and Mrs Dixon, at St Andrea. Edward's assurance, in response to Napier's request, that he would take all precautions to avoid the little girls' mother, Anastasia, knowing of their departure, seems heartless and somewhat underhand, but Anastasia does not appear to have been part of the children's lives since Napier and Elizabeth had taken full charge of them, and it is likely that Napier wanted to avoid upsetting the little girls by any confrontation which might ensue. Anastasia would no doubt have thought that her daughters living in England would be a wonderful outcome for them.

As we know, Anastasia had been Napier's mistress before his marriage to Elizabeth. Edward Beasley writes:

> Early on he took as his mistress a Greek nationalist named Anastasia …
> Napier also told his sister that he would have left the girls with Anastasia
> if she had wanted them, although it would have broken his heart. But he
> added that in fact Anastasia did not want them … They were brought to
> England by his kinsman Edward Curling.[275]

At the same time the dispute between Napier and Sir Frederick Adam had come to a head in England. Napier had raised the matter with Lord Goderich and had also published, in newspapers, rebuttals of Adam's accusations. The compromise which Napier was offered was the post of Resident on Zante. In his view, as we know, accepting it would amount to admitting that his behaviour in Kefalonia had been wrong, something which he felt passionately was not the case. So he rejected the suggestion and in doing so finally abandoned hope of returning to Kefalonia as its Resident. It was therefore clear that he would need to make arrangements to bring his daughters to England. Once again, Napier (and probably Elizabeth) found a solution which benefited both his own arrangements and those of Edward. Napier asked Edward to bring Emily and Susan to England. Although Edward wrote that

---

[274] BL Add MS 54536 ff. 120, 121.
[275] *The Chartist General:* pp. 67, 69, 93. Edward Beasley, Routledge, 2017.

he had decided to leave Rosa with the Dixons, it would have been very difficult for him to have cared for the little girls adequately on the three-week journey without a woman's help. Napier would have felt a responsibility for Edward's circumstances and authorised Edward to pay for his and Rosa's fares as well as those of the children from the funds which Edward had been collating at the bank in Argostoli.

Argostoli Sept 7 1831

Dear Colonel

By the Ionian steamer which has just passed I have received an answer to my letter, from Mr Woodhouse, he tells me the English Packet is not expected at Corfu till the 27th inst and advises me to leave by the next turn of the steamer, therefore in 12 days hence we shall leave this___ I have not seen the children since I last wrote but Mrs [Erein] told me the day before yesterday that they were quite well___ I shall pass by Saint Andrea this evening___

I send you by this opportunity two Bills of Exchange of £100 each, and if I can succeed in collecting your interest due I shall be able to send you home another for the same sum and have sufficient besides to pay our passage money___ I have sold the white horse for 28 dollars the price you gave for him, and the small cow for 10$___ Dixon takes the large cow and I settle the price with him today___ Turk remains with Cambisi___

I wish you had left it at my discretion to go home in a [currant] vessel in case of a good opportunity___ we might sail in two or three days in a beautiful schooner especially fitted up for passengers, we should have arrived in England as soon as by waiting for the steamer and you would have saved more than £100___

I have no news of any kind to write you
With kindest love to my Aunt
I remain
Yours ever faithfully
Edw Curling[276]

I will address my letters to Cadogan Place as I do not know if by directing them "Maidenhead" they will reach you and [you] do not say where you are except near Maidenhead.

---

[276] BL Add MS 54536 ff. 122, 123.

The postscript tells us that Napier has at least been in or near Cookham, which is near Maidenhead, in the recent past. He and Elizabeth may have kept the Stone House property in Cookham after their marriage, or they may have been staying with their friends the Packes. This is Edward's last letter written from Cefalonia.

Twelve days later, on 19 September 1831, he, Rosa and Napier's little girls, Susan Sarah aged five and Emily Cefalonia aged four, left Argostoli. They docked at Corfu, where Edward and Rosa married on 26 September 1831, no doubt with the little girls in attendance.[277] A day or two later they continued the journey by sea to England.

The death throes of the colony had been protracted and must have been very stressful for Edward. It was extremely unfortunate that Napier had had to leave the island in May 1830 to take Elizabeth back to England: he had thus been absent for a year when the coup de grace was administered to the colony. His presence would almost certainly have prevented the ultimate outcome, but then many events would have been different had he been able to stay in Kefalonia. Napier's published records never show a single word of blame or frustration that his working life at this period was so overshadowed by Elizabeth's health, but he cannot have been oblivious to the fact that it had a bearing on how his plans for Kefalonia, in particular the colony and his relationship with the Ionian government, played out.

When Edward left, he had been in Kefalonia for just over three years. He took with him letters from four residents of Kefalonia addressed to him, each with the intention that they should be passed on to Napier when he arrived in England. The four letters were signed by Giovani [sic] Combatecra, Demetrio Cambici, L. Reginis and Cristodulo Metaxia Anguria. Only Reginis wrote in English. He said

> I have the honor to beg you will have the goodness on your safe arrival in England to present my best respects to the Colonel and his Lady, and tell them that the voice of gratitude makes a very narrow and almost imperceptible path to pierce through a thick crowd of ungrateful flatterers, in order to travel many a mile and reach its destination![278]

The remaining letters were written in Italian. Cambici in particular expressed his sadness that Napier would not be returning, regretted that Napier was not given the respect due to him and sent greetings to Napier and the Kennedy men declaring that everyone in his house was their friend.

Napier never had the opportunity to return to Kefalonia, but the island was dear to his heart for the rest of his life.

---

[277] Copy of Marriage Certificate obtained from the General Register Office, June 2017. Historical Corfu records are held as part of the UK overseas military records.
[278] BL Add MS 54536 f. 128.

As a postscript to the Kefalonia years, the Dicksons continued for a time to teach in the Ionian Islands although Napier's school for the girls did not long survive his departure. The Dixons had one child, a son, Thomas, born in Kefalonia. When the girls' school closed they moved to Argostoli, where they set up a school for the poor. From there they moved to Zante (Zakinthos), where they taught for another four years. Wishing to see their parents, they obtained permission to return to Scotland for six months, but en route, George Dickson developed a fever, and died at Leghorn (Livorno) in August 1836. Mrs Dickson did not complete the journey, but returned to Zante and devoted the rest of her life to teaching in various schools in Greece.[279]

[279] *One Woman's Mission – A Memorial of Mrs Harriet E Dickson*, Rev A N Arnold, DD, publisher Henry A Young and Co., Boston, 1871 https://bit.ly/Ch15HDickson

Appendix 1a – A description of Kefalonia in Napier's time

Kefalonia is in the twenty-first century still comparatively unknown apart from its role as the setting of Louis de Bernière's book *Captain Corelli's Mandolin* and the subsequent film.[280]

Marine painter Joseph Cartwright (1789–1829) was the paymaster-general to the garrison at Corfu between 1816 and 1820. He published his *Views in the Ionian Islands* in 1821. They include his view of the *Town and Harbour of Argostoli, (Cephalonia)* (Fig. 25 p. 121). To accompany his illustrations, he provides the following contemporaneous information on the then British protectorate called 'the United States of the Ionian Islands'.[281]

Fig. 35.   The Ionian flag adopted in 1815 [282]

The Ionian Islands

These United States were in 1815 placed by the Treaty of Paris under the immediate protection of Great Britain, and the representative of the protecting Sovereign is styled "His Majesty's Lord High Commissioner". They are composed of Corfu, Cephalonia, Zante, Santa Maura, Ithaca, Cerigo, Paxo and their dependancies [*sic*].

The established religion is orthodox Greek, the religion of the high protecting power is exercised with the fullest liberty, that of the Roman

---

[280] *Captain Corelli's Mandolin*, Secker & Warburg, 1994, London, UK. The film of the same name was first shown in 2001 http://www.imdb.com/title/tt0238112/

[281] All twelve of Cartwright's images are available on https://bit.ly/App1aCartwright

[282] Image of flag from Wikipedia https://bit.ly/App1aIonianFlag

Catholic is specially countenanced, and all other forms of worship are tolerated.

The Civil Government of the States is composed of a Senate, a legislative Assembly and a Judicial Authority.

The Military Command of the Islands is placed in the hands of the Commander of His Britannic Majesty's Forces.

The Ionian flag is the lion of Saint Mark and bears, as a proof of especial protection, the British Union in the upper corner; its appearance in those Seas was hailed as the signal of dissolution to the numerous hordes of Pirates, who have for ages lurked among the rocks, mutilating and putting to cruel torture their unfortunate Captives.

Cephalonia

Is the largest of the Seven Ionian Islands; latitude 38.11.02; longitude 20.28.37. It is 180 miles in circumference, and contains about 55,000[283] inhabitants. The exports of the Island are chiefly Oil, Wine, and Currants. The crop of the last-mentioned article, in a favorable season, sometimes exceeds four millions of pounds.

The harbour of Argostoli is excellent, and sufficiently capacious to contain the whole Navy of Great Britain. About two miles up, on the left of the entrance, stands the town of Luxuri, principally inhabited by Cephaloniote Mariners. They are extremely numerous, upwards of one hundred and fifty vessels being fitted out from this Island, the greater part of which are employed in bringing corn from the Black Sea, and from Alexandria.

Extensive remains of ancient buildings are scattered about, particularly in the vicinity of Samos, which is directly opposite the Aitos of Ithaca.

There is considerable diversity of scenery in Cephalonia, and from the summit of the Black Mountain, which is nearly five thousand feet above the level of the Sea, may be seen Corfu, Paxo, Santa Maura, Ithaca, Zante, Acarnania and the Morea.[284]

---

[283] current population 35,801 (2011)
[284] BL 001812860 Cartographic Items Maps. 145.e.12 Joseph Cartwright *Views in the Ionian Islands*.

Appendix 1b – Napier's achievements in Kefalonia

After his departure from Kefalonia Napier found himself again on half-pay, with time on his hands, so he wrote a book about his time there, including a list of his practical achievements. [285] He had, he said,

> built spacious streets in place of 'dirty narrow lanes', two market places with associated markets, created a neat piazza, flagged and chained, extended Argostoli towards the bridge and 'formed a pretty street on what was previously beach; the houses and the ground now between it and the sea were also my doing'.[286]

He had also, as we know, set up a model farming colony to show the Greeks how they could improve their farming methods. In addition he had paved all the narrow lanes, built a mole (stone pier) in Lixouri, a girls' school, a prison, a quarantine hospital (required at all ports round the British empire, because there were fears of leprosy, plague and other infections), two lighthouses, a theatre and a quarry at Lixouri, and he had 'opened the ports of Algo, Guiscardo [Fisgardo], Samos and Pronos'. Above all he had introduced a programme of road building in which every man on the island, in a system known as the corvée, was obliged to participate: aristocrats could buy themselves exemption by paying a labourer to take their turn, but otherwise everyone did the work, even the Greek Orthodox priests (although they were somewhat reluctant) and Napier himself.[287] By this method he oversaw the building of more than one hundred miles of road.

The source for this information is in his book *The Colonies*. It could be said that his was a biased account, but the evidence of his partnership with Captain John Pitt Kennedy in engineering all these works remained after he had left the island.

[285] *Memoir on the Roads of Cefalonia*, Charles James Napier 1833.
[286] *Life and Opinions* pp. 388–391.
[287] *The Roads of Cefalonia*, Helen Cosmetatos, pub. Corgialenios Museum, Kefalonia, 1995, p. 69.

Appendix 1c – Nineteenth-century places in Pronos, Kefalonia

As soon as I learned, from Edward Curling's letters and journal in the British Library, of his time in Kefalonia I was keen to visit the island to see what traces I could find, if any, of his work there. My first obstacle was my own ignorance in every relevant area, not least my lack of linguistic skills in Greek, which made explaining what I was looking for, and why, very complicated. Gradually, over the next dozen or so years, supported by lessons in basic Greek and by making contacts on the island, the geography and history began to clarify.

Since discovering Edward's journal I have visited Kefalonia several times and until recently had reluctantly concluded that any traces of Agios Nikolaos, as it was in his time, and of the Maltese colony had probably slipped away into the two-hundred-year fissures of history and I would never know their exact location. On each visit I drove to the villages whose names are mentioned in the journal and letters, but without success. Edward recorded a 'fountain' at Agios Nikolaos on which he had had a mason build a 'reservoir'; he had had a chimney built for his house there, and developed a fruit and vegetable 'garden'. Napier wrote of finding 'a green and fertile tract of land' for his colony, and John Pitt Kennedy, in his letters to Napier, identified 'Racli' as the place where the colony was sited. But I knew neither what I was looking for nor whom to ask for clues. On my earlier visits I did ask the owners of my accommodation, the shopkeepers in the Poros supermarkets and the local bookshop, but although they were interested and wanted to help they had no concrete leads for me to follow. Most perplexing was that no-one had heard of a place called Racli or Rakli.

By Spring 2022, I had finished what I thought was the final draft of the present volume, but still had questions in my mind. So, when the Covid-19 pandemic travel restrictions lifted, I planned another visit to Greece, a week in Kefalonia and a week in Athens. The silver lining of advancing years is that physical limitations force one to ask for help and an apparently unrelated change can open whole new vistas. Driving had become a painful business, so for the first time I hired a driver.

Polydoros Stellatos, bilingual in Greek and English, knows the whole area very well and together we looked for the places that Napier, his subordinate and friend John Pitt Kennedy, and Edward Curling described. Polydoros did far more than drive me from point to point. I sent him brief extracts of the book including quotations from Edward's and Napier's writing, and he then, having discussed them with his father, Marinos Stellatos, took me not just to the present-day villages but to the ruins of earlier settlements which Mr Stellatos senior had told him how to reach.

In many European countries villages grew up around churches, and in agricultural communities the name of the church was also not only the name of the village but of the wider area, particularly as farming families were necessarily scattered and remote from each other. There is no word equivalent to 'parish' in Greek, but Polydoros confirmed that 'community' would be used in a similar way, and later, in Athens, my friend Alison Scourti spoke of 'settlements' in a related context. At last I understood fully that the names of the places mentioned in the letters were not necessarily the names of villages but might refer to scattered communities or settlements which might not properly have been called villages.

Polydoros told me that in the wake of the 1953 earthquake the formerly scattered agricultural communities in the mountains moved down from the highest lands and consolidated into more clearly delineated villages. With government funds they built small earthquake-proof bungalows to one of two patterns provided by the government.

Marinos Stellatos, who had lived in the Agios Nikolaos community before the 1953 earthquake, told Polydoros about some ruins there, above the present-day village of the same name. We visited these ruins and found there a water 'source'. Polydoros told me that in the Greek language natural water outflows of various kinds are called 'sources', and that this word might apply to what in English might be called a spring, a fountain or even a small waterfall.

Edward had written that he was building a reservoir. What we found near the little church of Agia Panagia, close to the ruins of old Agios Nikolaos, did not match my mental image of a reservoir – an expanse of water open to the sky like the great reservoirs I knew from my early adulthood in West Yorkshire – but it turned out to be a tank built into the mountainside with a piped outflow (Fig. 36).

Fig. 36. Water tank at Agia Panagia, near Agios Nikolaos, Kefalonia

Polydoros was able to decipher the whole of the inscription on the plaque on the back wall and gave me its translation. It says:

ΥΠΟΥΡΓΕΙΟΝ

ΚΡΑΤΙΚΗΣ ΥΓΙΕΙΝΗΣ & ΑΝΤΙΛΗΨΕΩΣ

1938

'Ministry of Government Hygiene & Perception 1938'.

Polydoros was unsure why the word 'perception' had been used, so he did a little research and found a paper[288] on the history of the Greek government health department. Polydoros deduced that the word ΑΝΤΙΛΗΨΕΩΣ had in this context been 'used more like "awareness" for the social issues of that era. Issues like the protection of war victims, charity foundations and protection of the poor'. He sent me the web link and (thank goodness for digital translation tools) I agree with him and think that the word we would use now is 'welfare'. In the UK an equivalent department might be Social Services. From the document which Polydoros found we learned that the Greek departments in charge of health and welfare morphed several times over the period 1833–1981, sometimes being separate from one another and sometimes merging.

There is a similar tank-style reservoir at Kambitsata, easier to see as it is free-standing (Fig. 37).

Fig. 37. Water tank at Kambitsata

---

[288] The document, a paper in Greek, is a pdf: https://bit.ly/App1cHealthPolicyDoc. A translation of its title is *The historical course of the Ministry of Health in Greece (1833–1981)* Theodore I. Dardavesis, Hygienist – Biopathologist, Ep. Professor of Medical School.

These installations would have been renewed several times over the years, so what we saw at Agios Nikolaos in April 2022 might not have been the original reservoir which Edward had his mason build. However, it was in all probability in the same location, rebuilt or reinforced as necessary after his departure. It would make sense for his reservoir to have been an enclosed tank, to prevent evaporation in the hot months and to minimize pollution from detritus. Dimitri Cambici may have taken the idea of a reservoir at Kambitsata from Edward's, but I am not at present able to confirm that these two water tanks were originally built in the late 1820s, let alone that they were the creations of Edward and Cambici.

The location of Napier's 'Racli' and of Cambici's house

The present-day village of Agia Eirini (or Irini) is 'also known by the name Arakli'.[289] It is in the Arakli valley, and linguistically 'Racli' is not a far stretch from 'Arakli'. One of the villages overlooking the Arakli valley is Kambitsata where in Napier's time Dimitri Cambici had his family home.[290] Polydoros and I drove up a steep incline out of the present-day village, and found a major group of ruined stone dwellings which clearly predated the 1953 earthquake and were probably nineteenth century if not earlier Fig. 38 and Fig. 39.

Fig. 38. Ruins at old Kambitsata (1)

---

[289] See the (Greek language) Wikipedia page at https://bit.ly/App1cIriniRakli
[290] See Napier's own painting, Fig. 9 Watercolour sketch 'Cambici's House Racli Cefalonia' p. 73.

Fig. 39. Ruins at old Kambitsata (2)

The blackened tree trunks in Fig. 39 bear witness to the extensive forest fires which swept the mountains in Kefalonia in the summer of 2021.

Old Agios Nikolaos

A similar collection of delapidated old stone buildings exists above today's village of Agios Nikolaos. Polydoros and I found several possibilities for Edward's home, all noteworthy for being built of stone, Fig. 40.

Fig. 40. Ruins of a house at old Agios Nikolaos

Sarakiniko

The port town of Poros (on the eastern coast of Kefalonia) boasts a fine ferry dock to the north of the town, which nestles in the crook of the Sarakiniko promontory.

Ferries sail up to three times daily, depending on the season, between Poros and Killini, on mainland Greece. In Fig. 41 the promontory can be seen running behind the ferry.

Fig. 41. The *Fior di Levante* docked in Poros

Sarakiniko promontory is probably still much as Napier found it, although there have been some modern additions. Fig. 42 Trees would have sheltered the Kefalonian look-outs from incoming enemy view in earlier centuries. In 1941 the British submarine *Perseus* was sunk by a German mine offshore, and only one man, leading stoker John Capes, survived. He was sheltered by Kefalonians for eighteen months, at great risk to themselves, because the Germans were occupying the island. There is an impressive memorial on the promontory. Fig. 43.

Fig. 42. Sarakiniko promontory with the *Perseus* memorial

Fig. 43. *Perseus* **Monument**

Inscribed in Greek and English with a quotation from the Odyssey and:

'Dedicated to the patriotic islanders who put courage before fear to shelter John H Capes, the sole survivor of the British submarine H.M.S. "Perseus", which was hit by a mine and sank on December 6 1941 off the coast of Mavrata, Kefalonia.'

Sailing away from the island on the ferry to Killini at the end of my 2022 visit, I looked at the coast with a greater understanding of the Pronos territory, Fig. 44.

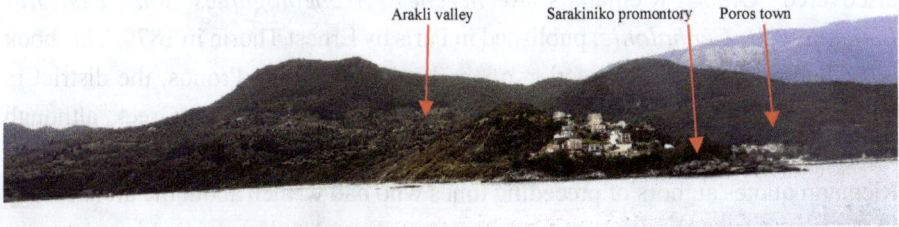

Arakli valley   Sarakiniko promontory   Poros town

Fig. 44. Poros Sarakiniko promontory and Arakli Valley from the ferry

As we rounded the promontory of Sarakiniko I could see exactly what Napier had described: a broad green and fertile stretch of land reaching back inland from the coast road to Skala. Take away the coast road, which was not there in Napier's time, and his decription fits exactly with the Arakli valley as I saw it, sloping downward to the shore.

Fig. 45. View of Arakli valley

187

The origin of the name 'Racli'

When the Ionian Islands were a British protectorate (1809–1864), the area in question had the English spelling 'Racli'. On my first trip to Kefalonia, in 2008, I tried to pinpoint where the area, as described by Napier in his book *The Colonies*,[291] would have been, but without success. The owner of the book shop in Poros hadn't heard of a place called Racli, or, as it would be spelt now, Rakli. She thought it might be the village of Arakli, but I couldn't find that on any map and my Greek wasn't good enough to follow directions. I also thought I was looking for a valley, not a village, so I abandoned that lead. Napier headed the relevant section of *The Colonies* 'Description of the district of Aracli, or Heraclea'.[292] But he gave no reference for his having made the link between the names Racli, Aracli and Heracles, and on my visits I did not come across anyone else who made it. I later discovered Othon Riemann's *Recherches Archéologiques sur Les Îles Ioniennes_ II: Céphalonie*, published in Paris by Ernest Thorin in 1879. This book is available online.[293] The section of the book concerning Pronos, the district in which Arakli is found, is headed 'Pronnoi', a transliteration from Greek, although Riemann's spelling is fluid and in his following paragraph he uses 'Pronoi'. Riemann quotes authors of preceding times who had written about the archaeology of the Ionian Islands, including several references to Napier's book *Memoir on the Roads of Cefalonia*. In the following paragraph Reimann is quoting Loverdos, an author who, it would seem, wrote anonymously, publishing his work in 1835 – but Reimann's enquiries in Kefalonia had revealed the name of its author. Loverdos wrote:

> Rakli ou Harakli doit être en effet une corruption de Ηράχλειον,[294] et l'on voit par les monnaies qu'il y avait un culte d'Heraklies à[295] Pronnoi. – Kiepert[296] dans une ancienne édition de son Atlas, indiquait, avec un point d'interrogation, une ville de Heracleia, qu'il plaçait assez loin de Pronoi. C'était la une erreur, qui ne se trouve plus sur l'éd. de 1872. Il ne devait pas y avoir à Rakli une ville distincte de Pronnoi, mais bien un

---

[291] See Chapter 1 – First love is the truest, p. 12 for full quotation of Napier's description.

[292] *Memoir on the Roads of Cefalonia*, Charles James Napier, James Ridgway, 1825.

[293] https://bit.ly/RecherchesCephalonie

[294] Transliteration: Irakleion.

[295] The printed original has grave rather than acute accents on this and a subsequent 'a'.

[296] Heinrich Kiepert was a renowned cartographer; the map in question can be seen on the David Rumsey Map Collection website: https://bit.ly/31XAHF4. On this map Kefalonia is named Kephallenia, and is on the western edge of the map; zoom right in to see Kiepert's label, 'Herakleia ?' Further information about Heinrich Kiepert and his son Richard can be found on the University of Chicago's web page https://bit.ly/App1cRaklinameorigin

sanctuaire d'Hérakles, faisant partie de cette ville. La vallée de Rakli était sans doute riante et fertile dans l'antiquité comme elle l'est aujourd'hui. Elle était protégée par deux forteresses, dont l'une, au N., dominait la gorge rocheuse qui déverse les eaux de cette vallée dans la mer, et dont l'autre, au S., commandait les routes de Valtes et de Skala, qui sont les deux entrées de la vallée de Rakli du coté du S.[297]

My understanding of Reimann's text is:

Rakli or Harakli must be a corruption of Ηράχλειον [Iracleion] and it can be seen from coins that there was a [religious] cult of Herakles at Pronoi. Kiepert, in an early edition of his Atlas, indicated with a question mark a town of Heracleia, which he placed not far from Pronnoi. This was an error which was not found in the later edition of 1872. There was not necessarily a town of Rakli distinct from that of Pronnoi, but certainly a temple of Herakles was part of this town. The valley of Rakli was without doubt a beautiful and fertile country in antiquity, as it is today. It was protected by two fortresses, of which one in the north dominated the rocky gorge from which the waters of this valley pour out to the sea, and the other, in the south, commanded the routes to Valtes and Skala, which are the two southern entrances to the valley of Rakli.

Reimann's mentioning that there were coins, presumably of ancient manufacture, which support the theory that there was a centre of devotion to Heracles, adds weight to Napier's writing of it in connection with his chosen area for the Maltese Colony. Reimann's footnote 4 on page 7 of his book says 'Ηράχλειον est le nom official, Rakli ou Arakli le nom vulgaire'. (Translation: Ηράχλειον is the official name, Rakli or Arakli the common name.)

Fig. 46 is an enlargement of the section of Kiepert's map of Classical Greece, showing 'Kephallenia', complete with question mark:

---

[297] *Recherches Archéologiques sur Les Îles Ioniennes_ II: Céphalonie*, p. 53.

Fig. 46. 'Kephallenia', from Kiepert's map[298]

[298] Enlargements of Kephallenia from Heinrich Kiepert's map of 'Lorris Attolia & Akarnia' from the David Rumsey Map Collection website: https://bit.ly/31XAHF4. On this map Kefalonia is named Kephallenia and is on the western edge of the map.

Further enlargement (Fig. 47) shows the label 'Herakleia ?' with its printed question mark more clearly:

Fig. 47. Kiepert map, further enlargement

Appendix 2 – Castlereagh's Cabinets of Weights

Edward Curling often mentioned weights and measures as he wrote about his crops, their cultivation and their sale. I had been wondering for some time exactly how much a bushel weighed in comparison to the weights used in the sale of vegetables or grain in the imperial measures which were still in use in the UK until the introduction of metric measures beginning in 1965.[299] So I searched online for 'bushel' and was surprised to learn that even within the UK the word meant different measures in different areas. I made the following notes:

It is difficult to pin down the equivalent metric weight for a bushel. Historically, across the UK, there were many different local weights with that name: see the Museum Association's page on Old Weights and Measures.[300] A London or Imperial bushel was equivalent to eight gallons. Imperial measurements of bushels and gallons were identical for liquid and dry weights. Other parts of the UK varied considerably from this; for example the Cornwall bushel, at 16 gallons, was twice the measurement of the Imperial. Quantities of dry goods were measured by capacity (volume) and not by weight.[301]

On a chance invitation from a friend in 2017 to visit Zaha Hadid's new mathematics gallery at the Science Museum in London, I discovered a wonderful treasure: *Lord Castlereagh's Consular Collection of Attested Foreign Standard Weights*. If you had told the teenage me that I would be wildly excited by a chest of weights in a gallery devoted to mathematics I would have been struck dumb with disbelief. But there was this beautiful wooden cabinet – well, two, standing side by side – full of little drawers, each numbered and all except one labelled with the name of a city. The exception was … the Ionian Islands. In a publicity video about the gallery, the curator of the Winton Gallery, Dr David Rooney, said

> At the heart of all science and all societies is the ability to measure accurately. In the early nineteenth century the Foreign Secretary, Lord Castlereagh, sent a message to all diplomats overseas, saying 'Send a set of the weights and measures for your area to London' so they could be compared accurately with Britain's standard pound weight. They were gathered together in a huge cabinet specially made for the purpose, and it's one of the stars on show. Castlereagh's cabinet was the beginning of an attempt to standardise weights and measures.[302]

---

[299] https://www.britannica.com/science/British-Imperial-System
[300] https://www.museumsassociation.org/download?id=77607
[301] https://physics.info/system-english/ is a jocular but thorough look at weights and measures nomenclature.
[302] 10 Objects Mathematics: the Winton Gallery. https://bit.ly/App2Winton

Fig. 48. Lord Castlereagh's collection of foreign standard weights[303]

I hadn't expected there to be a drawer for the Ionian Islands – but there it was, in the second row up from the bottom: drawer No. 32.

---

[303] Author's photographs, taken in the Winton Gallery of the Science Museum, London.

Fig. 49.   Close-up showing drawer no 32, Ionian Islands[304]

Even in 2017 international weights standardization was not universal, and in that year a different kind of cabinet, the Cabinet of the Bangladeshi government, issued the following press statement:

> The Cabinet [of the Bangladeshi government] today approved draft of the revised Standards of Weights and Measures Act, 2017 suggesting tougher punitive actions in its weekly meeting with Prime Minister Sheikh Hasina in the chair. "The Standards of Weights and Measures Act, 2017 is framed to upgrade the existing weight and measurement system to international standards," Cabinet Secretary M Shafiul Alam told a news briefing adding that the meeting today also endorsed two other proposed laws related to agriculture and industry. He said the draft on the new standardization law suggested higher amount of penalty for defiance of its provisions of the proposed act which was drafted modifying the 1982 Standard Weights and Measures Ordinance and translating it into Bangla.[305]

Seeing the Castlereagh cabinet, and knowing that there was no standard bushel, still left me wondering what the weights were that Edward Curling had used. So I emailed the archivists at the Science Museum and told them of my interest in the cabinet, wondering whether there was any associated documentation. Of course there was. They invited me to make an appointment to view the cabinet's technical

---

[304] As above.
[305] 30 March 2017, newspaper *Dhaka*: https://bit.ly/App2DhakaWeights

files.[306] I love visiting archives, so although I feared I probably wouldn't understand what I was viewing – 'technical files' sounded a bit daunting – I made the appointment, and a sunny June day in 2017 found me going through photocopies of original documents for each drawer. At the top of the pile were three summary sets of documents, none of which mentioned the Kefalonia drawer, and I was a bit dispirited by the time the bottom of the box hove into view without apparent success. But then, one set of documents up from the bottom, I found the paperwork associated with drawer 32. It is the work of Mr Woodhouse, then the auditor for the Ionian Islands. Mr Woodhouse did much more than describe the weights of the Ionian Islands: he detailed all coinage as well as 'weights and measures' and revealed a world akin to the archipelago in Ursula le Guin's *Earthsea* trilogy, where even within the Ionian island group there were many variations of measurement and coinage, stemming from the long and colourful history of what was known in the nineteenth century firstly as the Septinsular Republic (1800–1807),[307] and during the British protectorate (1807–1864) as the United States of the Ionian Islands.[308]

Woodhouse's jurisdiction included the whole of the Ionian Islands, the most southerly of which is Kythira, variously spelt even now as Kythera, Kithira and Cythera, and in Woodhouse's time known as Cerigo. We must remember that the bushel was a measurement of capacity, not weight. Woodhouse did not begin by recording capacity, but this was the measurement I was particularly interested in. We will look at the other measurements and coinage too, to demonstrate just how complex these were in this one small corner of the British Empire. Imagine Castlereagh's task in standardizing such ingrained complexities across the globe.

Each island's *Measures of Capacity* had to be listed separately because of variations between them:

Corfu and Paxo Moggio or 8 Misura equal to 5 Winchester Bushels.

Zante	*Baccile should contain 72lbs. peso grosso of best quality wheat & estimating the Bushel at 60lb. Avoirdupois, the relation will be 1 Baccile = 1¼ Bushels*
Cephalonia	*Baccile should contain 80lbs peso grosso of Wheat of best quality or according to foregoing Scale 1⅔ Bushel*
Sta. Maura	*Cado – 4 Cadi are equal to 3 Moggie, consequantly the Cado contains 3¾ Bushels.*

---

[306] Technical documents relating to the Castlereagh Cabinet of Foreign Weights T/1932–193 to 245. Dana Research Centre of the Science Museum Archives.

[307] http://www.strangehistory.net/2016/04/19/republic-seven-islands/

[308] https://atcorfu.com/ionian-state/

Ithaca	*Baccile – equal to 1 Chilo, 5 of which make 1 Moggio, therefore this Bacchile corresponds with an English Bushel*
Cerigo	*Chilo, equal to 1 Bushel English.*

Regarding coinage, he recorded that *accounts are kept in Dollars and Cents*, but his coinage record also includes Oboli and to complicate matters further he wrote

> *In the distant Island of Cerigo, Turkish Piastres & Paras are still Current, there necessarily being great intercourse with the neighbouring Continent, moreover those Islanders carry on a considerable fishery up the Archipelago, the produce of which is Salted and sold at Smyrna, Monte Athos &c, for Turkish Currency where not exchanged for grain.*

Woodhouse also mentioned that *A Coinage of Quarter Cents, or 400 p^r. Dollar, is in a state of great forwardness, the pieces being cut from the Gazzettes* [sic] *formerly current in this Island at 330 & 343 Pr. Dollar, and stamped to correspond with the Oboli.* Clearly the British were hoping to simplify coinage in circulation on the islands. The complexities for weights were even greater, and having to employ the smallest imperial measurement, the grain,[309] as a measure of comparison might seem quaint, not to say impossibly confusing, to us in the twenty-first century. Under *Weights* he wrote

> *The Pound Peso Grosso, or great weight of 12^{oz} is equal to 7384 grains troy, i.e. 94^{lbs}. ⅘ are equal to 100lbs. Avoirdupois.*
> *The Pound Peso Sottile, or small weight, for precious Metals and Drugs, is ⅓ lighter than foregoing 12 oz. peso sottile corresponding with 8 oz. Peso grosso.*
> *The Oke used in the Islands to the Southward weighs about 18,900 grains or 2lbs. 7/10 Avoirdupois _ the Levant Cantar, or Quintal, should contain 44 Okes.*
> *The Migliago (1000lbs) for Currants in the Island of Zante is 10% lighter than for other Articles.*

---

[309] 'In both British Imperial units and United States customary units, there are precisely 7,000 grains per avoirdupois pound', see https://en.wikipedia.org/wiki/Grain_(unit)

The Corn measures are always in form truncated Cones, and the dimensions of a Corfu misura or ⅛ of a Moggio, proved to be as follows,

> Diameter at Top 11 Inches
> Idem .... Base 14 ½ .. d°.
> Depth ....10....... d°.

Corfu and Paxo 32 Quartucci = 1 jar and 4 jars = 1 Barrel containing 18 Gallons English Wine Measure.

Zante   120 Quartucci = 1 Barrel containing 17⅝ English

Cephalonia   2 Quartucci=1 Boccali

                12 [Boccali]=1 Secchio

                6 [Secchio]=1 Barrel containing 18 Gallons English

Sta. Maura   6 Secchi = 1 Barrel containing 18 Gallons English

Ithaca   2 Quartucci = 1 Boccali

                54 [Boccali]=1 Barrel of 18 Gallons English

Cerigo   2 Aga... =1 Bozia

                30 [Bozia] =1 Barrel of 18 Gallons English

Corfu and Paxo 4 Quartucci =1Miltre

                24 [Miltre]=1 Jar

                4 [Jars] =1 Barrel of 18 Gallons English

Zante   Lire = 1 Barrel containing 17⅝ d°.

Cephalonia   9 Pagliazza =1 Barrel of   18   d°.

Sta. Maura   21 Succhali =1 Barrel of   18   do.

Ithaca   6 Secchi = 1 Barrel of   18   do.

Cerigo   24 Bozie = 1 Barrel of   14⅖ do.

Appendix 4 – The death of Henry Kelly (1797–1826)

Henry Kelly had moved on from his initial army service in the 102nd regiment under Napier's protection, first to the 59th Regiment of Foot, and in August 1826 he was promoted to captain, and moved from the 59th to the Royal African Colonial Corps, as this newspaper announcement in the *Waterford Mail* of 2 August 1826, (no doubt relayed from the *London Gazette*) records:

> Royal African Colonial Corps … To be Captains, without purchase---
> Lieutenant Henry Kelly, from the 59th Foot, vice Rainey, promoted;

Kelly's transfer and his promotion from lieutenant to captain being made 'without purchase' probably meant that he had been promoted on merit. Any pleasure he might have felt was short-lived. Although the death announcement quoted in Chapter 4 [page 34] says that Henry was 'of the Royal African Corps', I learned from an online article[310] by Pat Irwin of the South African Military History Society that this regiment had been disbanded in 1821, but a new regiment, 'The Royal African Colonial Corps', was formed in about 1823. Irwin reports that the earlier corps had been one of a group of military units known as 'condemned' or 'penal' regiments. He quotes as follows, including interjections of his own in square brackets:

> The Corps was a disciplinary regiment as far as whites were oncerned: That is to say, it was composed principally of deserters, convicts, [which often included culprits from the hulks[311]] and men whose sentence of punishment [including those with life imprisonment or awaiting execution] had been commuted for services in Africa.[312]

As we know from Samuel Laing, Henry died in Sierra Leone. Being posted there was fraught with dangers of all kinds, but perhaps worst of all was the unhealthy climate and the fear of contracting 'the fever', probably malaria. The following extract of a report, made the previous year, gives a fair impression of the prevailing conditions.

> On the 9th September despatches were received from the town of Bathurst in the Island of St Mary's (River Gambia), stating that the whole

---

[310] http://samilitaryhistory.org/jnl2/vol186pi.html

[311] In a footnote Pat Irwin writes 'After the American declaration of independence in 1776, they closed their ports to the transportation of British Criminals. To accommodate the criminals, Britain converted old naval and merchant ships into floating prisons known as 'hulks'. They were notorious for the poor living conditions on them.

[312] Irwin's reference: *Royal African Corps 1800–1821* p. 213, J J Crooks (Major), 1925 and an article, *Disbanded Regiments,* in the *Journal of the Society for Army Historical Research 14*: 233–235, W Y Baldry, 1935.

detachment of the Royal African Corps, in garrison there, amounting to one hundred and thirty-four soldiers with eight women and seventeen children, which were landed only in June, had all died of fever excepting thirteen soldiers, and these were in hospital, unfit for duty ... On the 20th September the *Surrey* sailed with the detachment she had on board, of about 100 men, seven women and nine children, to replace those who had died at Bathurst. On her arrival there, on the second of October, was found lying at anchor, the *Swinger* gun-brig, protecting the place. Her Commander, Lieut. Poingdestre, and seven of the crew, had died of fever; also Ensign Stapleton, of the Royal African Corps.[313]

Returning to Pat Irwin's article, he has the following footnote:

In 1826 the British practice of dispensing with military offenders by sending them to unhealthy climes, including West Africa, was stopped by an army General Order[314] but it took another four years for this decision to work through the system. Until then the death toll amongst those sent there from elsewhere was horrendous, the actual death rates ranging from 75–80%. ... Generally, of those sent to West Africa, one half died in the first three months and the average duration of life did not exceed 15 months. Malaria and yellow fever accounted for 85% of all deaths.[315]

Ironically, this army General Order was made in the very year that Henry Kelly was appointed to the Royal African Colonial Corps. It has not so far been possible to find primary source evidence for Henry Kelly's death, but it is more than likely that he died of 'the fever'. Appointed in August 1826, his death only three months later on 30 November made him a text book illustration of Curtin's assertion that half those sent to West Africa died within the first three months.

---

[313] The *London Courier and Evening Gazette* of Monday 21 November 1825.
[314] *The auxiliaries: Foreign and miscellaneous regiments in the British Army 1802–1817*, p. 12, R L Yaple, 1972, taken from an article in the *Journal of the Society for Army Historical Research 50*: 10–28.
[315] *Disease and Empire: The health of European troops in the conquest of Africa*, p. 5, Philip D Curtin, Cambridge University Press, 1998.

Appendix 7a – Packet ships

The English packet boat system began as early as the Tudor era,[316] and it developed worldwide. By the nineteenth century, it had become a complex network of British ships which transported mail around the empire.[317] The vessels varied considerably in size, some being ocean-going ships for which carrying the mail was only part of their remit and others being much smaller, unassuming vessels, as in Turner's painting of the Cologne packet, Fig. 50:

Fig. 50. Cologne, the arrival of the packet, evening, J M W Turner 1826 [318]

In the Mediterranean a succession of elegant packet ships, only lightly armed, sailed between the packet ship stations[319] and Spain, Malta and Corfu. As an example, HMP *Lady Mary Pelham* (Fig. 51) was in His Majesty's packet ship service at the time of Edward's outward and return sailings in 1828 and 1831. Instead of the ship prefix HMS (His Majesty's Ship), the prefix HMP (His Majesty's Packet) was used for these vessels from 1823 when the Admiralty took

---

[316] https://en.wikipedia.org/wiki/Post_Office_Packet_Service
[317] See https://www.postalmuseum.org/collections/mail-by-sea/
[318] The Frick Collection.
[319] Dover, Harwich, Great Yarmouth, Falmouth, Plymouth, Milford Haven, Holyhead.

over control of the service from the Post Office. The original title bar of the painting verifies this.

Fig. 51. H M Packet Lady Mary Pelham[320]

To make them commercially viable, these vessels provided services for passengers too. In 1838 'The British Post-office Mediterranean Steam-packets go and return once a month from Falmouth to Corfu, touching at Cadiz, Gibraltar and Malta.'[321]

The nineteenth-century historian and travel writer Sir John Gardner Wilkinson's *Modern Egypt and Thebes* (1843) was written twelve years after Edward's 1831 return journey, and indicates that by the later date Kefalonia had been added to the packet ship's schedule. In the preface we find booking procedures and fare information for the Mediterranean packets. The administration was highly organised, and Wilkinson's detailed information includes a nice indicator of where the modern 'visa' may have had its roots:

---

[320] Nicholas Cammillieri (1777–1860) National Maritime Museum, Cornwall.
[321] *An Hand-book for the Travellers on the Continent*, p. xxxvi, author unknown, John Murray and Son, 1838. This work was regularly updated and republished. The material appears to have been provided by several anonymous authors and the editor is not named. The publication was a hugely successful series, being published simultaneously in twenty-one other European locations as well as London.

A British Government Steamer leaves Marseilles once every month direct for Malta. … it reaches Malta in from 70 to 77 hours. The fare is 9*l*.[322] for first class passengers. Berths may be secured on board, or at the Agent's, M. Mallet, wine merchant, No. 9. Rue de Haxo, at Marseilles.

Three packets are employed on this service, … [and] also run between Gibraltar and Malta, and Malta and the Ionian Isles. The traveller must send his passport to the British Consulate and to the Board of Health at Marseilles, to be *visé*, before he can embark. This will be arranged by a commissioner of his Hotel, or by the Agent, M. Mallet; and two charges of 5 and 2 francs are made for it.

The same Agent has published the following *Tarif*[323] for the payment of boatmen and porters:-

"On arriving by the English Steamers:-

"1. *Going to the Custom House,*

Landing a passenger	0	50
For each box	0	50
Carpet bag or lady's band-box	0	25

"2. *From the Custom House to the Hotel,*

For a box	0	50
Carpet bag, lady's band-box	0	25
Four-wheeled carriage, including the pontoon, men and custom-house	25	0
Two-wheeled carriage	15	0
For embarking a passenger and his luggage	1	50

The implication is that the well-to-do would travel south through Europe in their own carriage to Marseilles (now Marseille), taking their carriage by ferry to their next destination. Wilkinson also provides a timetable showing the dates each month when the packet departed from Malta for Gibraltar, mail for England being forwarded from there on the P&O Company's steamer to Southampton. In Wilkinson's time the packet sailed again for Malta ten days after arrival in Gibraltar,

---

[322] 9*l* = £9.00 sterling.
[323] The currency for this tariff was presumably French francs and centimes.

calling on the return trip at Patras, Zante, Kefalonia and Corfu, and back to Malta.[324]

---

[324] *Modern Egypt and Thebes* John Garner Wilkinson, John Murray 1843 https://bit.ly/MaltaPacketSchedule1843. In Edward's day the packet did not call at Kefalonia.

Appendix 7b – Quarantine in Kefalonia in 1828

Edward Curling, in common with all visitors arriving at the island of Kefalonia, would have had to endure quarantine in the lazaretto[325], a building designed and built by Napier and Kennedy for the purpose. Another traveller, Jonathan P Miller,[326] arriving earlier the same year, recorded his visit to the island, giving a detailed account of the trials of the lazaretto in his journal,[327] from which we can also glimpse life in the Napier household:

Arrive at Cephalonia

> *Feb. 7._ The wind abating a little to-day, Mr. Wolfe[328] sent on shore a letter of recommendation which he had to the British resident, Col. Napier. The boat brought back a polite note from Col. N. informing us that our quarantine would be twenty-five days, that the Lazaretto was a very miserable place, and that he was fearful we should repent our resolution of getting pratique[329] from this island but at the same time offering us the best accommodation in his power.*

Perform quarantine at the Lazaretto.

> *February 8._ Got under way, and entered the harbour at an early hour this morning, and after being examined by the police physician,*

---

[325] In February 1827 Kennedy wrote to Napier *We have got the better of the plague in the Lazaretto* (BL Add MS 54535 ff. 23–24). This was the quarantine building which Napier had had built as one of his earliest projects, in 1822,see *Life and Opinions* pp. 307–8.

[326] A representative of the Executive Greek Committee of New York travelling in Greece to distribute clothing and supplies to non-combatant Greeks affected by the war with the Ottoman Empire.

[327] *The Condition of Greece in 1827 and 1828*, pp. 179–188, Jonathan P Miller, 1 January 1828, J. & J. Harper. Miller had been commissioned by the 'Executive Greek Committee of the city of New-York' to sail to Greece with consignments of 'clothing and provisions sent from the United States to the old men, women, children and non-combatants of Greece'. Miller describes the book as '*an Exposition of the poverty, distress, and misery, to which the inhabitants have been reduced by the destruction of their towns and villages, and the ravages of their country, by a merciless Turkish foe*'. The section headings used in these extracts are in the original publication available online; https://bit.ly/App6bMiller

[328] Wolfe was a fellow traveller of Miller's, a Christian missionary.

[329] Pratique: 'the licence given to a ship to enter port on assurance from the captain to the authorities that it is free from contagious disease. The clearance granted is commonly referred to as Free Pratique. A ship can signal a request for pratique by flying a solid yellow flag, letter Q in the international maritime signal flags. Flying it has also become an invitation to Customs to inspect vessels for dutiable goods or contraband: https://bit.ly/App6bPratique

we were shown by Dr. Muir, Superintendent of the Health Office, to our quarters in the Lazaretto. ...

Our quarters consisted of a room about twenty feet square, and nearly the same in height, without floor, furniture, or fire-place.

As we had eaten nothing of any consequence for the last twenty-four hours, our first business was to get some food, and we were soon presented with half a dozen of wine and a bottle of brandy, from Dr. Muir. Col. Napier sent us a file of Galignani's Messenger, in one of which, the number for 1st January 1828, I had the pleasure of seeing the message of the President of the United States to both Houses of Congress, delivered in the preceding November.

Establishment of Schools in the island of Cephalonia.

February 11._ We had a call to-day from Mr. Dixon, a Scotch gentleman, who has come to this island for the purpose of establishing schools. The Government has given him a monastery and its revenues, for the purpose of enabling him to prosecute his work. The monastery is situated at St. Andrea, five miles distant from Argostoli, the principal town in the island.[330] [Strangely, quarantine does not seem to have prevented visits from those already on the island. LAC] ...

Col. C. Napier

February 21._ Col. Napier called upon us to-day. He appears to be a man of good sense and much discernment. He is forty-six years of age, of a slender form, and about five feet eight inches in height.

Saturday, March 1, 1828 ...
Prospect of release from the Lazaretto.

Having had a visit from the physician of the Lazaretto to-day, we are informed, that if the Resident gives his consent, we shall be set at liberty to-morrow. We waited with no small anxiety until eight o'clock in the evening, when I received the following note from Col. Napier.

My Dear Sir_ I wish you joy of your probable evacuation of the Lazaretto. Pray do me the favour to dine with me on Monday, at five o'clock.

---

[330] See **Chapter 3 – How excellent & how perfect he is** pp. 43 ff. for details of this school.

Your humble servant,
C. Napier
Saturday evening, March 1, 1828.

Released from the Lazaretto.

Sunday March 2._ We were dismissed from the Lazaretto this morning, having performed a quarantine of twenty-two days. We called upon Col. Napier who received us with kindness, and introduced us to his lady. He offered me a lodging in his house, as Mr. Wolfe [Miller's travelling companion] *was going to St. Andrea to visit Mr. Dixon. ...*

March 3. ... We settled to-day the expenses of our quarantine, amounting to one hundred and one dollars, the half of which ($50½) [sic] *I paid. ...*

Mr. Wolfe, two English, and two Austrian officers, dined here [Napier's house] *to-day. At table it was reported as certain, that the British frigate Cambrian had been lost; but that the officers and crew were all saved in the boats of other ships. ...*

I am upon further acquaintance more and more pleased with Col. Napier. I think him one of the cleverest men I have ever met with. ...

March 4_ Mr. Wolfe gave a short and interesting history of his travels and missions to a number of officers, assembled at the house of Col. Napier ...

March 6._ I rode out with Col. Napier in a carriage, the first I have been in since I left the United States. We proceeded to the distance of six or seven miles in a circular direction around the island by a very good road.

The Col. informed me, not as a report but as a fact, that the English army suffered more in America, in proportion to the numbers opposed to them, than what they had in any other country.[331]

Leave Cephalonia, and put back in a Storm.

March 7._ Fearful that the steam-boat would not arrive, we took passage in a small boat for Corfu.

---

[331] Napier had been involved in British military actions in Chesapeake, the Carolinas and Nova Scotia in 1813.

Col. Napier, Mr Augustus Thompson from New-Brunswick in North America, and Captain Canida, accompanied us to the shore, where we had a friendly parting from men who had treated us with every possible attention. Our boat was small and crowded with passengers.

We set sail about noon, and began beating out of the harbour of Argostoli, which is one of the finest in the world. We had but just effected our object when a violent storm arose, and we were obliged to put back to Cephalonia.

Miller's account gives us a good insight into the quarantine process which Edward Curling would have experienced. What's more, Miller allows us to eavesdrop on dinner-table conversations when Charles and Elizabeth were entertaining visitors; Elizabeth must have relished the opportunity to socialise in this way, meeting people from different countries and many walks of life, after the years of austerity, financial anxiety and social isolation she had endured as Kelly's wife.

Appendix 8 – Charcoal burning

Charcoal burning is a time-consuming and complex process, in use since the iron age, for turning low-grade wood into charcoal. In the twenty-first century it still has a variety of uses, notably for millions of barbecues at family summer parties, but also widely in industry and by artists for their charcoal sketches.

> Its history was linked with the smelting of metals for which it was an ideal fuel because it produces an intense smokeless heat. Charcoal is made by heating wood in a furnace where air is restricted to reduce the rate of burning. The aim is to remove unwanted elements, such as water, creosote and tar and to leave pure black carbon. This can be used as a fuel without imparting impurities into the products which are being smelted.[332]

Removing 'unwanted elements' makes charcoal much lighter than the wood from which it was made. In earlier centuries there was no ready-made furnace. Equal lengths of wood were built into a stack which was carefully shaped to enable the protracted process. Artist Louis-Jacques Goussier (1722–1799) and French engraver Robert Bénard (1737–1777) illustrated the stages in two prints: see the three details in Fig. 52, Fig. 53 and Fig. 54 which each have a sequence of figured and/or lettered diagrams showing the process in its various stages.

Fig. 52. Œconomie Rustique, Charbon de bois [detail 1][333]

The first Bénard/Goussier image illustrates the process by which a central pole was temporarily placed to enable the stack to be built round it. The pole was removed when the stack was complete, leaving a central air vent which ran the full height of the stack; see letter 'C' in Fig. 52. The wood was stacked around this pole in tiers. The stack was then covered except for the air vent, with natural materials, to make it airtight, with a top layer of turf or soil. The pole was then removed, leaving the top of the air vent open. When the stack was ready a small fire was lit at the top, near the air vent opening. The burning material was dropped down the vent, which was then covered with a piece of turf, the only air source then being a hole made at the bottom. The burning of the stack was managed by making further holes in the cover – initially just one near the base, but as the process progressed many holes were made at intervals round the stack and at different levels (Fig. 53). These holes controlled the temperature and the speed of the burn, and were resealed if necessary. In order to achieve conversion from wood to charcoal the temperature had to reach 450–510° C, and if the temperature was not carefully controlled the stack could explode.

Charcoal burners knew from the smoke's colour how the burn was progressing. The burn had to be monitored day and night, and took several days.[334]

Fig. 53. Œconomie Rustique, Charbon de bois [detail 2]

---

[334] The detail of the process is clearly described on the Wikipedia page *Charcoal Pile*: https://bit.ly/App8CharcoalPile which includes two German videos of a modern reconstruction of the process of building and burning of a stack.

There were several methods of building the stack. The cross-sections of two are illustrated in this further detail (Fig. 54), the square one labelled 'O', being the base of the square pyramid 'Q':

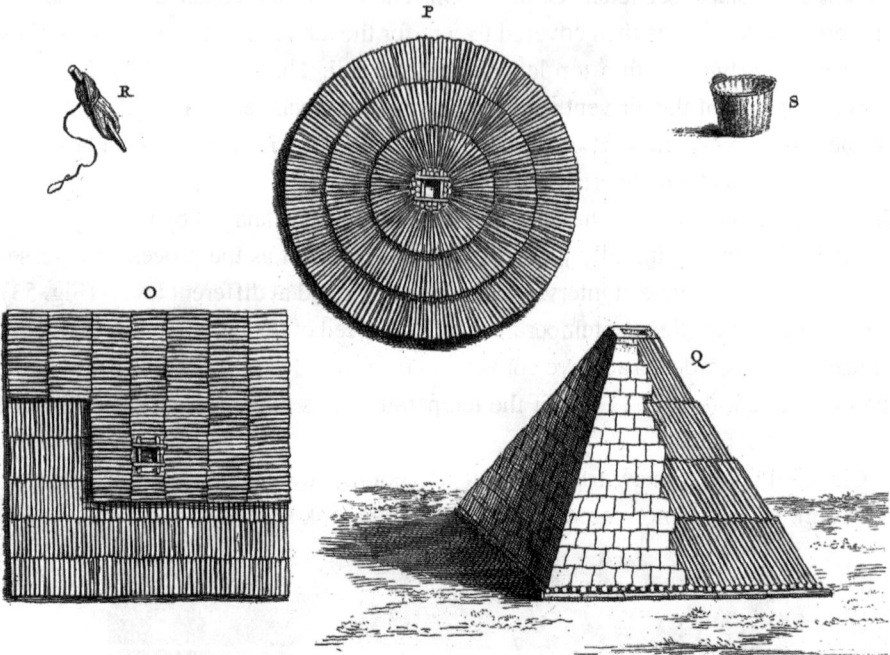

Fig. 54. Œconomie Rustique, Charbon de bois [detail 3]

Photographs of charcoal stacks of other shapes can be found on the Revolutionary Players' website, https://bit.ly/App7aCharcoal

Appendix 9a – Temperature tables, April–October 1829

Edward Curling began to keep a regular record of air temperature from the last week of April of 1829, but there are big gaps. The charts which I have created with his data show Fahrenheit temperature bar charts for the months of April to October 1829, with a monthly average in each, based on the data in Edward's journal entries. The most complete months are June and July.

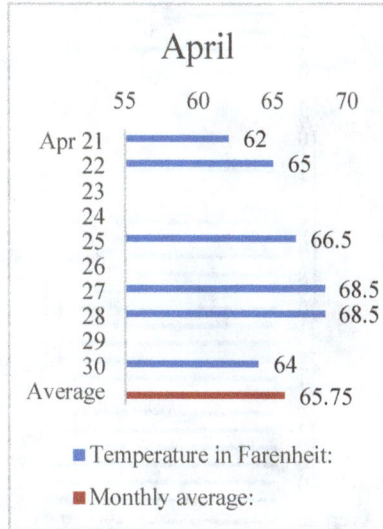

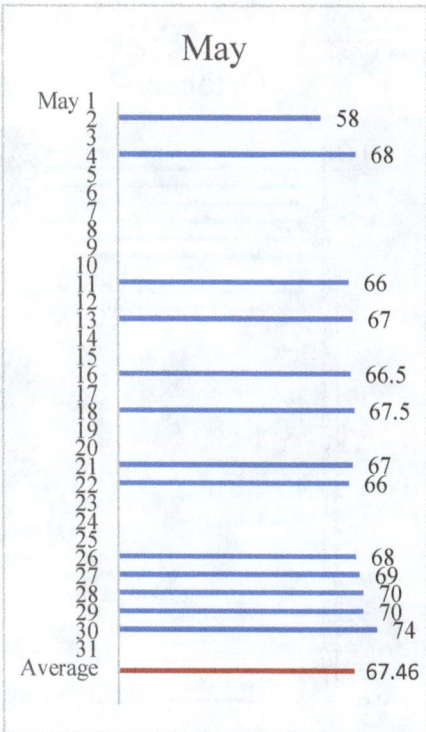

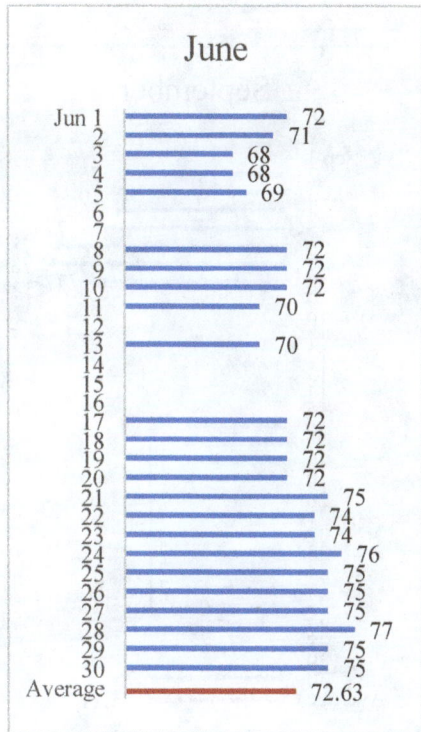

April

Day	Temperature in Fahrenheit
Apr 21	62
22	65
23	
24	
25	66.5
26	
27	68.5
28	68.5
29	
30	64
Average	65.75

■ Temperature in Farenheit:
■ Monthly average:

May

Day	Temperature in Fahrenheit
May 1	
2	58
3	
4	68
5	
6	
7	
8	
9	
10	
11	66
12	
13	67
14	
15	
16	66.5
17	
18	67.5
19	
20	
21	67
22	66
23	
24	
25	
26	68
27	69
28	70
29	70
30	74
31	
Average	67.46

June

Day	Temperature in Fahrenheit
Jun 1	72
2	71
3	68
4	68
5	69
6	
7	
8	72
9	72
10	72
11	70
12	
13	70
14	
15	
16	
17	72
18	72
19	72
20	72
21	75
22	74
23	74
24	76
25	75
26	75
27	75
28	77
29	75
30	75
Average	72.63

211

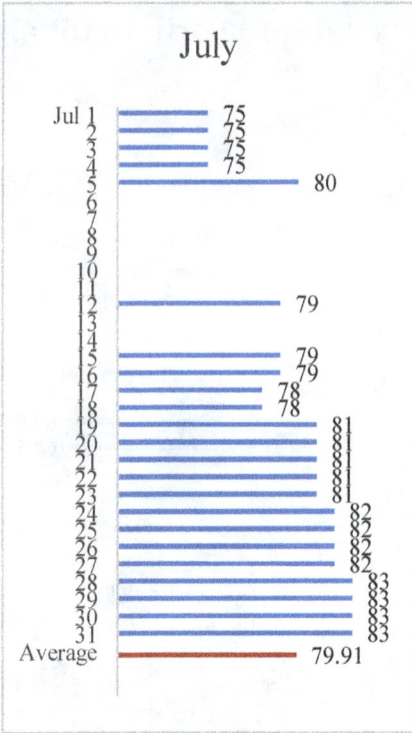

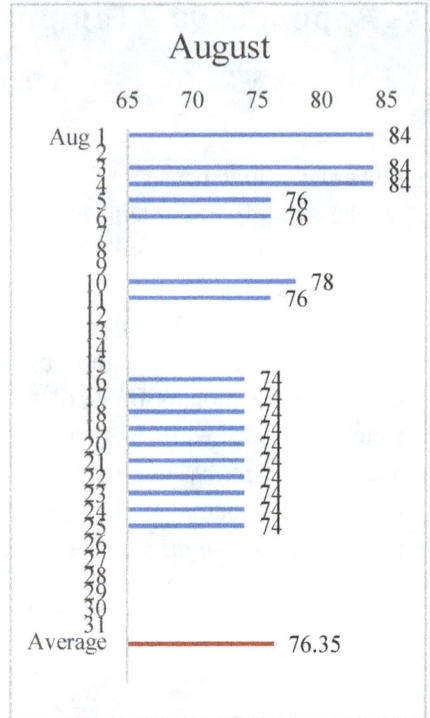

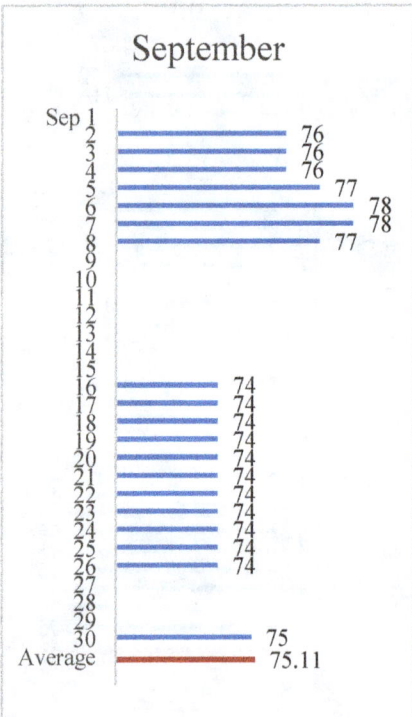

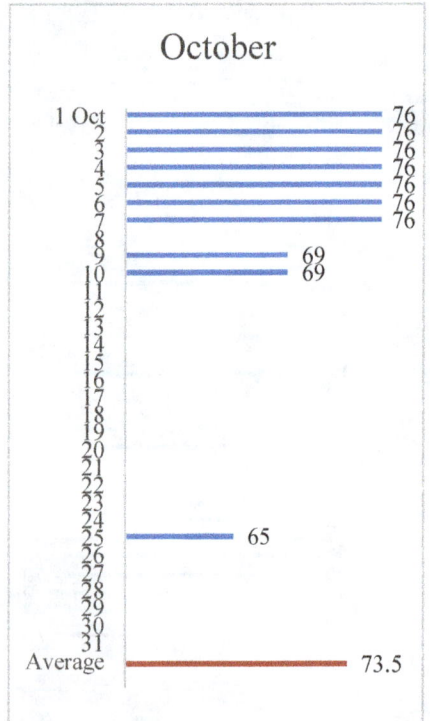

Appendix 9b – Beekeeping

Beekeeping in England changed little until the late nineteenth century, when modern movable-frame hives were introduced. In northern Europe, early hives were skeps – baskets inverted onto a flat surface – made first of woven wicker and later of coiled straw: Fig. 55. Modern hives were introduced in England in 1860.[335]

Fig. 55. The Beekeeper's Daughter[336]

---

[335] *The History of Beekeeping in English Gardens*, Penelope Walker and Eva Crane, journal article, *Garden History* vol. 28, No. 2, pp. 231–2, available on JSTOR: https://bit.ly/App9bBeekeeping

[336] Henry Bacon (1839–1912). Image courtesy of Caldwell Gallery Hudson, Hudson, New York. Bacon was an American artist who studied painting at the École des Beaux Arts in Paris. (Information from the website of the Smithsonian American Art Museum, https://americanart.si.edu/artist/henry-bacon-194)

The skep was the kind of hive which Edward would have known from childhood, very different from the Maltese method he described in his journal (p. 108–109). However, the stone hive appears to have been used also by local people on Kefalonia and further afield in the Ionian Islands and beyond. Georgios Mavrofridis in his article, *Stone beehives on the islands of the eastern Mediterranean*, writes:

> On the island of Kefalonia, … their traditional hives were … horizontal and were built out of slate. They were usually stand-alone structures, but sometimes stood in groups of two, or one next to the other. The roof was usually made out of tiles, while in some cases, a horizontal stone slab served as a roof. Slate and tiles were bonded together using a bonding material (some type of lime-based mud) so as to create a single entity. The length of the hive reached 30–40 cm, its internal width was approximately 30 cm, while its height exceeded 30 cm. The hive was closed from the front and back using two stone slabs. The front slab was permanently attached and had an opening at its base for the entrance of the bees. The rear slab was movable, so it could be removed during harvesting and when other work on the hive had to be carried out.[337]

Fig. 56 shows individual hives on Levkas, another Ionian island. The hives in this photo look quite like Edward's description of the beehives made by his Maltese workers, although he mentions slate as the material rather than stone slabs. The other main difference is that they appear to be missing one 'wall'. This would presumably be the wall which the beekeeper would have left detachable in order to access the honey. We do not know the exact date of these hives. It is possible that they predate Edward's time on Kefalonia, but another possibility is that the hives are of a later date and the method used by the Maltese in 1829 gradually spread out over the island.

---

[337] *Stone beehives on the islands of the eastern Mediterranean*, Georgios Mavrofridis, a presentation to the symposium *Beekeeping in the Mediterranean from Antiquity to the Present*, edited by Fani Hatjina, Georgios Mavrofridis, Richard Jones, © Chamber of Cyclades Division of Apiculture; Hellenic Agricultural Organization "Demeter", Greece; Eva Crane Trust, UK.

Fig. 56. Stone beehives of Lefkas[338]

I have not been able to find any scholarly references to individual stone hives on Malta, although there is a long history of beekeeping there. Even the name of the island is said to originate in its fabled honey:

> The most common etymology is that the word Malta is derived from the Greek word μέλι, meli, "honey". The ancient Greeks called the island Μελίτη (Melitē) meaning "honey-sweet", possibly for Malta's unique production of honey … The Romans called the island Melita, which can be considered either a Latinization of the Greek Μελίτη or the adaptation of the Doric Greek pronunciation of the same word, Μελίτα.
>
> Another conjecture suggests that the word Malta comes from the Phoenician word Maleth, "a haven", or 'port' in reference to Malta's many bays and coves. Few other etymological mentions appear in classical literature, with the term Malta appearing in its present form in the Antonine Itinerary (Itin. Marit. p. 518; Sil. Ital. xiv. 251).[339]

---

[338] As above. Photo: Ch. Lazaris.
[339] Wikipedia: https://en.wikipedia.org/wiki/Malta

Fig. 57 shows a stone hive with its front wall intact:

Fig. 57. Stone horizontal hive from Tinos[340]

Although Edward's description of the Maltese hives most closely resembles those in Fig. 56 and Fig. 57, there were many other types of hive used in the Mediterranean in the nineteenth century, made of stone, slate or terracotta or a mixture of these materials, and including 'apartment blocks' of hives such as this one in Fig. 58. Note the tiny bee entrance in each of the cells. The walls are made of porous stone and the 'roof' is terracotta tiles.

Similar 'bee room' apartments can be found in Malta. In the early nineteenth century, between 1798 and 1801, Rear Admiral Alexander Ball was the first British civil commissioner (governor) of the island.[341] He promoted schemes to encourage the islanders to develop agriculture. He appointed a network of men with the title 'Luogotenente'[342] to 'facilitate the implementation of legislation by informing the locals in their own language rather than in the heavy-handed manner of the French and the Knights before them.'[343] 'To 'entice the most learned individuals' in each locality to apply for these posts, he set up a network of gardens, which were to be

---

[340] As above. Photo N Karagiorgis.
[341] See Maltese History & Heritage blog, https://bit.ly/App7bBallGdns
[342] Literally 'place holder', from Italian, and like the French 'lieu tenant', which the British and Americans purloined for their military designation 'lieutenant'.
[343] MaltaHeritage blog: https://bit.ly/App8Tal-Kmand

managed by the Luogotenenti. He used the gardens as experimental sites to see which produce would thrive on the island: 'Of particular note is that the introduction of the potato in the Islands came about following experiments in these gardens to see whether this crop would give a larger yield than cotton (which was the main crop grown at that time).'[344] Another area which was of interest to him was apiculture, and he included apiaries in some of the gardens.

Fig. 58. Block of stone hives with terracotta tile 'roof'[345]

Ball, having been taken away briefly from his duties as civil commissioner to resume naval ones, was again appointed civil commissioner from 1802 until his death in 1809. Seven years is not particularly long to create a lasting impact, but several of his gardens have survived to the present day. The gardens as a group are called *Ġonna tal-Kmand* (transl. Commander's gardens).

In the present day, Ray Sciberras and Denise Camilleri of Golden Island Ltd, Malta, run a group of apiaries, some of which they use to monitor the relationship between pollution and bee health. Ray very kindly visited Safi Garden (one of the Commanders' gardens) specially to take photographs for me of the garden, and particularly its apiary. The garden is enclosed in beautiful honey-coloured sandstone walls, with a handsome dressed stone gateway.

---

[344] As above.
[345] Photograph kindly provided by G Mavrofridis.

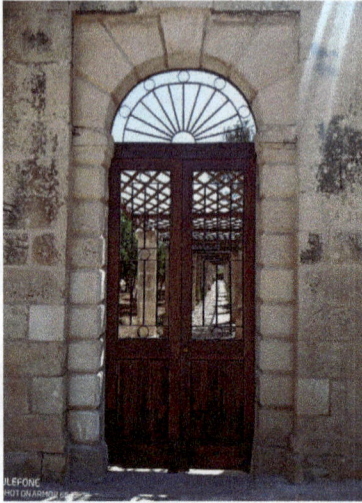

Fig. 59. Gateway to the Commander's garden at Safi[346]

Fig. 60. Pergola walkway, the Commander's garden, Safi[347]

Through the gate we find a path running under a handsome pergola with stone pillar supports – see Fig. 60 – and somewhere along the path there is the apiary room, off to the left, Fig. 61. Finally, Ray gives us a close-up of the bee entrances on the other side of the block of hives, Fig. 62:

Fig. 61. Apiary, the Commander's garden, Safi[348]

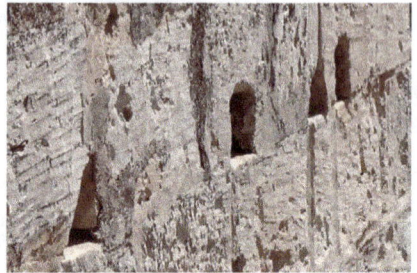

Fig. 62. Bee entrances to the apiary[349]

---

[346] Photograph Ray Sciberras.
[347] As above.
[348] As above.
[349] As above.

Appendix 11 – The carob tree

Fig. 63. Ceratonia Siliqua, Johannisbrot[350]

The Carob Bean Tree (Ceratonia Siliqua) is a Leguminous tree, wild and extensively cultivated in the countries bordering on the Mediterranean. It has a fleshy fruit, which is imported into this country in considerable quantities for cattle feeding. The seed was the original carat of jewellers … It forms a branching tree about 30ft. in height, having wood of a pretty pinkish hue. Its pinnate leaves are composed of two or three pairs of oval blunt-topped leaflets, of a leathery texture, and a shining dark-green colour. The flowers are in small red racemes, and are succeeded by flat

---

[350] From Dr. Willibald Artus' *Hand-Atlas sammtlicher mediinisch-pharmaceutischer Gewachse*, (Handbook of all medical-pharmaceutical plants), Jena, 1876. Wikipedia, creative commons: https://bit.ly/App11CarobCeratonia

pods, from 6 in. to 1 ft. in length. Besides the name of Carob Beans, these pods are also commonly called Locust pods, or St John's Bread, names by which they are well known in this country.[351]

Fig. 64. The Carob Harvest of Cyprus[352]

The carob tree is ubiquitous in southern Europe. This description of the August carob harvest in twenty-first-century Portugal could apply as well to nineteenth-century Greece:

> There is no precise date to mark the start of carob harvesting, which is done by using long poles to beat the tree branches and loosen the pods. However, towards the end of July, you are likely to see people out all over the region with their poles. The sound of the poles hitting the tree branches is as typical of the Mediterranean region as carob itself ...
>
> This is a very old process and it is very hard work. The poles are made of wood or cane. They are used to shake the branches to loosen the fruit, which then falls off on to canvas or cloth sheets spread out on the ground beneath the trees.
>
> Carob harvesting begins early in the morning, when the summer heat is not as intense, and it goes on all day long! In the past, it was the men's job to knock the pods off the trees and the women were responsible for

---

[351] *The Garden* journal 4 May 1878.
[352] *Illustrated London News*, 4 May 1878, with thanks to John Weedy.

bagging them in linen or sackcloth sacks, sometimes weighing as much as 50 kg! Nowadays, thanks to mechanization and automation, the process is much easier and less time-consuming …

At the end of the long day's work, the carob pods are transported to a warehouse where the bags are stored, ready for sale. In the past, the loads were carried by donkeys and mules, but farm tractors now do this job.

The carob pods are sold to traders in sacks weighing 15 kg, a unit of weight that is called "arroba" in Portuguese. After the seeds have been taken out, the pods are dried and roasted to be ground and turned into carob flour.[353]

From Fig. 64 we can see that the above description exactly matches how carob was harvested 150 years ago, and in all probability much earlier than that too.

[353] Carob World website: https://www.carobworld.com/en/carobharvest/

Appendix 12 – Life in nineteenth-century Malta

As we know that Rosa Mallia's family were bakers for the Maltese Colony, I imagine that they would have held a similar status in their home town of Siggiewi before embarking for Kefalonia. The closest I could get to an image relating to bakery in nineteenth-century Malta is this one by Brocktorff of a Maltese eating shop, Fig. 65.

Fig. 65. Maltese eating shop[354]

---

[354] Artist Charles Frederick de Brocktorff (born sometime between 1770 and 1785, died 1850). Image from the Heritage Malta blog, *Taste History*: https://tastehistory.mt/

The *Taste History* website says

> This watercolour by Charles Frederick de Brocktorff literally opens a
> window into a 19th century 'Maltese eating shop' to offer precious
> insights into food, dress, customs and aspects of daily life. It is very much
> a product of its age. To date this is the oldest known image of pasta being
> eaten in our capital city.[355]

Brocktorff was living and painting in Malta in the first half of the nineteenth
century, contemporaneously with the Mallia family, so his images are particularly
telling for our story.

As mentioned earlier, when I first learnt about the Maltese Colony on Kefalonia
I wondered what would have induced these 300 people to leave their homes and
everything familiar for a new life about which they knew virtually nothing. The
title of an article in *The Times of Malta*: *Apalling poverty in Malta in the early 19th
century*[356] by Giovanni Bonello provides the probable answer. Bonello draws
together the writings of nineteenth-century visitors to Malta to illustrate the
veracity of his article's title. He quotes an American traveller, Charles Rockwell:
'Never have I seen elsewhere so much squalid wretchedness, beggary and woe as
everywhere one meets in Malta.'[357]

Bonello's main argument is that the unprecedented poverty was the fault of the
British, who had taken Malta on as a protectorate in 1800. I have used Bonello's
article and quotations as a guide in writing this appendix, although I have followed
up each of his quotations to its source and included other extracts.

Andrew Bigelow, in his book *Travels in Malta and Sicily* about a journey he took
in 1827, a year after the Mallia family left for Kefalonia, wrote 'A large part of the
people are without money, without employment and, so far as I can see, without
bread or habitations.'[358]

Later in his book Bigelow provides a vivid illustration of a family with nowhere
to go but 'the cold bare pavement':

> I look out of my window and there I behold a wretched family group, a
> mother and several children, all in tatters, nay, with scarcely tatters
> enough to cover their nakedness – stretched on the side pavement by

---

[355] Taste History blog as above.

[356] I am very grateful to Leonard Callus of the National Archives of Malta for
recommending this article, which can be read online: https://bit.ly/App10ToMPoverty
and to Giovanni Bonello for permission to quote his material.

[357] The quotation is from *Sketches of Foreign Travel and Life at Sea vol. II*, p. 119,
Charles Rockwell, Tappan and Dennet, 1842.

[358] *Travels in Malta and Sicily with Sketches of Gibraltar in MDCCCXXVII*, pp. 115 and
121, Carter, Hendee and Babcock 1831.

yonder wall. The mother – I have frequently dropped a carlin into her hands, and that heart must be of stone that would not have done it – looks the image of famine and despair. "Why talk of petty inconveniences and magnify them into troubles, when there is perfect misery? Her home is that spot which she occupies. For her children she can hope no better lot. One is a baby lying on her withered arm, the other a feeble child with only a thin cotton wrapper about it, asleep on the cold, hard pavement!"[359]

As Giovanni Bonello writes:

Almost without a single exception, all the contemporary observers of the Malta scene attributed the flawless misery of the Maltese to the greed and mismanagement of their new colonial masters. With the start of the British connection, Malta was overrun by British immigrants seeking employment, advancement and money – all hoovered from the scarce resources and revenues of Malta. Within a short while, the new settlers had edged the Maltese out of almost every lucrative employment or job which had so far always been the preserve of the local population – ever since the times of the Knights.

A royal commission was set up in 1836 to look into a sequence of petitions which had been sent to England.[360] Bonello quotes directly from the report, saying

positions previously always held by Maltese had been 'abandoned for the most part to persons who had been unable to succeed in their respective professions in England'

and

'the business of a principal office filled by an Englishman had been performed by one of his Maltese subordinates – so the revenue had been burdened by a high salary paid to a useless principal'.

The person who had been appointed Governor of Malta in 1823 was none other than Sir Thomas Maitland, who held this title simultaneously with his duties as Lord High Commissioner of the Ionian Islands and who had been Napier's first boss when he arrived in Corfu in 1819.

---

[359] As above, p. 177.
[360] 'The Maltese Liberal Movement, The Royal Comission of 1836 and the New Council of Government' from an online paper in a course entitled *Maltese History: Political and Constitutional Developments*.

If the Maltese economy was in such a parlous state as these quotations describe it is hardly surprising that an enterprising family would seize the opportunity to leave. Impoverished people do not have the money even for basic necessities such as bread, and the Mallias would have hoped for better opportunities for themselves and better markets in Kefalonia.

Looking for illustrations which might hint at what my great-great-grandmother Rosa would have looked like, I thought that as the family were bakers they would possibly have been considered to belong to the same social group as other artisans in the community, so we're going on a little diversion here. Cotton was the major crop in Malta at this time. There is an endearing set of images of people from a range of backgrounds executed by Vincenzo Fenech, an artist active in Malta in the late eighteenth and early nineteenth centuries.[361]

We will look at some of Fenech's watercolours illustrating the different processes of spinning cotton. He seems to have used the same model for all these paintings and he did not give his pictures titles, so as I have no expertise in spinning I consulted Sue Chitty of Hilltop Spinning and Weaving Centre,[362] not far from where I live. She very kindly put the images in process order for me, told me what each process was and gave me some technical terms. In each painting the young woman is slightly differently dressed, and we can imagine that Rosa's outfits when Edward first knew her in Kefalonia might well have been similar to these. I was particularly taken with these little illustrations, as they are as close as we are likely to get to a portrait of Rosa in her youth. Sue Chitty tells me that blue is a difficult colour to dye. Fabric of that colour appears in each of these portraits, perhaps indicating the skill of the artisans involved.

The historical processes of turning cotton bolls (raw cotton) into thread were similar to those used for making wool yarn.

---

[361] These images are from a collection of Fenech's work, *Malta Costumes 1833*, held by the National Library of Malta, Valletta. My thanks to librarian Maroma Camilleri for drawing them to my attention.

[362] https://handspin.co.uk/

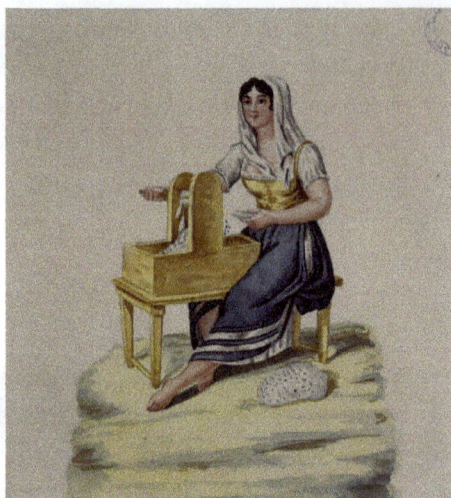

Fig. 66. Maltese girl ginning cotton

In Fig. 66 the girl is deseeding the raw cotton using a hand gin. This process is called 'ginning'. Her next job is to card the fibres.

In Fig. 67 she is using two carders – toothed paddles. The ginned cotton is laid across the teeth of one carder, and the other is pulled through the cotton, rather like combing hair, to straighten the fibres and remove any remaining field debris. You can see the pile of ginned cotton on the ground, and the finished neat squares of carded cotton stacked on the stool beside her. She has her left foot resting on the bottom rung. Her cat is giving the artist an inscrutable stare.

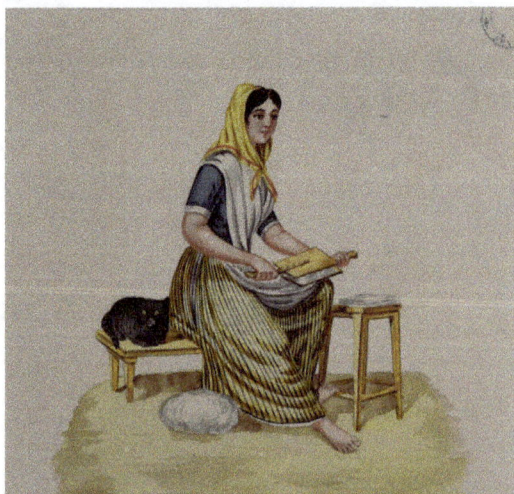

Fig. 67. Maltese girl carding cotton, Vincenzo Fenech

There are then several ways in which she can twist the fibres together to make a continuous thread, two of which are illustrated.

In Fig. 68 she is holding a distaff of carded cotton fibres in her left hand, and using a whorl spindle dangling from her right hand to spin the fibres into a single length of yarn.

Fig. 68. Maltese girl with distaff and whorl spindle

In Fig. 69 she is using a spinning wheel, which speeds up the spinning process. Sue Chitty says 'The foot is tensioning the whole process of spinning and building up the quantity of yarn on a spindle. Clever use of the foot controls the evenness of the yarn on the spindle, layering it rather than just letting it run any old how. It is being spun "long draw" as the cotton fibre is so short; that is why her arms are up in the air.'

Fig. 69. Maltese girl with spinning wheel

The mechanism in Fig. 70 is called an 'umbrella swift' or a 'yarn swift'. It is not entirely clear to me whether our spinner is using it to wind yarn into a hank on it or to wind the hank of yarn from the swift into a ball. The latter technique is demonstrated by the modern hand-spinner Barbara Benson in her video *Using an Umbrella Swift to Wind Yarn*.[363]

Fig. 70. Using an 'umbrella swift' [364]

---

[363] https://www.youtube.com/watch?v=VfEkmFnVi8o
[364] From *Malta Costumes 1833*, National Library of Malta, Valletta.

Fig. 71 is a bit of a mystery. Sue Chitty says: '3 yarns are being held together into one revolution of the niddy noddy (skeinholder) to lie beside each other. This does not make sense, as to twist yarns together needs a drop spindle to twist or spin. Laying yarns together is unhelpful for onward processes. I think this is called a winding process, as in the industrial process.'

Fig. 71. Winding the yarn onto a niddy noddy

One of the most endearing features of these paintings is the minimal settings which Fenech manages to include. He shows us that simpler spinning tasks could be carried out quite casually, sitting indoors with your cat for company, or on a sunny morning in the yard with the hens. Incidentally a Fenech family was among those on the list of Maltese Colony arrivals in 1826.

Appendix 13 – Government in the Ionian Islands

The history of the Ionian Islands is one of successive invasions and rule by different nations. Like shuttlecocks, the islands were tossed hither and thither in varying groups between several players, who saw them as strategic assets in centuries of maritime conflicts. Following early settlement by Greece, there were periods under the Romans and Byzantines. Gradually they were acquired by the Venetians between the thirteenth and fifteenth centuries, a dominion which lasted until Napoleon conquered Venice in 1797. The French had only held the islands for a year when in 1798 the Russian Admiral Ushakov captured them and united them as 'the Septinsular Republic', but they were passed back to the French in 1807. Two years later the British navy 'captured Kefallonia, Kythera and Zakynthos', and 'took Lefkada in 1810'.[365] When Napoleon was finally defeated at Waterloo the seven Ionian Islands were declared to be a single, free and independent republic, under the protection of England.[366] In practice this meant they were part of the British Empire. In 1817 a constitution was granted to the islands by the British government, setting forth the mode in which they were to be governed. In April 1819, the final arrangement was made by a treaty between England and Turkey in which the latter renounced all claim to the islands.[367]

The civil government set up by the British consisted of a legislative assembly, a senate, and a judicial authority. The legislative assembly consisted of forty members including the president. Of the forty, eleven were 'integral members' and the rest were elected, for a five-year term, from the islands in proportion to the size of their population. The Senate was the executive power, composed of the president and five senators elected from the legislative assembly, again in proportion to the population of each island. The Lord High Commissioner of the Ionian Islands was appointed by the British Crown. He in turn appointed a 'Resident' or representative, who was the field officer of the regiments on duty in the island. To 'balance' the British control, five appointments were in the gift of the senate, 'subject to the approbation of the Lord High Commissioner'. Napier was the 'Resident' on Kefalonia for ten years from 1821.[368]

---

[365] As above.

[366] 'Peace of Paris '1815.

[367] Notes taken from *The History of the British Colonies*, vol. V, p. 300. R Montgomery Martin, Cochraine & Co., London 1835. (https://bit.ly/App11IonianIslesMartin) The so-called 'four great powers' were Great Britain, Austria, Prussia and Russia.

[368] As above.

Appendix 14 – Final report on the Maltese Colony

Edward Curling submitted the following lengthy report to Colonel Conyers, Acting Resident appointed in Napier's absence. Edward highlighted the reasons for the colony's existence, the deficiencies in the Greek farming methods of the time and his solutions, drawing on current agricultural practice and making experiments of his own according to the conditions he found in Pronos. The letter follows on immediately in the original from his letter to Napier of 3 July 1831.

Copy of my letter to Colonel Conyers

"Sir

As you requested I now report to you for the information of the general Gov^t an account of the Colony_ i.e. my opinion as to its object, the manner it has hitherto been conducted, its present state, and its future prospect of success_ The object of the Colony has always appeared to me to be, to prove to the Greeks by example the advantage of good Agriculture, by putting in practice, the long established maxims of England and other countries, thereby to communicate the present system practised in the country_ that this system is capable of amelioration appears from these points,_ the Greeks cultivate the soil to no depth merely in fact scratching the surface, they scarcely make any use of manure, and have not the least idea of a succession of crops_ convincing proofs I think that Agriculture is at its lowest ebb in Cefalonia_ The object was also to show the best modes of rearing, feeding and fattening cattle, to introduce the best breeds of stock, and also to prove the capability of the island to produce plants and vegetables hitherto unknown in it_ I leave others more capable of judging, to appreciate the advantages of this project in a country like Cefalonia where so large a portion of land is uncultivated and so immense a proportion of capital expended in the importation of corn and cattle_ To effect the objects Government brought over a number of Maltese undoubtedly under the idea that they understood farming, whereas, as has been since proved they received a set of men, collected from the streets and hospitals of Malta and with scarcely an exception wholly incapacitated for the purpose intended_ Is it surprising then, that with such men a number of expenses should have been incurred_ Any one who has seen the land at Pronos where every inch of ground must be worked by the pickaxe must be persuaded that without any additional disadvantages it must be some years before it could pay the expenses *of its cultivation_ how then could it be expected that it would pay for building houses, farm yards, pig sties etc. that it could pay for the rations of a number of almost useless people, that it could pay for ~~purchasing of~~[369] tools, for the purchase of cattle and for the plantation of [Nua Papa] before that plantation produced fruit, that it could pay hospital bills, passage money, keep a Priest and Doctor, and in fact support the whole multitude of expenses heaped upon it_ Most of these expenses were of course unavoidable, but it should not be expected, that the land should, in three or four years pay for all when as I said before it could not for some time pay for itself_ That the produce has not hitherto been great is true, but it is such as might have been expected from a clayey soil (which requires more cultivation than any other) without manure, and before it had been brought into a proper state_ These appear to me to be the reasons why there has not hitherto been so great a result as has been too eagerly anticipated, and has induced many thoughtless persons, without local knowledge, without a knowledge of Agriculture, I was going to add, without common sense, to condemn the object of the Colony as impracticable_ but let me now consider the present state of the Colony_ there are as near as I can judge about 100 acres of land cleared from roots_ 15 acres of this are planted with [Nua Papa] and about 12 acres I have this year properly cultivated, that is worked it deeply, manured it and terraced a considerable portion of it, and from these 12 acres I therefore hope important results, the remainder from not having sufficient manure or strength I can only cultivate in the Greek mode, it is cleared from roots, but requires manure before it can be expected to return much profit to Government_ Our expenses for labour for the last three months have been £31.1^s.5^d reduced by the sale of produce to £21.19^s.8$^{3/4d}$ and this is a fair average of the expense that will in future be incurred_ Our produce this year will I calculate be about $500_ it would certainly have much more than have covered the expenses had Gov^t allowed me at once to have acted according to my proposal, but I had diminished my number of labourers so considerably that not letting the land to Greeks as I proposed, a great portion of the Colony necessarily remains uncultivated_ Next year I pledge myself if the Colony continues that the produce shall considerably more than pay the expenses_ in two years the Nuo Papa itself will almost cover them,*

---

[369] Edward Curling's strikethrough.

*but under any circumstances at the present rate of expense it is impossible the loss can be great to Government_ That great sacrifices have been made is evident, but why should Gov^t relinquish a project so useful in itself, just at the time when no more sacrifice is requisite_ from manure alone we could hope to succeed, to obtain manure has always been my object, and that manure I have now begun to collect_ for the present we have sufficient ground cleared, no more buildings are required, we have nearly cattle sufficient, in a word I may say no more expense is necessary except for seeding the land & harvesting the produce_ And here I think I cannot do better than repeat the proposal I made to his Exc^y Sir F Adam some time since_ viz to reserve to ourselves only the land already manured and in good condition and so much more as with our present labourers we could terrace & manure for instance, this year I have terraced and manured more than 12 acres, next year after cropping this I shall be able to terrace 12 acres more or as much in addition as there will be manure for_ the remainder I proposed should be let to Greeks from which we should receive without any expence one half the produce, they of course cultivating it under my superintendence and I humbly submit whether in this manner without further sacrifice on the part of Government we cannot carry into effect the great object of the Establishment and by degrees reduce the whole of the Colony into a good state of cultivation_*

Endpapers of address page:

I leave Government therefore to consider whether it is advisable now to relinquish the project and to abandon all its improvements_ the example set has already begun to influence the Greeks and the country around to receive the benefit_ I appeal to Mr Cambisi[370] if these are not facts_ I say again that Gov^t cannot lose much in continuing the project and in abandoning it it loses everything_ You can easily imagine, Sir, that I can have no interested motives in making this report, neither the Salary I receive, nor the situation of the place, are sufficient to cause them_ I am only anxious that the Gov^t should have a right view of the Establishment under my charge and not abandon it from the report of persons who without any knowledge of Agriculture & from not having seen the place or works must be wholly incompetent to judge of the probability or

---

[370] As well as being a close neighbour of the colony and a good friend to Napier and Edward, Cambici was a member of the local government.

*improbability of success_ Let any competent person see and make his report and I have no fears as to the result_ I refer you to the accompanying paper for an account of the produce for the two years which the Colony has been under my superintendence_*

I have the honour to be &c &c E.C.

The above was Edward's copy of his letter, made for Napier, to whom he added a postscript about three men, presumably formerly under Napier's command, and a word about Napier's horse, Turk. He still had responsibility for some Maltese men and boys:

PS Let me know when you write whether you approve of this report and if in some measure it does not make up for my not keeping my journal_ Hay too, and Haynes are well, the latter only gets drunk now & then_ Turk gets on famously he is still at St [Mails] and I pay Gov^t as usual_ Rankin was an inhabitant of Kennedy Castle for 20 days a short time since for striking a constable_ My Maltese labourers are receiving 1½^d per man & 1^d a boy for their maintenance til the answer comes from Corfu respecting them_ the R[371] could not undertake greater responsibility_ however they must not complain as they are much better treated than I [am] now,[372][373]

Napier annotated this letter above its address panel:

An invaluable letter Curling about the Colony proving that Adam well knew he was doing mischief to the public out of jealousy of me. July 3rd 1831.

---

[371] R was probably the Regent.
[372] Edward was now unemployed and was therefore without an income.
[373] BL Add MS 54536 ff. 110–111.

Main index

A

agricultural tools, 93, 132
  flails, 97, 126
  harrows, 87
  hoes, 77, 78, 84
  pickaxes, 87, 91
  ploughs, 77, 79–82, 87
  seed drills, 82
agriculture, 46, 64–66
  calendar, 72
  diversification, 15
  education in, 73
  harvesting, 97, 220
  improvements in, 47, 75, 158
  land clearing, 83, 87, 95, 101–2, 126, 131
  manuring, 75, 77, 79, 102–4
  market gardens, 82, 93
  model farms, 131, 159
  pests, 87
  reaping, 97
  scientific, 12, 15
  seasonal routines of, 75
  skills in, 126
  soil improvement, 102–4
  threshing, 97–98, 126
  tools, 18
  traditional methods of, 76
  water management, 94, 109, 119, 132
  winnowing, 98–99
  see also crops; fertilisers; Maltese Colony.
arbitration, 43
archives, museums and galleries
  Argostoli, 17, 136
  British Library, 4, 32, 35
  Dana Research Centre, Science Museum, 192, 194
  London Metropolitan Archives, 42
army regiments and establishments
  4th Regiment of Dragoons, 150

235

59th Regiment of Foot, 198
Royal African Colonial Corps, 34, 198
Royal Staff Corps, 10, 33, 36

B

battles and wars
   Battle of Navarino, 1827, 51–52, 106
   Greek War of Independence, 8, 51–52, 171
   Napoleonic, 53, 230
   Second World War, 186
birds
   eagles, 107
   hens, 91, 92
   herons, 107
   woodcock, 88
blackmail, 42
boats *see* vessels.
building, 85, 88, 91, 109, 110–11, 119
   flooring, 94
   plastering, 110
   terracing, 93, 111, 132
   see also walls.
business, failures in, 43, 57, 62, 146–48

C

careers *see* occupations.
charcoal production, 75, 89–91, 126–27, 208–10
charities, 53
children, 28
   abandonment of, 48, 51, 54–63
   care of, 20
   cruelty to, 60
   health of, 141, 156
   illegitimate, 19–21, 23, 31, 48, 55
   labour of, 77, 83, 85
clothing, 100
convents *see* monasteries.
cotton, 113, 225–29
court cases, 45, 59–61
crime, 92
crops, 47, 75, 77, 82, 118–19, 120–22, 131, 161
   almonds, 91
   barley, 87, 104
   beans, 84, 120
   cabbages, 82, 120

237

I

illness, 29, 41, 43, 115–16, 133, 154
   fever, 198
   of Maltese Colony workforce, 74, 77, 78, 100–101
   plague, 69
   quarantine, 69, 115, 151, 204–7
infrastructure
   development of, 10
   roads, 9, 27
inheritance, 39–40, 53
   conditional, 66
irrigation, 94, 109, 132
Italian language, 69

J

justice, 9, 62, 135, 163

K

kelp, 46

L

labour, 18–19, 91–92
   of children, 77, 83, 85
   manual, 93
   of women, 77, 83, 85
livestock, 103–4, 161, 173, 175
   bees, 108, 213–18
   bullocks, 88, 94, 103, 110, 112, 132
   cattle, 47, 78, 82, 102, 104, 108, 110, 143
   goats, 113
   hens, 91, 92
   horses/ponies, 104, 107, 143
   mules, 83
   pigs, 91, 104, 110, 143
   poultry, 104
   sheep, 46, 47, 113
love, 40, 135–39, 154–55

M

Maltese Colony, 68, 73–92, 93–109, 110–15
   barns, 95–97
   building work, 85, 88, 91, 109, 110–11, 119
   closure of, 118, 131, 134, 157–64, 176

Locations index

L

M

N

O

Names index

A

Adam, Sir Frederick, 12, 49, 115, 122, 144, 158
   Ionian Islands, departure from, 151, 163, 168, 173
   and Maltese Colony, 15, 82, 105, 112, 121, 131–35, 142–43
   and Napier, Charles James, 117–18, 153, 171–72, 174
Ali Pasha of Ioannina, 7
Allen, William, 49–50
Anastasia (mistress of Charles James Napier), 19–22, 23, 48, 51, 174

B

Bacon, Henry, 213
Baldock, William, 66
Ball, Alexander, 216–18
Bathurst, Henry, 3rd Earl Bathurst, 49
Baynes, Mr (overseer, Kefalonia), 74–75, 150, 161, 163
Becker, Jane II *see* Rowcroft, Jane.
Becker, Mary (later Delmar), 66, 67
Becker, Michael III, 66, 67, 68, 134
Bénard, Robert, 208
Bennet, Mary & Caroline, 31
Blencowe, Frances (later Napier), 155
Brocktorff, Charles Frederick de, 222
Bunbury, Richard Hanmer, 106
Bunbury, Sir Henry, 155, 156

C

Cambici, Demetrio, 133, 168, 176
   and Curling, Edward I, 70, 86
   hospitality of, 105–6
   house of, 74, 184
   irrigation system of, 94, 184
   and Maltese Colony, 15, 18, 19, 21–22, 27, 74, 122
   and Maltese Colony closure, 161, 163
   scientific agriculture, support for, 76, 113, 143, 151
Camilleri, Denise, 217
Cammillieri, Nicholas, 201
Carter, Thomas, 54, 56–58, 60
Cartwright, Joseph, 121, 178
Chervet, Mr, 55

D

Debonos, Angelos, 113
Delmar, Charles, 65, 67
Dickson, George, 50, 130, 135, 156–57, 165–66, 173, 177
Dickson, Harriet, 50, 130, 135, 166–67, 173, 177
Dickson, Thomas, 177
Dobson, Mr (school usher), 59, 60

E

Elphinstone, Sir Howard, 43, 44
Evans, Mr (father of Robert), 54–63
Evans, Robert, 54–63

F

Fenech, Vincenzo, 225–29
Fereday, R. P., 43
Ferguson, Sir Ronald, 43, 44
Frost, Susan, 20

G

Gatfield, Charles, 55–56, 60
Goderich, F. J. Robinson, 1st Viscount, 134, 153, 174
Goussier, Louis-Jacques, 208

H

Hassell, J, 147

I

Imber, Edward, 42

J

Jarvis and Waddington (apothecaries, Margate), 149
Johnston, Sir Alexander, 40, 41, 44, 45

K

Kelly, Agnes (later Laing), 32, 33, 36–37, 41
Kelly, Arthur, 36, 37
Kelly, Eliza, 37, 39, 40, 43, 67
Kelly, Elizabeth *see* Napier, Elizabeth.
Kelly, Francis John, 16, 33, 35, 36–37, 37, 40, 42, 43

O

Oakley Curling, Thomas II *see* Curling, Thomas II Oakley.
Oakley, Anne (later Mantell), 35, 42
Oakley, Catharine *see* Curling, Catharine I, 235
Oakley, Elizabeth *see* Napier, Elizabeth.
Oakley, Thomas II, 35, 43

P

Packe, Reverend Christopher, 23, 25, 28, 43
Packe, Tomazine Gentile, 23–25, 43
Pitt, Colonel (interim Resident of Kefalonia), 133, 161

R

Rankin, Mr (Kefalonia resident), 142, 151, 167
Rawlinson, Mr (magistrate), 60–61, 61
Reginis, L. (Kefalonia resident), 176
Reid, Mr (Kefalonia resident), 151, 173
Reinagle, George Philip, 52
Robertson, Lewis, 42
Rowcroft, Charles, 53–63, 65, 133, 144–48
Rowcroft, Jane (formerly Curling, née Becker), 53, 65, 67, 144, 145–48, 151–53
Rowcroft, Thomas, 53–54

S

Sciberras, Ray, 217
Scourti, Alison, 182
Smithson, Mr, 169
Staines, W. T., 58–59
Staples, Louisa (née Stewart, later Napier), 6
Stellatos, Marinos, 181, 182
Stellatos, Polydoros, 181, 182
Stevens, Mr (Kefalonia resident), 119, 132, 144, 158, 162
Stewart, Anne Louisa (later Staples, Napier), 6

T

Travers, Robert, 8
Turner, J M W, 200

V

Valsamachi, Paulo, 163

W

Y

Sources index

A

Administration of Col. Charles James Napier in the Island of Cefalonia, The (Heron), 51
'Appalling poverty in Malta in the early 19th century' (*Times of Malta*), 223–24
Autobiography (Laing), 32, 34, 36, 37, 43, 47
Auxiliaries, The (Yaple), 199

B

Belfast Commercial Chronicle (newspaper), 60
Blue Anchor Corner (blog), 66

C

Calcutta Annual Register and Directory, 150
Cephalonia of Old Volume I, Argostoli (Corgialanios Foundation), 69
Charles Napier, Friend and Fighter (Lawrence), 38, 39, 48
Chartist General, The (Beasley), 133, 174
Colonies at Home (Allen), 49, 50
Colonies, The (Charles James Napier), 12–13, 18, 22, 64, 68, 71, 101, 118, 124, 134, 188
Condition of Greece in 1827 and 1828, The (Miller), 204
Curling Wisps vol. 1 (Curling), 33, 35, 53, 64–66, 64, 65, 66, 75, 149

D

Dhaka (newspaper), 194
Diaries of John Helder Wedge, 72
Disbanded Regiments (Baldry), 198
Disease and Empire (Curtin), 199
Domestic Encyclopaedia, 82

F

Field Clearing (Gage), 102
From observatory to dominion geopolitics (Zarokostas), 69

G

Garden, The (journal), 125, 220

H

I

J

K

L

M

O

P

R

S

T

V

W

Other publications from Ōzaru Books

Ōzaru Books is a boutique publisher based in the Thanet village of St Nicholas-at-Wade. Our primary focus is on books with a local connection, ranging from creative writing by East Kent authors to (occasionally niche) scholarly tomes about Kentish history, but we have a secondary interest in works in translation, particularly from Eastern languages, and also tales from East Prussia. Some of our profits go to support gorilla charities, which is the origin of the name Ōzaru ('Great Ape') and our logo.

Curling Wisps & Whispers of History

Vol. 1: Thanet to Tasmania

LucyAnn Curling

If family history is about gathering as many ancestors as possible, this book fails: it focuses on just three generations of the author's paternal side, between 1780 and 1826. At first nothing stirs the still waters of centuries of East Kent farming tradition. Men organize parish affairs, women follow domestic routines, boys attend a boarding school in Ramsgate, and only grandma seems interested in socializing or travel. Why then did Thomas Oakley Curling uproot everything and take his family on a marathon five-month voyage to Van Diemen's Land? Why leave one child behind? And where does Sir Charles fit in?

Curling Wisps & Whispers of History
Vol. 1: Thanet to Tasmania

LucyAnn Curling

The genealogical quest starts naturally with a family heirloom, but soon tangential questions emerge, as multiple threads are collated and woven into one story. 'Georgian & Regency ancestors' might sound remote, removed from our reality, but the individuals' letters draw us into their world, and copious illustrations punctuate the text, animating the environments in which they lived. For fellow seekers there are also abundant indices, references, and lists of archives.

"a superbly-produced family history, using an impressive range of sources and archives ... Well-illustrated, and with no less than one hundred pages of appendices covering many ancillary topics, this is an essential read for anyone who has Curling and Oakley ancestors in their family, as well as everyone who has an interest in life in Kent in the 18th and 19th centuries. A highly-recommended read; roll on Volume Two!" (Kent Family History Society)

"It is a very impressive piece of work, full of research and brimming with interesting insights not just of these Curling family members but of life in the early 19th century. I found it particularly fascinating to read about the pressures to emigrate – and the risks therein. I think the appendices are a great idea: allowing the story to rattle along and readers to explore around it at leisure. The illustrations are a superb addition to the whole package." (Tim Albert)

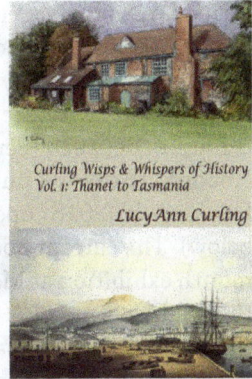

ISBN 978-1-915174-02-4

Animal Guising and the Kentish Hooden Horse

An Exhibition at Maidstone Museum

James Frost

Hoodening is an ancient calendar custom unique to East Kent, involving a wooden horse's head on a pole, carried by a man concealed by a sack. The earliest reliable record is from 1735, but little serious research had gone into the tradition between Percy Maylam's seminal work "The Hooden Horse", published in 1909, and George Frampton's 2018 update, "Discordant Comicals" (see below). The current book, published to accompany a four-month exhibition at Maidstone Museum, further expands the field.

The text, accompanied by over 60 full colour illustrations, describes what hoodening was, what the hooden horse is, and how it can be seen in the national context of animal guising. It covers historical records and artifacts, revival groups, 'Autohoodening' performances which reimagine the old tradition in a modern context, and related practices such as the Mari Lwyd, Obby Osses, various northern beasts, and stag guising. Appendices contain the text of numerous contemporary verses and plays.

The author, James Frost, is a Lecturer in Performing Arts at Canterbury Christ Church University, as well as a Senior Fellow of the Higher Education Academy.

ISBN 978-1-915174-06-2

Discordant Comicals – The Hooden Horse of East Kent

George Frampton

Other than Percy Maylam's 1909 classic "The Hooden Horse" (republished in an annotated edition in 2021: see below), specialist books on the old Kentish tradition of the Hoodeners have been virtually non-existent.

George Frampton has rectified this, by cross-referencing dozens of newspaper reports, census records and other accounts to build a comprehensive picture of who the Hoodeners were, why (and where) they did it, and how it related to other folk traditions.

He then goes beyond Maylam to look at the 'demise' of Hoodening in around 1921, its widely heralded 'revival' in 1966, and discovers that this narrative is in fact quite misleading, as several Hooden Horses were still active throughout that period. He includes descriptions of the current teams, and supplies plentiful appendices detailing past participants, places visited, songs performed, events on Hoodening's timeline, and the horses themselves.

Full indices make it easy for modern Men and Maids of Kent to check whether their ancestors might have been involved, and detailed references make this an invaluable resource for social historians too.

The book features over 70 full colour illustrations.

"a good read for the interested layman as well as a valuable resource for anyone interested in the custom" (The Morris Dancer)

"very readable research [...] backed up with generous quotations [...] reveals a tale of rich cultural heritage." (The Living Tradition)

"thoroughly researched [...] well presented [...] full of previously un-published interviews [...] in depth analysis [...] extremely interesting" (Around Kent Folk)

"provides a sense of the scope and history of the rarely studied practice of hoodening [...] offers the most up-to-date and comprehensive starting point for any scholar interested in the practice" (The Journal of Folklore Research)

"attractively published in hardback with numerous colour illustrations [...] A lot of admirable spadework and academic endeavour [...] copious references are given throughout" (Master Mummers)

"Frampton has left no stone unturned in his research [...] there is a very useful index, which helps make this a book to dip into profitably" (Archæologia Cantiana)

"profusely illustrated and printed in colour, it's a treat for the eyes [...] meticulous and detailed [...] a compelling and intriguing volume" (Tykes' News)

ISBN: 978-0-9559219-7-3

The Hooden Horse of East Kent – Annotated Edition

Percy Maylam

Percy Maylam's "The Hooden Horse: an East Kent Christmas Custom" was long the definitive work on Hoodening – indeed, the only full-scale study of the custom. It covered the current practice in Thanet at the start of the 20th century, past printed records, theories about its possible demise, similar customs in other parts of England and Germany, and speculation about its ancient, possibly pagan origins.

Although Frampton has arguably superseded Maylam as the authority on Hooderers and their activities, his book still takes Maylam as a basis to explore what happened since his time. Maylam's original work is indispensable even now, but the first format is very rare, as only 303 copies were printed, and only a reduced edition appeared later.

This new eBook includes the whole of Maylam's text, with numerous features to help those wanting to push the research further – even those lucky enough to have a copy of the 1909 hardback. There are copious annotations, internal hyperlinks, images of and external links to original sources, and appendices with contemporary reviews. The eBook naturally allows readers to search the whole text, yet the page numbers are still present to enable cross-referencing to Frampton and others (N.B. some of the functionality may vary, depending on the device used to read the book). The list of subscribers (which was omitted from another edition) is present, along with brief biographical notes on many of them, to show who was reading Maylam and what impact he would have had at the time.

The book is therefore a vital source of information for anyone interested in folk drama, including mumming. It is rigorously academic by the standards of the day, but also remains readable for general fans of the genre. This edition also contains updated versions of the early 20C photographs.

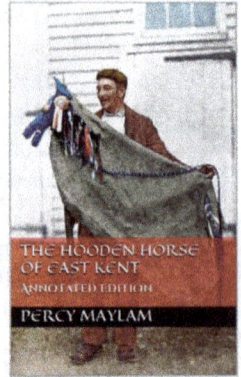

Available on Kindle

The Margate Tales

Stephen Channing

Chaucer's Canterbury Tales is without doubt one of the best ways of getting a feel for what the people of England in the Middle Ages were like. In the modern world, one might instead try to learn how different people behave and think from television or the internet.

However, to get a feel for what it was like to be in Margate as it gradually changed from a small fishing village into one of Britain's most popular holiday resorts, one needs to investigate contemporary sources such as newspaper reports and journals.

Stephen Channing has saved us this work, by trawling through thousands of such documents to select the most illuminating and entertaining accounts of Thanet in the 18th and early to mid 19th centuries. With content ranging from furious battles in the letters pages, to hilarious pastiches, witty poems and astonishing factual reports, illustrated with over 70 drawings from the time, The Margate Tales brings the society of the time to life, and as with Chaucer, demonstrates how in many areas, surprisingly little has changed.

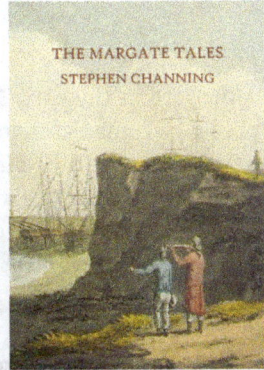

"substantial and fascinating volume...meticulously researched...an absorbing read"
(Margate Civic Society)

ISBN: 978-0-9559219-5-7

Turner's Margate Through Contemporary Eyes

– *The Viney Letters* –

Stephen Channing

Margate in the early 19th century was an exciting town, where smugglers and 'preventive men' fought to outwit each other, while artists such as JMW Turner came to paint the glorious sunsets over the sea. One of the young men growing up in this environment decided to set out for Australia to make his fortune in the Bendigo gold rush.

Half a century later, having become a pillar of the community, he began writing a series of letters and articles for Keble's Gazette, a publication based in his home town. In these, he described Margate with great familiarity (and tremendous powers of recall), while at the same time introducing his English readers to the "latitudinarian democracy" of a new, "young Britain".

Viney's interests covered a huge range of topics, from Thanet folk customs such as Hoodening, through diatribes on the perils of assigning intelligence to dogs, to geological theories including suggestions for the removal of sandbanks off the English coast "in obedience to the sovereign will and intelligence of man".

His writing is clearly that of a well-educated man, albeit with certain Victorian prejudices about the colonies that may make those with modern sensibilities wince a little. Yet above all, it is interesting because of the light it throws on life in a British seaside town some 180 years ago.

This book also contains numerous contemporary illustrations.

"profusely illustrated...draws together a series of interesting articles and letters...recommended" (Margate Civic Society)

ISBN: 978-0-9559219-2-6

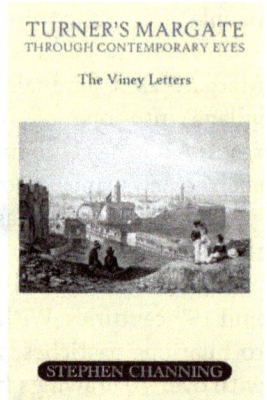

A Victorian Cyclist

– Rambling through Kent in 1886 –

Stephen & Shirley Channing

Bicycles are so much a part of everyday life nowadays, it can be surprising to realize that for the late Victorians these "velocipedes" were a novelty disparaged as being unhealthy and unsafe – and that indeed tricycles were for a time seen as the format more likely to succeed.

Some people however adopted the new-fangled devices with alacrity, embarking on adventurous tours throughout the countryside. One of them documented his 'rambles' around East Kent in such detail that it is still possible to follow his routes on modern cycles, and compare the fauna and flora (and pubs!) with those he vividly described.

In addition to providing today's cyclists with new historical routes to explore, and both naturalists and social historians with plenty of material for research, this fascinating book contains a special chapter on Lady Cyclists in the era before female emancipation, and an unintentionally humorous section instructing young gentlemen how to make their cycle and then ride it.

A Victorian Cyclist features over 200 illustrations, and is complemented by a fully updated website.

"Lovely...wonderfully written...terrific" (Everything Bicycles)
"Rare and insightful" (Kent on Sunday)
"Interesting...informative...detailed historical insights" (BikeBiz)
"Unique and fascinating book...quality is very good...of considerable interest" (Veteran-Cycle Club)
"Superb...illuminating...well detailed...The easy flowing prose, which has a cadence like cycling itself, carries the reader along as if freewheeling with a hind wind" (Forty Plus Cycling Club)
"a fascinating book with both vivid descriptions and a number of hitherto-unseen photos of the area" ('Pedalling Pensioner', amazon.co.uk)

ISBN: 978-0-9559219-7-1
Also available on Kindle

Bicycle Beginnings

The Advent of the Bicycle or Velocipede… and what people of the 19th century were really saying about it

Stephen Channing

Cycling is such a natural activity for millions of people around the globe now, it is difficult to imagine that a little over a century ago many regarded it as reprehensible, revolting, or indeed revolutionary. The best way to get a feel for what early 'velocipedists' encountered is to read the words of the times, and this book gathers into one volume the most enlightening, entertaining and extraordinary insights from contemporary sources.

The mammoth work (over 190,000 words, covering the period 1779 to 1912) contains race reports, legal developments, technical innovations and inventions, records, advertisements, acrobatics, clothing, poems, arguments for and against the new-fangled vehicles, debates over women cyclists, and a long travelogue, " Berlin to Budapest on a Bicycle" capturing the excitement of a forgotten age of adventure on two wheels.

Not all the inventions were two-wheeled, however. This book also reveals the numerous variations that came into being before makers standardized on the shapes we commonly see nowadays: tricycles, ice velocipedes, water-paddle hobby-horses… These are explained with the aid of numerous illustrations, covering the gamut from cartoons to technical drawings and photographs. Even the race reports demonstrate far more variety than we are accustomed to seeing: 'ordinaries' (penny farthings) versus 'safety' bicycles versus tandems, monocycles, dwarf cycles, tricycles, double tricycles, four-wheel velocipedes, horses, ice skaters, steamships…

Rather than a single narrative to be read in one go, it is an anthology of fascinating glimpses into cycling's 'golden age', providing a new understanding of a bygone age of experimentation and much amusement, whenever the reader dips into it.

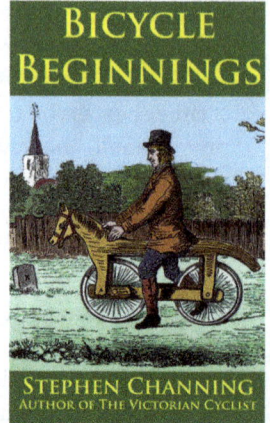

ISBN: 978-1-5210-8632-2
Also available on Kindle

The Call of Cairnmor

Book One of the Cairnmor Trilogy

Sally Aviss

The Scottish Isle of Cairnmor is a place of great beauty and undisturbed wilderness, a haven for wildlife, a land of white sandy beaches and inland fertile plains, a land where awe-inspiring mountains connect precipitously with the sea.

To this remote island comes a stranger, Alexander Stewart, on a quest to solve the mysterious disappearance of two people and their unborn child; a missing family who are now heirs to a vast fortune. He enlists the help of local schoolteacher, Katherine MacDonald, and together they seek the answers to this enigma: a deeply personal journey that takes them from Cairnmor to the historic splendour of London and the industrial heartland of Glasgow.

Covering the years 1936-1937 and infused with period colour and detail, The Call of Cairnmor is about unexpected discovery and profound attachment which, from its gentle opening, gradually gathers momentum and complexity until all the strands come together to give life-changing revelations.

"really enjoyed reading this – loved the plot...Read it in just two sittings as I couldn't stop reading." (P. Green – amazon.co.uk)

"exciting plot, not a book you want to put down, although I tried not to rush it so as to fully enjoy escaping to the world skilfully created by the author. A most enjoyable read." (Liz Green – amazon.co.uk)

"an excellent read. I cannot wait for the next part of the trilogy from this talented author. You will not want to put it down" (B. Burchell – amazon.co.uk)

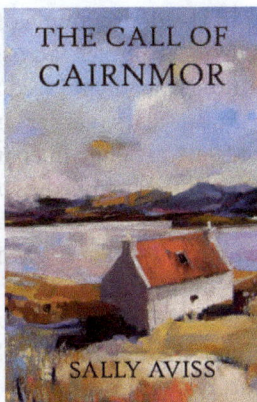

ISBN: 978-0-9559219-9-5
Also available on Kindle

Changing Tides, Changing Times

Book Two of the Cairnmor Trilogy

Sally Aviss

In the dense jungle of Malaya in 1942, Doctor Rachel Curtis stumbles across a mysterious, unidentifiable stranger, badly injured and close to death.

Four years earlier in 1938 in London, Katherine Stewart and her husband Alex come into conflict with their differing needs while Alex's father, Alastair, knows he must keep his deeper feelings hidden from the woman he loves; a woman to whom he must never reveal the full extent of that love.

Covering a broad canvas and meticulously researched, Changing Times, Changing Tides follows the interwoven journey of well-loved characters from The Call of Cairnmor, as well as introducing new personalities, in a unique combination of novel and history that tells a story of love, loss, friendship and heroism; absorbing the reader in the characters' lives as they are shaped and changed by the ebb and flow of events before, during and after the Second World War.

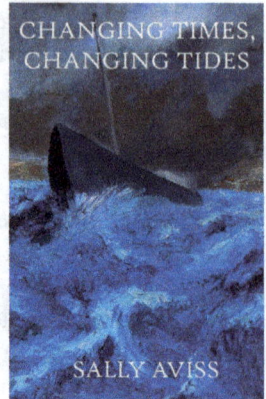

"I enjoyed the twists and turns of this book...particularly liked the gutsy Dr Rachel who is a reminder to the reader that these are dark days for the world. Love triumphs but not in the way we thought it would and our heroine, Katherine, learns that the path to true love is certainly not a smooth one." (MDW – amazon.co.uk)

"Even better than the first book! A moving and touching story well told." (P. Green – amazon.co.uk)

"One of the best reads this year...can't wait for the next one." (Mr C. Brownett – amazon.co.uk)

"One of my favourite books – and I have shelves of them in the house! Sally Aviss is a masterful storyteller [...She] has obviously done a tremendous amount of research, judging by all the fascinating and in-depth historical detail woven into the storyline." ('Inverneill' – amazon.co.uk)

ISBN: 978-0-9931587-0-4
Also available on Kindle

Where Gloom and Brightness Meet

Book Three of the Cairnmor Trilogy

Sally Aviss

When Anna Stewart begins a relationship with journalist Marcus Kendrick, the ramifications are felt from New York all the way across the Atlantic to the remote and beautiful Scottish island of Cairnmor, where her family live. Yet even as she and Marcus draw closer, Anna cannot forget her estranged husband whom she has not seen for many years.

When tragedy strikes, for some, Cairnmor becomes a refuge, a place of solace to ease the troubled spirit and an escape from painful reality; for others, it becomes a place of enterprise and adventure – a place in which to dream of an unfettered future.

This third book in the *Cairnmor Trilogy*, takes the action forward into the late nineteen-sixties as well as recalling familiar characters' lives from the intervening years. *Where Gloom and Brightness Meet* is a story of heartbreak and redemptive love; of long-dead passion remembered and retained in isolation; of unfaltering loyalty and steadfast devotion. It is a story that juxtaposes the old and the new; a story that reflects the conflicting attitudes, problems and joys of a liberating era.

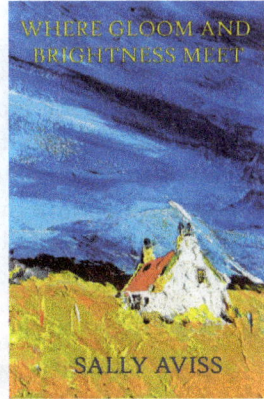

"the last book in Sally Aviss's trilogy and it did not disappoint...what a wonderful journey this has been...cleverly written with an enormous amount of research" (B. Burchell – amazon.co.uk)

"I loved this third book in the series...the characters were believable and events unfolded in a beguiling way...not too happy ending for everyone but a satisfying conclusion to the saga" (P. Green – amazon.co.uk)

ISBN: 978-0-9931587-1-1
Also available on Kindle

Message from Captivity

Sally Aviss

When diplomat's daughter Sophie Langley is sent on an errand of mercy to the Channel Island of St Nicolas in order to care for her two elderly aunts, she finds herself trapped in an unenviable position following the German invasion.

In the Battle for France, linguist and poet Robert Anderson, a lieutenant in the Royal Welch Fusiliers, finds himself embroiled in an impossible military situation from which there seems to be no escape.

From the beautiful Channel Islands to the very heart of Nazi-occupied Europe, Message From Captivity weaves factual authenticity into the fabric of a narrative where the twists and turns of captivity, freedom and dangerous pursuit have unforeseen consequences; where Robert's integrity is tested to the limit and Sophie needs all her inner strength to cope with the decisions and challenges she faces.

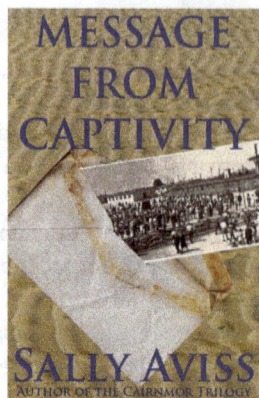

"The structure of the book takes you between the main protagonists and weaves their lives together as the story unfolds, add to that authentic research on the events of the period and you have a great story which keeps you guessing to the end." (P. Green – amazon.co.uk)

ISBN: 978-0-9931587-5-9
Also available on Kindle

The Girl in Jack's Portrait

Sally Aviss

When struggling barrister Callie Martin encounters soldier Jamie Rutherford on ceremonial duty near Horse Guards Parade, her life is changed forever. When Edie Paignton's ex-husband deprives her of alimony, she puts her lovingly restored Victorian house up for sale and finds her life transformed by a chance meeting with architect Ben Rutherford, Jamie's father. When successful businessman Erik van der Waals discovers an unknown name and telephone number on a piece of paper, he determines to meet the owner. And when mental health nurse, Sarah Adhabi, embarks on a dangerous new relationship, she discovers she is more than a match for the new man in her life.

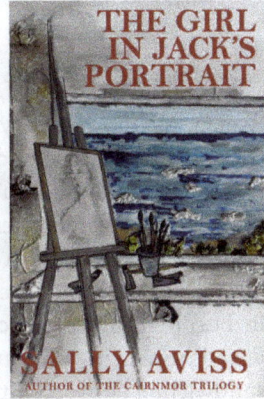

Six people seeking an escape from their pasts; six people seeking redemption in the present; six people who find their lives interwoven and their secrets revealed.

But just who is the Girl in Jack's Portrait?

ISBN: 978-0-9931587-6-6
Also available on Kindle

Reflections in an Oval Mirror

Memories of East Prussia, 1923–45

Anneli Jones

8 May 1945 – VE Day – was Anneliese Wiemer's twenty-second birthday. Although she did not know it then, it marked the end of her flight to the West, and the start of a new life in England.

These illustrated memoirs, based on a diary kept during the Third Reich and letters rediscovered many decades later, depict the momentous changes occurring in Europe against a backcloth of everyday farm life in East Prussia (now the north-western corner of Russia, sandwiched between Lithuania and Poland).

The political developments of the 1930s (including the Hitler Youth, 'Kristallnacht', political education, labour service, war service, and interrogation) are all the more poignant for being told from the viewpoint of a romantic young girl. In lighter moments she also describes student life in Vienna and Prague, and her friendship with Belgian and Soviet prisoners of war. Finally, however, the approach of the Red Army forces her to abandon her home and flee across the frozen countryside, encountering en route a cross-section of society ranging from a 'lady of the manor', worried about her family silver, to some concentration camp inmates

"couldn't put it down...delightful...very detailed descriptions of the farm and the arrival of war...interesting history and personal account" ('Rosie', amazon.co.uk)

"Anneli did not fully conform but she still survived, and how this happened is the real gem...There is optimism, humour, great affection and a tremendous sense of adventure in a period when this society was hurtling towards disaster." ('Singapore Relic', amazon.co.uk)

ISBN: 978-0-9559219-0-2
Also available on Kindle
German translation (with colourized photographs) available as ISBN 978-1-915174-00-0

Skating at the Edge of the Wood

Memories of East Prussia, 1931–1945…1993

Marlene Yeo

In 1944, the twelve-year old East Prussian girl Marlene Wiemer embarked on a horrific trek to the West, to escape the advancing Red Army. Her cousin Jutta was left behind the Iron Curtain, which severed the family bonds that had made the two so close.

This book contains dramatic depictions of Marlene's flight, recreated from her letters to Jutta during the last year of the war, and contrasted with joyful memories of the innocence that preceded them.

Nearly fifty years later, the advent of perestroika meant that Marlene and Jutta were finally able to revisit their childhood home, after a lifetime of growing up under diametrically opposed societies, and the book closes with a final chapter revealing what they find.

Despite depicting the same time and circumstances as "Reflections in an Oval Mirror", an account written by Marlene's elder sister, Anneli, and its sequel "Carpe Diem", this work stands in stark contrast partly owing to the age gap between the two girls, but above all because of their dramatically different characters.

"Marlene Yeo's account of living on a well to do farm is very engaging and her description of some of the small details of picking mushrooms in the woods, baking rye bread and skating in winter all brought the great political tragedy of the region down to an understandably human level for the non German reader … the description of desolation at the end of the book was heart breaking. " (Jonathon M Stenner, amazon.co.uk)

"Fantastic autobiography – beautifully written! Gives real insight into life and times in rural East Prussia in 1930s and 1940s. One of the best of several autobiographies of this period that I have read." (Mrs C.J. Pedley, amazon.co.uk)

" Fascinating look at a brutally ethnically cleansed province … This book was so interesting, I read it very quickly … The author does a great job of describing farm life in East Prussia as well as the chaos and insanity in that province in the waning days of the war. Gripping and highly recommended." (R. Miller, amazon.com)

ISBN: 978-0-9931587-2-8

Also available on Kindle

German translation (with colourized photographs) available as ISBN 978-1-915174-01-7

Ichigensan

– *The Newcomer* –

David Zoppetti
Translated from the Japanese by Takuma Sminkey

Ichigensan is a novel which can be enjoyed on many levels – as a delicate, sensual love story, as a depiction of the refined society in Japan's cultural capital Kyoto, and as an exploration of the themes of alienation and prejudice common to many environments, regardless of the boundaries of time and place.

Unusually, it shows Japan from the eyes of both an outsider and an 'internal' outcast, and even more unusually, it originally achieved this through sensuous prose carefully crafted by a non-native speaker of Japanese. The fact that this best-selling novella then won the Subaru Prize, one of Japan's top literary awards, and was also nominated for the Akutagawa Prize is a testament to its unique narrative power.

The story is by no means chained to Japan, however, and this new translation by Takuma Sminkey will allow readers world-wide to enjoy the multitude of sensations engendered by life and love in an alien culture.

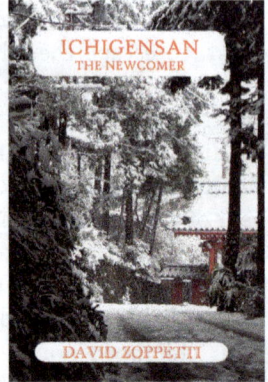

"A beautiful love story" (Japan Times)
"Sophisticated...subtle...sensuous...delicate...memorable...vivid depictions" (Asahi Evening News)
"Striking...fascinating..." (Japan PEN Club)
"Refined and sensual" (Kyoto Shimbun)
"quiet, yet very compelling...subtle mixture of humour and sensuality...the insights that the novel gives about Japanese society are both intriguing and exotic" (Nicholas Greenman, amazon.com)

ISBN: 978-0-9559219-4-0
Also available on Kindle
German translation available as ISBN 978-1-915174-05-5

Sunflowers

– Le Soleil –

Shimako Murai
A play in one act
Translated from the Japanese by Ben Jones

Hiroshima is synonymous with the first hostile use of an atomic bomb. Many people think of this occurrence as one terrible event in the past, which is studied from history books.

Shimako Murai and other 'Women of Hiroshima' believe otherwise: for them, the bomb had after-effects which affected countless people for decades, effects that were all the more menacing for their unpredictability – and often, invisibility.

This is a tale of two such people: on the surface successful modern women, yet each bearing underneath hidden scars as horrific as the keloids that disfigured Hibakusha on the days following the bomb.

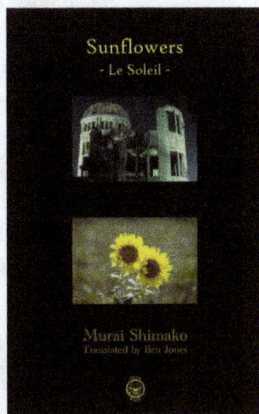

"a great story and a glimpse into the lives of the people who lived during the time of the war and how the bomb affected their lives, even after all these years" (Wendy Pierce, goodreads.com)

ISBN: 978-0-9559219-3-3
Also available on Kindle and Google Books

The Body as a Vessel

Approaching the Methodology of Hijikata Tatsumi's Ankoku Butō

Mikami Kayo
An analysis of the modern dance form
Translated from the Japanese by Rosa van Hensbergen

When Hijikata Tatsumi's "Butō" appeared in 1959, it revolutionized not only Japanese dance but also the concept of performance art worldwide. It has however proved notoriously difficult to define or tie down. Mikami was a disciple of Hijikata for three years, and in this book, partly based on her graduate and doctoral theses, she combines insights from these years with earlier notes from other dancers to decode the ideas and processes behind butō.

ISBN: 978-0-9931587-4-2

Courtly Feasts to Kremlin Banquets

A History of Celebration and Hospitality:
Echoes of Russia's cuisine

Mikami Oksana Zakharova and Sergey Pushkaryov
Translated & adapted by Marina George

This is a book not only for lovers of food but also for those with an appetite for adventure and a thirst for the discovery of exciting gastronomic delights.

Russian history presents us with a rich tapestry of extravagant ceremony, characterized not only by the magnificent grandeur of individual courtly feasts but also by successive generations of nobility actively vying with each other to surpass the splendour created by their predecessors. Russian hospitality has always exuded a special vitality and sense of warm-hearted sociability. In Old Russia there was also a significant link between hospitality and the teachings of the Orthodox Church.

The political and social history of Russia has seen some very violent changes. The more shocking the political events of a country, the more brutal the cultural changes can be. At times, the differences between the past and the present are so extreme that one is faced with completely different worlds. Despite dramatic and often heart-breaking upheavals, we do surely have a duty to remember those distant roots that helped to nourish the present.

"Modern society contemptuously dismisses and sneers at the former way of life and deliberately breaks any connection with the past, which would always have been held to be so dear at the time." These words of writer, historian and theatre critic Yevgeny Opochinin† were published in 1909 before the full horror of the revolutionary upheaval. The relevance of such remarks is surely as valid now as then.

Throughout history, special events have been an important way of imparting tradition from one generation to another, and symbolic meanings can still be found, if one knows the stories from the past. One just has to know where to look.

So, it is time to raise a toast in memory of bygone custom and tradition and to celebrate that great warm-hearted generosity of the Russian people.

ISBN: 978-0-9931587-8-0

Watch and Ward

A History of Margate Borough Police 1858 to 1943

Nigel Cruttenden

A comprehensive history of Margate Borough Police from its inception in 1858 until its amalgamation into Kent County Constabulary in 1943. It covers the origins of the modern police force, detailing the influence of local councillors, JPs, solicitors and freemasons, as well as central government and world events such as the Boer War and two subsequent world wars.

Alongside its new prosperity, the up-and-coming Victorian seaside resort also had an underbelly watched over by the boys in blue. The borough's residents and visitors encountered issues similar to those of today, ranging from nuisance dogs and speeding vehicles through to mental health, alcohol abuse, domestic violence and assault – even the occasional murder. This book therefore also serves as a social history of East Kent, offering local, social and police historians copious material for research. Whenever an incident occurred in Margate, a policeman would be lurking nearby: a police man, indeed, as there were no warranted female police officers until after amalgamation. Women did however also play an important role within Margate Police, as the book shows.

This is also an invaluable reference work for genealogists or other enthusiasts researching family history in and around Thanet. Family Trees are all very well, but they do not put the flesh on the bones, and even internet searches are quite limited. Full indices make it easy for modern Margatonians and Thanetians to check whether their ancestors might have been 'involved' with the police – on whichever side!

"without a doubt this book raises the bar ... a well-researched and comprehensive account ... not a cheap book, but in terms of value for money, serious students ... will not be disappointed ... impressive book" (Police History Society)

ISBN: 978-1-915174-03-1

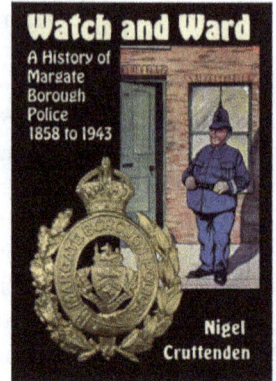

Misadventures at Margate – A Legend of Jarvis's Jetty

Thomas Ingoldsby
illustrated by Ernest Jessop

This lavishly illustrated facsimile edition comprises a humorous story about the adventures of a 19th century London gentleman visiting the seaside resort of Margate. There he naively befriends a poor 'vulgar boy', only to have his trust betrayed... A quaint fable from the Victorian era, or a cautionary tale for modern-day DFLs coming 'down from London' to explore Thanet's nooks and crannies (and crooks and nannies)? Some of the faces depicted in Jessop's wonderful cartoons can still be found in the side streets around Margate Pier and the Turner Contemporary art gallery! The verse – in rhyming couplets throughout – forms part of the ever popular Ingoldsby Legends. An appendix also explains the witty references that pepper the poem, and some terms that may be unfamiliar to modern readers.

ISBN: 978-0-9931587-9-7

www.ingramcontent.com/pod-product-compliance
Lightning Source LLC
Chambersburg PA
CBHW070152310326
41914CB00089B/864